DATE			

*f***P**

Cooking with Love

Comfort Food That Hugs You

Carla Hall

with Genevieve Ko

FREE PRESS

New York London Toronto Sydney New Delhi

FREE PRESS
A Division of Simon & Schuster, Inc.
1230 Avenue of the Americas
New York, NY 10020

First Free Press hardcover edition November 2012

FREE PRESS and colophon are trademarks of Simon & Schuster, Inc.

For information about special discounts for bulk purchases,
please contact Simon & Schuster Special Sales
at 1-866-506-1949 or business@simonandschuster.com.

The Simon & Schuster Speakers Bureau can bring authors to your live event.
For more information or to book an event contact the Simon & Schuster Speakers Bureau
at 1-866-248-3049 or visit our website at www.simonspeakers.com.

DESIGNED BY ERICH HOBBING

Greg Powers: Photographer; Ceci Loebl: Food Stylist; Grace Knott: Prop Stylist; Charles Lee: Retoucher.

Manufactured in the United States of America

1   3   5   7   9   10   8   6   4   2

Library of Congress Cataloging-in-Publication Data
Hall, Carla.
Cooking with love : real comfort food from Carla's kitchen / Carla Hall with Genevieve Ko.—First [edition]
p. cm.
Includes index.
1. Cooking, American—Southern style. 2. Comfort food—Southern States. I. Ko, Genevieve. II. Title.
TX715.2.S68H35 2012
641.5975—dc23
2012013725

ISBN 978-1-4516-6219-1
ISBN 978-1-4516-6221-4 (ebook)

*To Granny, for all the love she brought
to the table and to my life*

Contents

Introduction

Hootie hoo! Welcome to my very first cookbook. I've been a chef, a caterer, a lunch lady, a dancer, a runway model, a reality show star, a daytime cooking show host, even an accountant (really!)—and now I'm a cookbook author. But most of all, I'm a simple Southern girl who loves to cook and who cooks to love. What you've seen on *The Chew* and *Top Chef* isn't a gimmick, or an act, or something that ends when the dishes are cleared. That's who I am and what I cook. Food that hugs you. What could be better than that?

Now, giving a hug is easy, but making food that hugs requires a little bit of practice, but it's actually easier than most people think—and so much more fun! Whether you're starting to cook for the first time or you've been in the kitchen forever, I'm here to give you the techniques, the recipes, and the confidence you need to cook with love.

As you'll see, my food comes from all over the place. I draw as much comfort from Italian flavors as I do from Japanese ones. But at the end of the day, much of my inspiration comes from the American South. I grew up in Nashville, Tennessee, home of the Grand Ole Opry and the Titans. But my grandmother's house is my favorite spot in town. Every week of my childhood, I was smothered with a giant food hug at my Granny's Sunday supper. I can't say that I learned how to cook at Granny's side, though. Most of the time when we went to her house for a family meal after church, the closest I came to cooking was making mud pies.

Then one afternoon, Granny asked me to help harvest collard greens from the garden. Like any kid, I tried to beg my way out: "Really? Do I really have to pick the greens?" My complaining didn't get me anywhere, so I relented and did it. I wasn't happy about it. When we sat down to eat, I had to make sure I wasn't asked to pick the greens again and informed everyone, "I don't know what you're eating. I couldn't tell the difference between the greens and the weeds. You might just be eating weeds right now."

I've learned a lot since then: the difference between greens and weeds, the fact that, of course, Granny knew which was which and cooked only the collards, and how much the memories from our Sunday suppers have defined me. Granny's weekly ritual started long before I came around. She was born Freddie Mae Price to Jessie, who came from a family that was spread across South and North Carolina, Georgia, Mississippi, and Tennessee. Jessie had been bought as a slave by the Price family and was among the last to be freed. In her 102 years on this earth, she lived to see generations of change in the South. She also passed on to Granny the depth and breadth of great Southern black cuisine. I wish every person in America could have sat at Granny's table and been transformed by her cooking, warmth, and hospitality. I'm writing this book to honor Granny—and the women who came before her—and to give you a taste of just how much joy can be had in the kitchen and at the table.

I'm even giving you some of Granny's treasured recipes, like her buttery pound cake and juicy smothered pork chops, and passing on my interpretations of soul food. Sure, I cook my collard greens low and slow, but guess what? I also sauté them quickly and top them with gremolata, an Italian parsley-lemon-garlic mix. And I do a mean French bouillabaisse sauce of fennel and tomatoes to serve with a roasted whole snapper. Yep, I do all that. I've been cooking professionally for years (and I mean years!) and travelling and eating around the world. I've discovered that I can draw comfort from all types of cuisines. Here I've created a collection of my all-time favorites. Sort of an "all you'll ever need" repertoire of global comfort food. Because it's not the geographic origins of the food that matters, it's the heart you put into it.

And the book is about making comfort food good for your heart, too. I never count calories or sacrifice flavor. Instead, I boost flavors by using just the right amount of butter (which I love!) and the ideal cooking technique. I say "no" to nothing. It's all about moderation. For example, I always make sure that both my pan and the oil are hot enough when cooking cornmeal-crusted Southern fried catfish. That way, the cornmeal doesn't soak up the oil, it just gets super crisp in it. My dishes end up being naturally nutritious. My goal is to create the most delicious, comforting dishes possible, but I'm also always thinking of ways to lighten ultrarich soul food classics and other soulful hearty favorites. It's a way of bringing out the fresh, natural flavors in great ingredients, but my motivation hits closer to home.

While living abroad, I received a call and found out that my mama was seriously ill. I flew home right away and was relieved to find that her emergency surgery had been a success. Since that experience, I'm constantly tinkering with dishes to make them lighter, healthier for Mama. Even when I started my first "professional" cooking company, delivering lunches using a retired mail truck and sheer grit in getting my food out through rain, sleet, and snow, I was providing options far superior to the surrounding fast foods, both in flavor and nutrition. With my company, The Lunch Basket (which I later renamed The Lunch Bunch), I became the lunch lady of Kennedy Street in Washington, D.C., a primarily African American neighborhood with lots of beauty salons, barber shops, florists, and doctors' offices.

Even though I didn't realize it at the time, my decision then to not use beef or pork (though some of my recipes here do) came from a desire to show people how tasty food could be without those things. I stuffed my biscuits with lean smoked turkey and put together fresh green salads, seasonal fruit, and rich veggie soups. At the end of the day, I'm giving you delicious fresh food—whole ingredients, lovingly prepared. I'm making dishes good for my family, in every sense of the word, and I'm here to help you do the same for your family and friends, too.

The act of cooking for and feeding loved ones yummy wholesome food is deeply fulfilling. I didn't completely understand that until I was an adult well into my food career. I went through a heart-wrenching breakup (boyfriend left me for best friend—you know the story), so I poured myself into my lunch business to shield myself from the pain. By cooking for others, I was nurturing them with food, and in turn, felt nurtured myself. I expanded the lunch business into a catering company and called it Alchemy Caterers, because I needed it to change my life, to turn the lead in my hurt into gold. I wanted my food to do the same for others and be a conduit for healing. I don't know exactly what you need right now, but I do know that there's comfort in food. Alchemy is all about transformation, and I want to change the way you experience food by cooking with love.

The only way you can make transformative food, even if it's one of the simple dishes in here, is to cook it from the heart. You have to *want* to do it. If you're not in a good mood and don't feel like cooking, the only thing you should make is a restaurant reservation. And you can't cook with fear. I didn't grow up in the kitchen and I know how it feels to be intimidated by a recipe and be immobilized by that fear. I'm here to tell you it's okay to mess up! I'll help you avoid screwing up and tell you what to do in case something does go wrong.

Now, it's time to have fun! I'm going to make sure you enjoy cooking for family and friends by sharing easy entertaining tricks I've learned from decades of catering. When you're armed with tips from a pro, cooking *with* and *for* friends is the best way to have fun in the kitchen. One of the happiest moments in my life—my wedding day—came from doing just that. My husband, Matthew, and I celebrated our marriage with forty friends and family and a group of us prepared the food together. I didn't stress over the planning or micromanage the meal. I just let everybody express themselves in the kitchen and it was awesome. I felt like I was on top of the world and I honestly can't imagine a more memorable wedding day. But take my advice as a former caterer: Please don't try this if you have hundreds of guests celebrating with you. LOL.

So, are you ready? With all my yummy recipes and tips, get excited to welcome friends and family over for big meals and good times!

❧A little note: Any brand names of products I use in this book are included just because I like them!

Cooking
with Love

Appetizers

Cheap and cheerful! That's my motto for starting a meal. I don't want to blow the bank on appetizers, but I want them to set the stage for a fun, inviting meal. Great starters get you ready for the main dish without upstaging it. As a caterer, I loved putting together little pinchy bites—the pretty individual servings that are as much about crafting as cooking. When I don't have time to make those, I always whip up at least a simple dip or bowl of seasoned nuts. Just be sure to make enough! Nothing's sadder than an empty appetizer dish. That's why when I'm serving, I divide my appetizers among a bunch of smaller dishes. That way, as soon as a dish is almost empty, I can swap the whole plate. Otherwise, I find it time-consuming and messy to try to refill a dish with the food, plunking down the pieces one at a time while my friends stand around. After all, the whole point of appetizers is to have a tasty nibble while casually hanging out with family and friends. My little dish-swapping trick will let you chat up the whole room to build up to the fun you'll all have at the table.

Down-Home Deviled Eggs with Smoky Bacon

Makes 24 egg halves

Growing up in the South meant being part of a wide and warm social circle. We were always visiting with friends and family at casual picnics, fancier teatime parties, and sit-down dinners. There was always a gracious spread of classic dishes and *always* a plate of deviled eggs.

I'll never forget the time my sister, Kim, and I arrived at a party and, after exchanging pleasantries with the hostess, found that there were no deviled eggs on the buffet. I don't know if the hostess ran out or never had them to begin with. Either way, we were scandalized. We ran to Mama and told her and there were a lot of whispers and raised eyebrows among the ladies after that. If you're a Southern hostess, you'd better have deviled eggs and lots of them.

They don't have to be fancy. In fact, I like to keep to the classic vinegar-mayo-mustard combo. My only addition here is to top them off with crunchy bacon. A small but worthy addition. You can easily double, triple, quadruple this recipe—make enough so you don't run out at your party!

> *3 strips bacon (regular, not thick-cut)*
> *12 large eggs*
> *Kosher salt*
> *1 tablespoon white vinegar or cider vinegar*
> *⅓ cup mayonnaise*
> *2 teaspoons Dijon mustard*
> *¼ teaspoon cayenne pepper or to taste*
> *¼ teaspoon freshly ground black pepper*

1. In a medium skillet, cook the bacon over medium heat, turning occasionally, until browned and crisp, about 10 minutes. Drain on paper towels. When the bacon is cool, crumble into small pieces and reserve.

2. Put the cold eggs in a large saucepan and add enough cold water to cover them by 1 inch. Add 1 tablespoon salt, then bring to a boil. Cover the saucepan and remove from the heat. Let stand, covered, for 10 minutes.

3. Fill a large bowl with cool water. Remove the eggs from the saucepan, gently roll on the counter to crack all over, then place them in the cool water. The water will get under

the membranes and make the eggs easier to peel. Once they've sat for a little while, peel them, one by one. Pat the eggs dry, trim a little slice from the top and bottom of each egg, then cut each egg in half crosswise. The trimmed tops and bottoms will help the egg halves sit up.

4. Carefully remove the yolks and transfer to a large bowl. Mash with a fork, then sprinkle the vinegar over the yolks. Add the mayonnaise, mustard, cayenne, black pepper, and ¼ teaspoon salt. Stir until well mixed and smooth. Taste and add more salt if you like.

5. Transfer the mashed yolks to a piping bag fitted with a plain or rosette tip. You can also use a resealable plastic bag; snip a hole in a corner. Pipe the yolks into the whites so the eggs look pretty. Garnish with the crumbled bacon.

Catering Like Carla

To serve the deviled eggs, you can wash dried black beans and dry them well. Spread them in a layer on a serving platter and nestle the eggs in them. The beans both make a beautiful, dramatic backdrop for the eggs and help them stay up. Plus, the beans are large enough to not stick to the eggs when they're picked up.

Old eggs are easier to peel. If you know when you're going to serve deviled eggs, buy a dozen a few weeks beforehand.

🐓 At Granny's Table

Granny, my mama's mama, influenced my career more than anyone else. (And it's not only because she helped pay for culinary school.) She was an amazing woman, in every sense of the word. Granny worked as a beautician and as a dietician and raised a family with my grandfather, whom we all called Doc. In Lebanon, Tennessee, Doc worked at the hospital and also dabbled in real estate. Out of the many properties he built, the most significant was the home he made for Granny.

We dubbed their first home the Big House. It was where Mama grew up, but Granny wanted something smaller, a little more manageable. She wanted Doc to build a home that was just hers. During construction, Granny asked Doc to create an open kitchen and great room. Though it's a popular layout now, Granny's request was cutting edge back then. But we weren't thinking about kitchen design. We just loved being able to see Granny cooking and she loved being able to see us. That being said, the room itself was beautiful. Doc installed a big latticework between the kitchen and the main counter on the other side. Along the adjoining wall, Granny hung decorative souvenir plates from different states, gifts from her many friends. The shelves overflowed with pretty glasses and jewel-toned tin cups in turquoise, yellow, and pink. Everywhere, she hung pictures. From the front entrance to the rear, she had photos of us growing up. Anyone coming into the house—close friends or deliverymen—would get the story of our family as told in that intimate gallery.

Those lucky enough to be invited to Granny's Sunday suppers would get a real taste of our family history. She always started with deviled eggs. For the main meal, she cooked smothered pork chops or country ham, the gnarly-skinned kind that you had to soak to get out the salt. It was dry yet moist and smoky and sweet all at the same time. Yum! My favorite accompaniment was her creamy mac and cheese, baked until bubbly and golden brown on top. She made her signature flaky buttermilk biscuits by hand, stamping out dough rounds with her tin cups, dented by years of use. And cornbread came one of two ways. For her hot water cornbread, she worked hot water, bacon fat, and salt into white cornmeal. She made the mixture into little patties and pan-fried them. They would get really crisp on the outside and nice and tender inside. I loved that! And I loved seeing the indentations of her long fingers in each patty. They were truly a sign that she had handled each one. If Granny didn't do those patties, she made what she called skillet egg cornbread instead. That was made not with white cornmeal but with yellow because, after all, eggs whip up yellow. She stirred the batter and baked it in a smoking hot cast-iron skillet only after we all arrived so that its crust would crackle when we cut into it, just the way we all liked it. So good!

And yes, there were greens. Granny was proud of her large garden and always put lots of vegetables on the table. Sometimes the produce came from neighbors and friends knocking on the back door to share their harvest. To season and complement her rotation of braised collards, kale, and turnip greens, Granny kept a jar of pickled peppers on the table. In the summer, she plucked ripe tomatoes and cucumbers from the garden, then peeled them and cut them into large chunks to toss with onions and vinegar. I'll admit I wasn't a big tomato lover back then (my sister was), but I knew the difference between home-grown tomatoes and store-bought. And I just knew we were the cat's meow to have *peeled* tomatoes.

When it came to dessert, it was all about indulgence. All of us Sunday supper regulars—me, my mama, sister, aunts, and cousins—had our favorites. My sister's was Granny's summertime peach cobbler, which had an unbelievably buttery crust. Mama preferred Granny's chess pie, with its tangy buttermilk filling, and I usually requested sweet potato pie. Come Christmas, Granny would make boiled custard and bake loaves of her wonderful five-flavor pound cake—my cousins' favorite. With vanilla, rum, coconut, lemon, and almond baked into buttery batter, the cakes would fill the whole house with the most amazing fragrance. We'd cut slices of the cake and dunk them into the custard. What'd I say? Pure indulgence.

Boiled custard was a holiday treat, but the cake itself, baked in classic ring molds, came around all year. When the grandkids had grown up and moved on, Granny made the cakes, wrapped them in wax paper, then paper towels, then plastic wrap, then bubble wrap, and shipped them off to us. While you unwrapped the package, you could feel Granny's arms wrapping around you. *That's* food that hugs you.

Sweet and Spicy Walnuts

Makes 4 cups

If you don't consider yourself a cook, you've got to start here. Seasoned nuts are the very first thing I tried that made me so proud as a young cook. Before I started to learn how to really cook, I considered sugary spiced nuts a delicious how-in-the-world-do-you-make-that sorta thing. That was my mind-set when I tasted the amazing nuts at an event celebrating the renowned cooking teacher and chef Anne Willan. That version was based on a recipe in one of her cookbooks. Those nuts were so good, I went home, got the book, and made the recipe. It was such a great feeling! I did it on my own and it was amazing! While I passed a bowl of 'em to my friends, I was like, "Ooh! Aah! Look at these nuts!" I blew myself away with the savory, sweet, spicy balance in the mix and how crisp they were. Not sticky or chewy at all. Nowadays, I whip 'em out as an easy app. (And they are, even if you've never tried them before.)

Over the years, I've played with the sugar-spice mix to suit my tastes. The three options below are among my favorites, but you can tinker with other spices, too. Just be sure to keep the proportions of nuts to egg whites to sugar the same for each recipe style below (sweet and spicy, savory, candied) if you want to get the right texture.

This all-purpose appetizer can also be made with almonds, pecans, cashews, or a combination of nuts. Serve them as munchies on their own or scatter them on salads or simply cooked veggies.

1 large egg white
4 cups walnut halves
½ cup granulated sugar
¼ cup packed light brown sugar
½ teaspoon ground ginger
½ teaspoon kosher salt
½ teaspoon coarsely ground black pepper

1. Preheat the oven to 300°F. Line a half sheet pan with a Silpat or other nonstick silicone baking mat, or parchment paper.

2. In a large bowl, beat the egg white until soft peaks form. Add the walnuts and toss gently until well coated. In a medium bowl, combine the sugars, ginger, salt, and pepper. Sprinkle over the walnuts and gently fold until the nuts are evenly coated. Spread in

a single layer on the pan. Bake, stirring every 10 minutes, until golden brown, about 45 minutes.

3. Transfer the pan to a wire rack. Separate the nuts with a fork and let cool completely in the pan. The cooled nuts will keep in an airtight container for up to 1 week, but are best when fresh.

Cinnamon-Cayenne Pecans

&•Substitute pecans for the walnuts. Stir 1 tablespoon melted butter into the egg white before tossing with the nuts. Substitute 1½ teaspoons ground cinnamon, ½ teaspoon cayenne pepper, and ½ teaspoon kosher salt for the sugars, ginger, salt, and pepper. Proceed as above.

Candied Almonds

&•Preheat the oven to 250°F. Substitute whole almonds for the walnuts. Beat 1 teaspoon water into the egg white. Omit the brown sugar, ginger, and pepper, then proceed as above.

Polenta Trio with Sun-Dried Tomato Pesto

Makes about 24 pieces

When I was catering, I had to come up with ways to make beautiful, delicious food in big batches ahead of time. This fits the bill! Stirring potent pesto and parm into mild polenta not only adds tasty pop, it also shades it the gorgeous colors of Italy's flag. These small bites are ideal as an appetizer, but you can also skip the stacking and enjoy the seasoned polenta soft and warm as a side dish.

> *Nonstick cooking spray*
> *10½ cups water*
> *Kosher salt*
> *2¼ cups white cornmeal (preferably stone-ground)*
> *6 tablespoons (¾ stick) unsalted butter, cut into large chunks*
> *Freshly ground black pepper*
> *¼ cup Basil Pesto (recipe follows)*
> *¼ cup Sun-Dried Tomato Pesto (page 130), plus more for serving*
> *¾ cup freshly grated Parmigiano-Reggiano cheese, plus more*
>   *for serving (optional)*

1. Line a half sheet pan with parchment paper and lightly coat with cooking spray.

2. In an 8-quart saucepot, bring the water to a boil. Reduce the heat to maintain a gentle simmer and add 1 tablespoon salt. Add the cornmeal in a slow, steady stream while stirring continuously with a wooden spoon. Reduce the heat to low, cover, and cook for 30 minutes, stirring and scraping the bottom of the pot every 5 minutes.

3. When the polenta is really soft and smooth, it should look like thin mashed potatoes and have lost its raw cornmeal taste and gritty texture. Stir in the butter, ½ teaspoon salt, and ¼ teaspoon pepper, stirring until the butter melts.

4. Divide the polenta among three bowls; you should have 2½ cups in each bowl. With separate rubber spatulas, stir the basil pesto into one bowl, the tomato pesto into another, and the parmesan into the third bowl. Stir each until very well mixed.

5. Grease an offset spatula with cooking spray. Spread the parmesan polenta in an even layer in the pan, using long, even strokes to rake it flat. If you'd like, you can spread some

up the sides of the rims of the pan. When that layer is firm, wash and respray the spatula and spread the tomato polenta over it. When the tomato layer is firm, finish with the basil polenta layer. Cover tightly with plastic wrap and refrigerate until very firm, up to 3 days.

6. When ready to serve, cut the polenta into 3-inch squares or triangles. Top each with a little dollop of sun-dried tomato pesto and, if you'd like, a sprinkle of parmesan. This is nice cold, but if you prefer it hot, lightly coat the cut pieces with cooking spray and brown them on top and bottom in a nonstick skillet over medium-high heat or under a broiler.

Catering Like Carla

To get the layers perfectly even for beautiful straight stripes in the stacks, cover the layer with plastic wrap, place another half sheet pan on top of the plastic wrap, and press down until the polenta is flat and even. Remove the plastic wrap before spreading and pressing the next layer.

Basil Pesto

Makes 1½ cups

3 cups packed fresh basil leaves
¼ cup extra virgin olive oil
2 garlic cloves, lightly crushed and peeled
¼ cup pine nuts, toasted (page 296)
¼ cup freshly grated Parmigiano-Reggiano
     or Pecorino Romano cheese
Kosher salt

In a large bowl, toss the basil with the oil. In a food processor, pulse the garlic, pine nuts, and cheese until finely chopped. Add the basil and oil and pulse to combine, then process until it forms a smooth paste. Season to taste with salt. You can keep the pesto in an airtight container in the fridge for 1 week or in the freezer for up to 3 months.

Smoked Trout Dip

Makes about 2½ cups

I could eat this creamy, smoky, savory dip all day long. Bright lemon zest and juice bring zing to this fresh, easy dish. I like the intensity of smoked trout, preferably the Ducktrap brand, but I make this with Spicy Hot Smoked Salmon (page 227), too, when I have it around. The classiest way to serve this is dolloped on blini, but you can also spoon it into endive leaves or set it out in a bowl with a crudité or cracker platter. For a light lunch, spread it on good bread to make an open face sandwich.

> ½ small yellow onion, finely diced (½ cup)
> ½ pound smoked trout, skin and bones removed,
>   flaked into small chunks
> 1 cup sour cream
> ¾ cup mayonnaise
> 2 tablespoons capers, rinsed, drained, and chopped
> 1 tablespoon fresh dill leaves, chopped
> 1 teaspoon freshly grated lemon zest
> 1 teaspoon fresh lemon juice
> 1 teaspoon Tabasco sauce
> ¼ teaspoon kosher salt
> ¼ teaspoon freshly ground black pepper

1. Bring a small saucepan of water to a boil. Add the onion and cook, stirring occasionally, for 1 minute. Drain well and rinse under cold running water. When cool, drain again and transfer to a large bowl.

2. Add the trout, sour cream, mayonnaise, capers, dill, lemon zest and juice, Tabasco, salt, and pepper to the onion. Stir until well mixed. You can serve this right away, but it's even better after you cover and refrigerate it for at least a few hours and up to a day. The flavors really develop and meld with time.

Bacon, Blue Cheese, and Apple Stacks

Makes 20 stacks

When I'm creating finger food recipes, I often take a big dish—in this case, a classic chopped salad with bacon, apple, and blue cheese—and make it bite-size. Cream cheese binds blue cheese, apple, and walnuts into a chunky, creamy mix for salty-sweet crunchy bacon strips. Then I take it one step further by layering the spread with fresh apple slices and chopped walnuts. Each bite's a wow of textures and a satisfying taste of fall.

> *1 to 2 tart apples (such as Granny Smith)*
> *4 ounces blue cheese, crumbled (about 1 cup)*
> *One 8-ounce block cream cheese, softened*
> *3 tablespoons half-and-half*
> *¼ teaspoon freshly ground black pepper*
> *½ cup plus 2 tablespoons walnuts, toasted and chopped*
> *(page 296)*
> *20 Maple-Glazed Bacon pieces (recipe follows)*

1. Core one apple and cut it in half. Cut one half of the apple into ¼-inch pieces. Wrap the other half tightly in plastic wrap and refrigerate.

2. Reserve 2 tablespoons of the blue cheese. Place the remaining blue cheese in a food processor along with the cream cheese, half-and-half, and pepper. Process until well blended and smooth, stopping to scrape the sides and bottom of the bowl occasionally.

3. Transfer the blended cheese to a large bowl. Stir in the diced apple and ½ cup of the nuts. Cover and refrigerate for at least 30 minutes and up to 1 day.

4. If the cut side of the reserved apple has browned, slice off the brown part. Cut the apple into 40 very thin slices. Use a second apple if needed.

5. Divide the cream cheese blend among the bacon strips and spread evenly. Sandwich between 2 apple slices. Garnish with the remaining blue cheese and walnuts. Serve immediately.

Maple-Glazed Bacon

Makes about 30 pieces

> 1 pound thick-cut bacon, cut in half crosswise
> ¼ cup maple syrup
> 1 teaspoon Dijon mustard
> 1 teaspoon packed brown sugar

1. Preheat the oven to 400°F. Line two half sheet pans with parchment paper.

2. In a small bowl, combine the syrup, mustard, and sugar until well blended.

3. Lay the bacon in a single layer on the pans. Bake until the fat renders, about 15 minutes. Carefully drain the rendered fat from the pans. (You can strain the fat, then refrigerate or freeze it for another use.)

4. Brush the glaze onto the bacon. Bake until browned, caramelized, and crisp, about 5 minutes longer. Transfer the bacon to wire racks and let cool completely.

Herb Focaccia with Ricotta and Olives

Makes one 13 by 9-inch or 14-inch-round loaf

If you've ever wanted to try making homemade yeast bread, but have been intimidated by the process, here's a good place to start. Sticking your fingers in soft dough is such a satisfying feeling, you should definitely try it. This dough rises quickly and simply needs to be pressed into a pan. You can sprinkle coarse salt on top, or add some herbs, or go all the way here and do the pesto, ricotta, and olives. I love this savory trio, with briny olives nestled in milky cheese over a tangy, tomatoey layer.

The basic focaccia recipe here without the toppings is a platform for you to create something uniquely yours. Check out suggestions based on my other faves below. You can use the bread plain for sandwiches, cut it into wedges or small rectangles for appetizers, or cut it into little cubes and fry or toast them into croutons.

> *3 tablespoons extra virgin olive oil, plus more for the bowl*
> *and pan*
> *1 packet active dry yeast (2¼ teaspoons)*
> *½ teaspoon sugar*
> *¾ cup warm water (110°F)*
> *2 cups all-purpose flour, plus more for kneading*
> *1½ teaspoons kosher salt, plus more for sprinkling*
> *½ teaspoon garlic powder*
> *½ teaspoon cayenne pepper*
> *¼ cup Sun-Dried Tomato Pesto (page 130 or store-bought)*
> *½ cup Homemade Ricotta (recipe follows) or store-bought*
> *whole milk ricotta*
> *¼ teaspoon dried rosemary leaves*
> *¼ cup pitted Kalamata olives, chopped*

1. Lightly oil a large bowl. In a small bowl, stir together the yeast, sugar, and water until the sugar dissolves. Let stand until foamy, about 5 minutes.

2. While the yeast stands, combine the flour, salt, garlic powder, and cayenne in a food processor. Pulse until well mixed. With the machine running, add 3 tablespoons oil, then pulse until fully incorporated. With the machine running, add the dissolved yeast, then pulse until the dough forms a ball around the blade. Or mix the ingredients in the order above by hand.

3. Transfer the dough to a lightly floured work surface and knead gently just until the dough is smooth, about five times. Transfer to the oiled bowl, cover with plastic wrap, and let stand in a warm place until the dough has doubled in size, about 1 hour.

4. While the dough is rising, preheat the oven to 400°F. Generously oil a 13 by 9 by 1-inch baking pan or 14-inch round tart pan.

5. Punch down the dough, cover with plastic wrap, and let stand for 5 minutes.

6. Transfer the dough to the pan. Use your fingertips to gently stretch the dough to the edges, pressing it into an even layer. Dimple the dough with your fingertips.

7. Gently spread the pesto evenly over the dough, then dollop the ricotta over the pesto. Carefully spread the ricotta into an even layer. Sprinkle the rosemary and a pinch of salt over the ricotta.

8. Bake until golden brown, about 25 minutes. Transfer the pan to a wire rack. Sprinkle the olives on top and let cool in the pan. Cut into pieces before serving warm or at room temperature.

&Here are just a few of the other toppings that I love for my focaccia.

SAVORY
- Maldon sea salt or fleur de sel with chopped fresh thyme and rosemary leaves
- Caramelized onions with sliced fresh sage leaves and lemon zest
- Roasted butternut squash cubes over ricotta

SWEET
- Grapes with vanilla sugar
- Fruit and honey over ricotta

Homemade Ricotta

Makes about 2 cups

>   1 quart whole milk
>   1 cup buttermilk
>   ½ cup heavy cream
>   1 teaspoon kosher salt

1. Line a fine-mesh sieve with four layers of cheesecloth. Set it over a bowl.

2. In a large saucepan, combine the milk, buttermilk, cream, and salt. Bring to a boil over medium heat, stirring frequently to prevent scorching, until the milk solids separate from the liquid.

3. Pour into the strainer. Let drain for 15 minutes.

4. Use the cheese in the sieve; discard the liquid in the bowl. If you prefer a creamier ricotta, you can pulse the cheese in a food processor until smooth. Homemade ricotta can be refrigerated in an airtight container for up to 1 week.

🦋 Toot Toot! Honk Honk! Ah-Ooh-Ga!

No trains coming through—that's just what I call out when I'm proud of something I've done. And my focaccia's one of them. In my cooking career, focaccia was the first dish that gave me that proud face. You know? That small smirk you're entitled to when you've just done something really well, when you can really say to yourself, "Hey, I'm good at what I do."

I was in the Bahamas, cooking as a private chef for a demanding boss. I took the job because I couldn't imagine anything wrong with getting paid to spend the winter in the Caribbean. Little did I know just how hard it would be. There were no nearby supermarkets, or any markets for that matter, so I had to plan my menus and weekly shopping trips very carefully. Not a problem—I'm the queen of organization!—unless, of course, the boss wants a sandwich. For lunch. Today.

I had some steak and grilled veggies from dinner the night before, but no bread. I had no bread! And there was no way I could make it to the market and back by the time they'd want to have lunch. And no, not making sandwiches was not an option. When I scanned my pantry and saw some yeast, I knew I could pull it off. Homemade bread! There was only time for focaccia, the perfect base for steak sandwiches.

The family, who called me Carla the Cook, raved about those sandwiches. And they're not the raving type. Yup, that's when I got my proud face on. Toot toot! Honk honk! Ah-ooh-ga! It's never easy or fun working for a difficult boss. But if you can make 'em happy, if you can fulfill an impossible request, that's something to smile about. And if you get a delicious recipe out of it, all the better.

Curried Beef Dumplings

Makes 40 dumplings

I first had shao mai (little open-topped dumplings) at dim sum, the Chinese-style brunch where you graze on lots of small dishes. I enjoyed the traditional pork and shrimp dumplings so much, I decided to do my own version with a curried beef filling. Curry powder is great! Because it's a blend of many different spices, you don't have to work as hard to get flavor. Plus, I love bringing Indian flavors into my food. The warmth and depth of spices add so much to the lean beef in this filling.

For this recipe, be sure to buy thin wonton wrappers made with an egg-based dough, not the thicker dumpling wrappers made from an eggless flour-based dough.

1 tablespoon minced peeled fresh ginger
1 garlic clove, minced
1 tablespoon curry powder
2 tablespoons cornstarch
1 teaspoon kosher salt
½ teaspoon sesame oil
2 large eggs
¾ pound lean (90%) ground beef sirloin
1 red bell pepper, stemmed, seeded, and finely diced
¼ cup thinly sliced scallions (green onions)
1 tablespoon water, plus more for cooking
Forty 3½-inch-diameter round wonton wrappers

1. In a small bowl, whisk together the ginger, garlic, curry powder, cornstarch, salt, sesame oil, and 1 of the eggs. In a large bowl, combine the beef, bell pepper, and scallions, then stir in the ginger mixture until well combined. Cover and refrigerate for 1 hour.

2. In a clean small bowl, whisk the remaining egg with the water. Lightly brush a thin layer of the egg wash on a wonton wrapper. Use a measuring tablespoon to scoop 1 tablespoon of the beef filling into the center of the wrapper. Hold the filled wrapper in the palm of one hand and pull the sides of the wrapper up around beef with the other hand while slowly spinning the dumpling in your palm. You should be gently squeezing the wrapper around the beef and pushing the beef up so that it's flush with the top of the wrapper. You're not really pressing the filling, just gently shaping it. The beef should be exposed on top and the whole dumpling should be in the shape of a wide cylinder. Place wrapped

dumplings on a wax paper- or plastic wrap-lined half sheet pan. Repeat with the remaining wrappers, egg wash, and beef filling. If you don't want to cook them immediately, cover tightly with plastic wrap and freeze for up to 1 month.

3. Heat a large nonstick skillet over medium heat. Add just enough dumplings so that you can space them 1 inch apart in a single layer. Cook until the bottoms are lightly browned, about 2 minutes.

4. Add enough water to come ¼ inch up the sides of the pan. Cover and cook until the water evaporates, about 2 minutes. Again add enough water to come ¼ inch up the sides of the pan. Cover and cook until the beef is cooked through, about 2 minutes more. You can tell when the beef is done when the dumpling feels very firm. If you want to be sure, cut one in half to check.

5. Transfer the cooked dumplings to a serving plate and tent loosely with foil. Repeat with the remaining dumplings. Serve hot or warm.

Catering Like Carla

To make this easy recipe even easier, set up an assembly line: Lay out 5 or more wrappers, brush them all with the egg wash, place a dollop of filling in the center of each, and wrap them up, one by one. Repeat until you're done.

There's little difference between making 25 and 125 of these once you've got your assembly line set up. So why not make more, since they're perfect for freezing? You can double, triple, or quadruple the recipe easily. Line half sheet pans with plastic wrap, place the dumplings on them, and freeze until very hard. Transfer them to resealable plastic freezer bags and freeze for up to 1 month. Cook them straight from the freezer. They'll take about 5 minutes longer than fresh ones to cook through.

Salads

It's all about the bits and bobs here. I love little treasures of fruit and cheese with the lettuce and other veggies, so I compose my salads thinking about how to make every bite a bit different. And I always need to have some crunch from goodies like bacon or nuts. Whether I'm serving a salad as a main or side dish, I want the whole thing to be satisfying. That's where well-balanced dressings come in. By building layers of savory and tangy flavors, I make sure my dressings are super tasty. Once everything comes together, it's a happy bowl of fresh zing that puts a huge smile on my face.

Arugula and Shaved Fennel Salad with Goat Cheese Croutons and Champagne Vinaigrette

Serves 6

I first developed this recipe for a cooking class—a good salad can teach you so much! One of the first things I show novice cooks is the importance of layering flavors. Even though this salad is simple, the molten goat cheese gives it a surprising and sophisticated twist. The anise scent of fresh fennel, which I love, is echoed in fennel seeds in the cheese.

When I was catering, I'd fry the little cheese parcels. But I bake them when I'm cooking healthier food at home. Baking is also ideal for entertaining. I don't want to stand over a pot, nursing a dish in its last stages, when I have friends coming over. Just don't forget to set the oven timer!

CHAMPAGNE VINAIGRETTE

1 tablespoon finely diced shallot

1 small garlic clove, minced

2 tablespoons champagne vinegar

1 teaspoon sugar

½ teaspoon freshly grated lemon zest

½ teaspoon Dijon mustard

¼ teaspoon kosher salt

¼ teaspoon freshly ground black pepper

2 tablespoons canola or other neutral oil

2 tablespoons extra virgin olive oil

SALAD

1 Ruby Red grapefruit

1 orange

½ cup all-purpose flour

½ teaspoon fennel seeds, toasted (page 296)

½ teaspoon fresh rosemary leaves, finely chopped

1 large egg

½ cup panko bread crumbs

8 ounces goat cheese

Two 5-ounce packages baby arugula
1 fennel bulb, cut in half and sliced paper-thin
½ cup sliced almonds, toasted (page 296)

1. To make the vinaigrette: Combine the shallot, garlic, and vinegar in a medium bowl. Let stand for 5 minutes.

2. Whisk in the sugar, lemon zest, mustard, salt, and pepper. Continue whisking while adding the canola oil and then the olive oil in a slow, steady stream. Whisk until completely emulsified. Taste and adjust seasonings. The vinaigrette can be transferred to a tightly closed jar and refrigerated for up to 1 week. (Shake well to reemulsify before using.)

3. To make the salad: Line a half sheet pan with parchment paper.

4. Slice off the top and bottom of the grapefruit so that it can sit flat on the cutting board. Using a sawing motion, slice off the peel and white pith in sections until the fruit is exposed all around. Holding the grapefruit over a bowl, slice between the membranes to release the segments into the bowl. Repeat with the orange.

5. Line up three small bowls: In the first, combine the flour, fennel seed, and rosemary. In the second, lightly beat the egg. Put the panko in a third.

6. Using a piece of single-thread kitchen twine or unflavored, unwaxed dental floss, divide the goat cheese into twelve even pieces. Roll each piece into a ball. If the cheese gets too soft, refrigerate until firm.

7. Roll a ball in the seasoned flour, then dunk in the egg. Let the excess egg drip off, then coat with the bread crumbs. Put on the pan. Repeat with the remaining balls and refrigerate until firm, up to 1 day. Preheat the oven to 375°F.

8. Bake the breaded goat cheese until the bread crumbs are golden, about 7 minutes.

9. Meanwhile, toss the arugula and fennel with the vinaigrette until evenly coated. Divide among six serving plates and top with the grapefruit, orange, and almonds. Arrange the goat cheese balls on top and serve immediately.

Mixed Greens, Strawberries, Pecans, and Ricotta Salata with Chocolate Vinaigrette

Serves 6

As a cooking teacher, I sometimes take my students on a journey I've never been on. That's what happened with this salad. For a Valentine's Day menu, I thought, "Chocolate in salad? Why not?" But the first incarnation of this dish had way too much chocolate and it was a gloppy mess. Here's what I do when I screw up: I figure out how to get out of it and make it a good thing. On my next chocolate salad attempt, I added just enough cocoa to the dressing for a subtle nuttiness. Because this vinaigrette packs a punch, add just a few drops at a time to the greens before dragging the dressing through by lightly turning the lettuce. You want the salad lightly dressed here.

CHOCOLATE VINAIGRETTE
2 teaspoons unsweetened cocoa powder
1¼ teaspoons packed brown sugar
½ teaspoon Dijon mustard
½ teaspoon minced shallot
¼ teaspoon minced garlic
2½ tablespoons balsamic vinegar
⅓ cup extra virgin olive oil
Kosher salt and freshly ground black pepper

SALAD
8 to 10 ounces mixed baby greens
1 cup sliced strawberries
One 2-ounce block ricotta salata
¾ cup Cinnamon-Cayenne Pecans (page 8)
Freshly ground black pepper

1. To make the vinaigrette: In a medium bowl, whisk the cocoa, sugar, mustard, shallot, and garlic until well combined. Alternately whisk in the vinegar and oil until the dressing is emulsified. Season to taste with salt and pepper. The vinaigrette can be transferred to a tightly closed jar and refrigerated for up to 1 week. (Shake well to reemulsify before using.)

2. To make the salad: In a large bowl, gently toss the greens and strawberries with vinaigrette until well coated. Divide the salad among 6 serving plates. Use a grater to grate the ricotta salata on top, then sprinkle the pecans over the salad. Grind black pepper directly over the salad and serve immediately.

Mixed Greens and Pan-Roasted Butternut Squash Salad with Apple Cider Vinaigrette

Serves 6

Fall in a bowl! I just love the start of the season. When the harvest rolls in, I take all that gorgeous stuff—the heirloom apples and the squash—and pair them with end-of-the-summer greens. (A mixture of baby greens, baby romaine, and frisée is ideal here.) To get even more out of the apples, I pick up fresh cider from local orchards and reduce it into a beautiful syrup for the dressing. To balance that sweetness, I top this all off with savory sharp aged cheese.

APPLE CIDER VINAIGRETTE

1 cup fresh apple cider
¼ cup cider vinegar
3 tablespoons minced shallot (from about 2 medium)
2 teaspoons Dijon mustard
½ cup canola or other neutral oil
Kosher salt and freshly ground black pepper

SALAD

One 1¼-pound butternut squash, peeled, seeded, and cut into
    ½-inch dice (4 cups)
Extra virgin olive oil
Kosher salt and freshly ground black pepper
8 cups mixed greens
2 crisp, tart apples (such as Granny Smith, Braeburn, Honeycrisp,
    or Stayman), cored and diced
2 ounces aged cheddar or Gouda cheese, shaved with a vegetable
    peeler or cheese plane
½ cup Sweet and Spicy Walnuts (page 7)

1. To make the vinaigrette: In a small saucepan, bring the apple cider to a boil and cook until reduced to ¼ cup. Let cool completely.

2. In a medium bowl, combine the vinegar, shallots, mustard, and reduced apple cider. Whisk well and continue whisking while adding the oil in a slow, steady stream until

emulsified. Season to taste with salt and pepper. The vinaigrette can be transferred to a tightly closed jar and refrigerated for up to 1 week. (Shake well to reemulsify before using.)

3. To make the salad: In a large bowl, toss the squash with just enough oil to lightly coat and season with salt and pepper. Heat a large nonstick skillet over medium heat. Working in batches, add the squash in a single layer, cover, and cook, stirring occasionally, until tender, about 5 minutes. Uncover and cook, tossing occasionally, until browned, about 2 minutes longer. Transfer to a plate. Repeat with the remaining squash. Let cool.

4. In a large bowl, combine the greens, apples, and squash. Gently toss with just enough vinaigrette to lightly coat. Any leftover vinaigrette can be refrigerated for up to 1 week. Divide among six serving plates and top with the cheese and walnuts.

Catering Like Carla

❧ Here's how to a tackle butternut squash: To easily peel the lumpy gourd, just use a vegetable peeler! You may have to go over it a few times to get all the skin off. Then cut it in half lengthwise and scoop out the seeds and pulp with a big spoon. Cut the squash into ½-inch-thick planks, stack 'em up, cut into ½-inch sticks, and finally cut crosswise to dice them.

Lemony Roasted Beets and Arugula with Herb Cheese

Serves 4

I've said it a million times and I'll say it again: "I love lemon." To get the most out of lemon here, I blend the whole fruit with oil. Yes, you really can throw it in a blender! That way, you totally infuse the oil with the floral zest and tart juice. (And you can't taste the bitter pith in the strained oil.) Of course this vinaigrette is great with the beets, homemade herb cheese, and arugula here, but I use it on everything from salads to grilled fish to sautéed vegetables.

ROASTED BEETS

1½ pounds beets, trimmed and scrubbed
2 garlic cloves, crushed and peeled
4 sprigs fresh thyme
1½ teaspoons extra virgin olive oil

HERB CHEESE

4 ounces goat cheese, softened
¼ cup fresh flat-leaf parsley leaves, finely chopped
1 teaspoon fresh thyme leaves, finely chopped
1 tablespoon fresh dill leaves, finely chopped
2 tablespoons freshly grated Parmigiano-Reggiano cheese
Freshly grated zest of ½ lemon
1 garlic clove, minced

LEMON VINAIGRETTE

1 lemon, cut into wedges and seeded
½ cup canola or other neutral oil
2 tablespoons fresh lemon juice
½ teaspoon sugar
¼ teaspoon kosher salt

1 orange
Two 5-ounce packages baby arugula
½ small red onion, very thinly sliced
Kosher salt and freshly ground black pepper

1. To make the beets: Preheat the oven to 350°F. On a large sheet of foil, combine the beets, garlic, thyme, and oil. Wrap tightly and bake until a knife easily pierces the beets, about 1 hour 10 minutes for small ones.

2. Unwrap and discard the garlic and thyme. When cool enough to handle, peel the beets and cut into ½-inch chunks. You can refrigerate the beets for up to 3 days.

3. To make the herb cheese: In a medium bowl, mix the cheese, parsley, thyme, dill, parmesan, lemon, and garlic until very well blended. Transfer to a sheet of plastic wrap and form into a log. Wrap tightly and refrigerate for up to 3 days.

4. To make the dressing: Combine the lemon and the oil in a stand blender. Puree until smooth, stopping to scrape down the sides of the bowl occasionally. Strain through a fine-mesh sieve. You should have ½ cup lemon oil. Transfer to a jar and add the lemon juice, sugar, and salt. Shake well. The dressing can be refrigerated for up to 1 week. (Shake well to reemulsify before using.)

5. Slice off the top and bottom of the orange so that it can sit flat on the cutting board. Using a sawing motion, slice off the peel and white pith in sections until the fruit is exposed all around. Holding the orange over a bowl, slice between the membranes to release the segments into the bowl.

6. In a large bowl, combine the orange, arugula, onion, and beets. Add just enough of the dressing to lightly coat and toss well. Season to taste with salt and pepper. Cut the cheese into ½-inch-thick slices and arrange on top of the salad.

Catering Like Carla

Wanna get fancy with this? You can turn the beets and cheese into sandwiches. Cut the roasted beets into ½-inch-thick slices, place a slice of cheese on one round, top with paper-thin red onion slices, and sandwich with another beet round. Toss the greens and orange with just enough dressing to coat, then drizzle the remaining dressing over the sandwiches. I think it's way too fussy for weeknights, but super fun for dinner parties.

Roasted Carrot Salad

Serves 4

When I go to picnics, I'm so happy when I see a salad like this on the table. It's hearty enough so that it doesn't get all sad and wilted in the sun, but it's not heavy, so you feel light enough on your feet to play around afterwards. The North African–Mediterranean blend of garlic and cumin soaks into the chickpeas and carrots as the salad sits, so it becomes more flavorful over time. It's great as a side dish, but I like to eat it as a light vegetarian lunch, too.

SPICY CUMIN VINAIGRETTE
½ teaspoon finely chopped garlic
⅛ teaspoon kosher salt
1 tablespoon cider vinegar
½ teaspoon Dijon mustard
½ teaspoon cumin seeds, toasted and crushed (page 296)
¼ teaspoon honey
⅛ teaspoon cayenne pepper
2 tablespoons extra virgin olive oil

One 15-ounce can chickpeas, rinsed and drained

SALAD
1 pound carrots (about 6), cut in half lengthwise then into
    ⅓-inch-thick slices at an angle
3 garlic cloves, smashed and peeled
1 teaspoon cumin seeds, toasted (page 296)
1 tablespoon extra virgin olive oil
½ teaspoon kosher salt, plus more to taste
1 cup walnut halves, toasted (page 296)
¼ cup crumbled feta cheese
¼ cup lightly packed fresh cilantro leaves
¼ cup lightly packed fresh mint leaves

1. To make the dressing: In a large bowl, combine the garlic, salt, and vinegar. Let stand for 2 minutes.

2. Add the mustard, cumin, honey, and cayenne. Whisk until well blended. Continue whisking and add the oil in a slow steady stream. When emulsified, add the chickpeas and stir well to coat. Let stand while you roast the carrots.

3. To make the salad: Preheat the oven to 400°F.

4. On a half sheet pan, toss the carrots with the garlic, cumin, oil, and salt until well coated. Roast, shaking the pan occasionally, until tender and browned, about 25 minutes.

5. Discard the garlic, if you'd like. (I love eating roasted whole cloves, but I know not everyone does.) Transfer the hot carrots to the bowl with the chickpeas. Toss until well mixed. Cool slightly, then toss in the walnuts, feta, cilantro, and mint. Season to taste with salt. Serve warm or at room temperature.

Catering Like Carla

❧ The dressed chickpeas and carrots can be refrigerated overnight. Be sure to bring to room temperature before serving.

❧ If you are making this for a picnic or making ahead for entertaining, add the nuts, cheese, and herbs just before serving.

Celery and Blue Cheese Slaw

Serves 4

I created this little slaw as a topping for my Buffalo Wing Burgers (page 211), then I found myself eating it on its own. Yum, yum! I couldn't stop munching on the tangy, savory crunch of the celery and onion with the fresh herbs. Even though I don't like eating blue cheese alone, I like the way the crumbles add a complexity to this simple slaw. The vinegar's nice here because its sharpness cuts through the heat of buffalo wings or any other spicy meat you're chowing down. The quantity here is just enough to top four burgers or to serve as a tidy side for a meal, but you can easily double, triple, or quadruple it.

> 4 celery ribs, thinly sliced at an angle
> ½ small red onion, very thinly sliced (½ cup)
> ½ cup fresh flat-leaf parsley leaves, chopped
> 1 tablespoon red wine vinegar
> 1 tablespoon plus 1 teaspoon extra virgin olive oil
> ½ teaspoon freshly grated lemon zest
> ¼ teaspoon kosher salt
> ⅛ teaspoon freshly ground black pepper
> ¼ cup crumbled blue cheese

In a large bowl, combine the celery, onion, and parsley. Add the vinegar, oil, lemon zest, salt, and pepper and toss well. Gently toss in the blue cheese.

Fennel and Napa Cabbage Slaw with Ginger and Lemongrass

Serves 6

Growing up, I did not like licorice. (In fact, I still don't like black licorice candy.) When I was at my first restaurant kitchen job, I was offered a taste of fresh fennel and was told that it tasted like licorice. I thought I'd hate it! But I immediately fell in love with its fresh crunch and faint sweet aroma. The fresh vegetable and candy share some flavor qualities, but if you hate licorice, you may very well love fennel. When the fresh bulb is thinly sliced and tossed with a fresh acid, it's a match made in heaven. It's most commonly paired with lemon juice, but I love it with lime juice, too—and all the other savory Asian flavors I've combined here. This one little veggie totally transforms Asian-style slaw and kicks it up to the next level of refreshing.

2 garlic cloves, minced
1 teaspoon minced peeled fresh ginger
1 teaspoon minced lemongrass (white and pale
 yellow parts only)
1 teaspoon chili paste
2 tablespoons sugar
½ teaspoon yellow curry powder
1 teaspoon soy sauce
2 tablespoons fresh lime juice
2 tablespoons canola or other neutral oil
2 carrots, peeled
½ small head napa cabbage, shredded (2 cups)
1 fennel bulb, thinly shaved
2 scallions (green onions), trimmed and chopped
½ cup packed fresh cilantro leaves, chopped
¼ cup packed fresh mint leaves, chopped
Kosher salt
2 tablespoons chopped salted peanuts

1. In a large bowl, whisk together the garlic, ginger, lemongrass, chili paste, sugar, curry powder, soy sauce, lime juice, and oil until well mixed.

2. Use a vegetable peeler to peel the carrots into thin ribbons. Add to the dressing along with the cabbage, fennel, scallions, cilantro, and mint. Toss until well mixed. Season to taste with salt. Top with peanuts and serve immediately.

Catering Like Carla

The fastest and simplest way to slice fennel paper-thin is to use a mandoline. You don't have to break the bank buying a fancy French version that takes up a lot of kitchen cabinet space. I prefer the more affordable small Japanese Benriner that fits nicely into a drawer and does the trick. Just be really careful when using any handheld slicer. You gotta keep those fingertips intact!

Sweet and Gold Potato Salad

Serves 6

I'm all about fresh, fresh, fresh. But there are some jarred products that just rock. Sweet relish is one of them. It saves you the hassle of finely dicing pickles and figuring out just how much sugar to add to balance a creamy potato salad. Of course, I've got to add my fresh here: celery, scallions, and herbs bring a bright note to this homey dish.

1 pound Yukon gold potatoes, peeled and cut into ¾ inch dice
1 pound red sweet potatoes, peeled and cut into ¾-inch dice
Kosher salt and freshly ground black pepper
4 large eggs
½ cup mayonnaise
½ cup sour cream
½ cup sweet relish
1 teaspoon Dijon mustard
½ teaspoon cayenne pepper
2 celery ribs with leaves, minced (¾ cup)
3 scallions (green onions), trimmed and finely chopped
¼ cup chopped mixed fresh herbs (preferably a combination
of parsley, thyme, tarragon, and basil)

1. Place all the potatoes in a large pot and add enough cold water to cover by 2 inches. Generously salt the water and bring to a boil over high heat. Reduce the heat to simmer until just tender, about 15 minutes.

2. Drain well, then spread in a single layer on a half sheet pan to cool.

3. Meanwhile, put the eggs in a small saucepan and add enough cold water to cover them by 1 inch. Bring to a boil. Cover the saucepan and remove from the heat. Let stand, covered, for 10 minutes. Don't overcook! Overdone green yolks in any Southerner's potato salad are just plain wrong.

4. Fill a large bowl with cool water. Remove the eggs from the saucepan, gently roll on the counter to crack all over, then place in the cool water. The water will get under the membranes and make the eggs easier to peel. Once they've sat for a little while, peel them. When they're cool, coarsely chop them.

5. In a large bowl, stir the mayonnaise, sour cream, relish, mustard, cayenne, and a pinch each of salt and pepper until well mixed. Add the celery, scallions, herbs, potatoes, and eggs and gently toss to combine. Season to taste with salt and pepper. Serve room temperature or chilled. You can prepare the whole salad, cover, and refrigerate it up to 1 day ahead of time.

Three Bean Salad

Serves 4

If you had to serve lunch to the Securities and Exchange Commission, what would you make? Not easy, right? I had this brilliant idea of bean salad with green beans cut into tiny coins. They're pretty that way and easy to scoop up. I chose color-complementary red beans because they're not so starchy, and limas to round out the dish. That would've been perfect except I thought I could thaw limas the way you do frozen peas—which, by the way, you can't. I wanted the limas just tender but on the crunchy side, but they were un-done-tay (the near opposite of al dente). I tend to err on the side of underdone, but this time, it was just an error. A pot of boiling water saved the day! Lesson learned: You have to blanch lima beans. The end result was a beautiful bean salad.

Kosher salt
½ pound green beans, trimmed and cut into ¼-inch-thick coins
One 10-ounce package frozen baby lima beans
1 garlic clove, minced
2 tablespoons cider vinegar
1 teaspoon Dijon mustard
1 teaspoon freshly grated lemon zest
¼ cup lemon oil (such as O brand Meyer lemon oil),
*   or extra virgin olive oil*
½ small red onion, finely diced (½ cup)
One 15-ounce can small red beans, rinsed and drained
¼ cup fresh dill leaves, coarsely chopped
Freshly ground black pepper

1. Fill a bowl with ice and water. Bring a medium saucepan of water to a boil. Add 2 teaspoons salt, then add the green beans. Cook, stirring occasionally, just until crisp-tender and bright green, about 4 minutes. Drain well and transfer to the ice water. When cool, drain again and transfer to a small bowl.

2. Repeat with the lima beans, cooking for 3 minutes and transferring to a separate container. The green and lima beans can be refrigerated for up to 1 day.

3. In a large bowl, combine the garlic and vinegar and let it sit for a few minutes so that the garlic can mellow out. Whisk in the mustard, lemon zest, and ½ teaspoon salt. Continue

whisking while adding the oil in a slow, steady stream until emulsified. Add the onion, red beans, and lima beans and toss until well mixed. Let stand for 1 hour.

4. When ready to serve, toss in the green beans and dill. (And I mean *really* ready to serve. As soon as the green beans touch the acid, they'll start to discolor.) Season to taste with salt and pepper and serve immediately.

🐕 *Everyday Eating*

Granny's Sunday suppers brought my extended family together once a week, and weeknight meals were bonding times for my mama, my sister Kim, and me. Mama wasn't as much into cooking as her own mama, but she put dinner on the table every night. After she and my dad—who was the *real* cook in the house—divorced, she worked a full-time job as a nurse, ran the household, raised my sister and me, and fed us her hearty ketchup-smothered meatloaf, Aunt Jemima pancakes, and special pot roast with chunks of potatoes and carrots. Somewhere between handling her own life and shuttling us to lessons all the time, Mama managed to sit us down to a proper family dinner every night. It may have all come from boxes and cans, but it was food to be shared together. Mama showed us her unique kind of love in the kitchen and I'm forever grateful.

On the days when she had to work late, my dad's mom would pick up my sister and me, bring us back to her place, and make us some good soul food. Her fried chicken was fantastic and I loved her Hoppin' John with black-eyed peas, too, but I loved even more that connection to my dad's side of the family. My dad and I have similar temperaments and I always had so much fun when he took me fishing. Other times, I would hang out at his father's five-and-dime shop, get a burger, onion rings, and lemon meringue pie and eat out back. Instead of working at his dad's shop, my dad waited tables in restaurants, charming customers with his energy and bright smile.

Young when my parents divorced, I never really knew another daily routine. They were so great about making sure my sister and I were happy and healthy and they kept up a strong friendship over the years. My folks had fallen in love young, participated in the sit-ins together, had my sister and then me, and even married again after their first divorce (only to divorce again a year later). I learned growing up that it didn't matter much what you ate or where you ate it—a family meal's a family meal if you're having it with family. And a family meal could mean just my sister and me and Mama, or grandma and us, or even me at my friend Karen's house. Gettin' people you love together at the table—eating, laughing, sharing—that's a family meal. One worth having every night.

Hoppin' John Salad

Serves 6

For generations, my family prepared Hoppin' John, a savory blend of rice and field peas, with fresh shell peas from their gardens down South. I can only imagine the amazing heirloom varieties of peas they must've grown and enjoyed! Nowadays, if I can get my hands on fresh black-eyed peas, I use them, but most of the time, I used dried beans. They still taste great with rice when doused with a dressing that also wilts the hearty collard greens I've added here. Along with the collards—or kale, if you like—crisp romaine turns this into a full-fledged salad.

Hoppin' John Black-Eyed Pea Confit (page 91)
1 teaspoon ketchup
1 teaspoon tomato paste
1 garlic clove, minced
⅛ teaspoon cayenne pepper, or to taste
¼ cup cider vinegar
1 bunch collard greens
1 romaine heart, thinly sliced crosswise
2 cups cooked long-grain white rice
Kosher salt and freshly ground black pepper

1. Drain the black-eyed peas, reserving the oil. Pick out the thyme and discard. Pick out the garlic and reserve for another use. Pull out the bacon and cut crosswise into ½-inch-wide pieces. Place the bacon in a skillet and cook until browned and crisp. Drain on paper towels and reserve.

2. In a large bowl, whisk the ketchup, tomato paste, garlic, cayenne, vinegar, and ¼ cup of the reserved oil from the peas. Refrigerate the remaining oil in an airtight container for another use.

3. Prepare the collards: Working in batches, hold the stems with one hand and the leaves with the other, folding up the leaves together like the wings on a butterfly. Pull the leaves down, leaving the stems clean. If the leaves are really large, cut them down the center. Stack a few leaves, then roll them like a cigar. Slice the roll crosswise into very thin shreds. Repeat with the remaining leaves.

4. Add the collards to the dressing along with the romaine, rice, and drained peas. Toss until well coated. Season to taste with salt and pepper. Let stand for 30 minutes to 1 hour.

5. Garnish with the crisped bacon and serve.

Catering Like Carla

You can use leftover rice for this salad, but make sure it's neither too sticky nor too dry. The former and your salad will be clumpy, the latter and it'll be hard.

Soups

If I had to create a single dish to tell my story, it'd be a soup, with all those layers of flavors. Soups seem so simple, but they're a "less-is-more" thing, allowing you to showcase seasonal veggies when no other technique makes sense. I like to keep the veggies chunky, suspended in chowders or delicate broths, and I also love to puree them until silky smooth. In both cases, soups are awesome because you can just drop and roll. Drop everything in a pot and roll on with whatever you have to do while they simmer.

The Saints' Gumbo with Andouille Sausage, Chicken, and Crayfish

Serves 6

During a Quickfire challenge on *Top Chef*, I won Super Bowl tickets for making this dish—in 20 minutes. No one in her right mind would even attempt a gumbo in such a short time. But I had no choice but to beat the clock (and the competition!). After that episode, every catering client requested this dish. I must have made a thousand gallons of this soup that year. This gumbo is down-home cooking at its best, but it's only as good as the ingredients you use. Look for high-quality crayfish. If you can't find them, substitute really fresh shrimp. And because much of the spice and smokiness comes from the andouille, it's worth seeking out really tasty sausage.

2 tablespoons unsalted butter
2 tablespoons all-purpose flour
1 tablespoon canola or other neutral oil, plus more for the sausage
1 small yellow onion, finely diced
2 teaspoons minced garlic
Kosher salt and freshly ground black pepper
1 celery rib, finely diced
1 red or yellow bell pepper, stemmed, seeded, and finely diced
1 green bell pepper, stemmed, seeded, and finely diced
1 jalapeño chile, stemmed, seeded, and finely diced
1 andouille sausage link, cut in quarters lengthwise then into
*   1-inch chunks*
12 ounces boneless, skinless chicken thighs, cut into ½-inch
*   chunks (1 cup)*
2 large collard green leaves, thinly sliced (1 cup; see Country Greens
*   on page 87)*
1 tablespoon fresh thyme leaves, finely chopped
1 tablespoon fresh oregano leaves, finely chopped
¼ teaspoon cayenne pepper
½ cup dry white wine
2 cups Chicken Stock (page 54) or store-bought unsalted chicken broth
1 pound shelled crayfish tails (thawed if frozen)
Cooked white rice, for serving

1. In a small saucepan, melt the butter over medium heat. Add the flour and cook, stirring, until well browned. Remove the roux from the heat.

2. In a large saucepot, heat the oil over medium heat. Add the onion and cook, stirring occasionally, until tender and translucent, about 5 minutes. Add the garlic, season with salt and pepper, and stir well. Add the celery, bell peppers, and jalapeño. Season again with salt and pepper and cook, stirring occasionally, until soft, about 10 minutes.

3. While the vegetables cook, heat a skillet over medium-high heat and add just enough oil to coat the bottom. Add the sausage. Cook, turning occasionally, until browned, about 5 minutes. Transfer the sausage to the saucepot of vegetables. In the same skillet, cook the chicken in the rendered fat over medium-high heat, turning occasionally, until browned and cooked through, about 7 minutes. Add to the vegetables and sausage.

4. Stir the collards, thyme, oregano, and cayenne into the meat and vegetables. Continue stirring until the collards wilt. Add the wine, bring to a boil, then simmer until reduced by a third.

5. Add the chicken stock, then stir in the roux. Season to taste with salt and pepper. Bring to a simmer.

6. Just before serving, throw in the crayfish. You don't want them to overcook! Heat them just until cooked through. Serve hot over rice.

Chicken Noodle Soup

Serves 8

A good chicken is worth every penny. My grandma Thelma, my dad's mom, used to buy really good chicken for her fried chicken and it made all the difference. Another way to show off chicken is in this pure, simple form. When you slowly simmer a chicken, you capture all its juicy tenderness. Yum! It's so good! And you get homemade stock out of it, too. Small hormone-free, antibiotic-free organic birds, preferably from a small farm near your home, are best.

That being said, you can throw together this soup if you start with an already cooked rotisserie chicken, too. Discard the skin, pull the meat for the soup, and use the bones and wing tips for the stock.

The seasonings here capture the essence of comfort-in-a-bowl. Ultraclassic and clean. But feel free to toss in other aromatics if you like. Sometimes, I'll stir in tarragon and lemon zest at the end.

> *2 teaspoons extra virgin olive oil*
> *2 medium yellow onions, cut into ¼-inch dice*
> *4 celery ribs, cut into ¼-inch-thick slices*
> *2 garlic cloves, minced*
> *Kosher salt*
> *2 quarts Chicken Stock (recipe follows) or store-bought*
> *   unsalted chicken broth*
> *1 whole cooked chicken (see Chicken Stock, recipe follows)*
> *3 cups extra wide egg noodles*
> *¼ cup chopped fresh dill leaves*
> *Freshly ground black pepper*

1. Bring a large pot of water to a boil for the noodles.

2. Meanwhile, heat a large saucepan over medium heat. Add the olive oil and swirl to coat the bottom of the pan. Add the onions, celery, garlic, and 1 teaspoon salt. Cook, stirring occasionally, until the onion is soft, about 7 minutes. You don't want hard onions here; they'll take away the pleasure of the soup.

3. Stir in the chicken stock and 1 teaspoon salt and heat to a simmer.

4. Remove and discard the skin and bones from the chicken. Pull the meat against the grain into large slivers. Stir the chicken into the soup and heat through.

5. Cook the egg noodles as the package directs. Drain and immediately stir into the simmering chicken soup, along with the dill.

6. Season to taste with salt and pepper and serve immediately.

Catering Like Carla

🍴Timing is everything when it comes to noodles. You don't want to throw them in too early and have them get all soggy and soft, but you also don't want to make them ahead of time and have them sitting around until you're ready to serve. If the cooked noodles get tossed into the soup right after being drained, they soak up the chicken broth and become even more flavorful. Then the whole thing should be served immediately.

🍴Here's what I do if I need to make this ahead: I keep my soup with all the veggies very gently simmering; I have my chicken meat shredded and my dill ready; and I keep a pot of water boiling. You can have this little setup going for half an hour or so while you mingle with your guests before dinner. A few minutes before I'm ready to serve, I cook the noodles in the boiling water, drain 'em, and get them into the soup, along with the chicken and dill. That way, everything tastes fresh and the textures are just perfect.

Chicken Stock

Makes about 3½ quarts

I once tasted some store-bought stock and gagged. I actually had to run to the sink to spit it out. It's not always so bad, but it's never going to be as good as homemade. It's not that stock from scratch is more flavorful (in fact, I leave it unseasoned until I use it); it's that it captures the flavors of whole, fresh ingredients. And that makes all the difference when you're cooking.

I get that stock can be a hassle to make. That's why I'll often make more than I need and freeze the rest in quart-size containers. You can easily double this recipe and use a large stockpot.

If you have a pressure cooker, use it for this recipe, carefully following the manufacturer's instructions. It concentrates the flavors under its ultratight lid and makes the process even faster.

> 1 medium yellow onion, coarsely chopped
> 2 celery ribs, coarsely chopped
> 3 carrots, coarsely chopped
> 1 leek, trimmed, coarsely chopped, and thoroughly rinsed
> 2 sprigs fresh thyme
> 2 fresh sage leaves
> 2 fresh or dried bay leaves
> 1 sprig fresh rosemary
> ½ teaspoon whole black peppercorns
> One 3½-pound chicken, including neck

1. In an 8-quart pot, combine half of the onion, celery, carrots, leeks, thyme, sage, and bay leaves. Place the chicken and its neck on top, then cover with the remaining onion, celery, carrots, leek, thyme, sage, bay leaf, and the rosemary and peppercorns.

2. Add just enough cold water to cover the vegetables on top. Bring to a boil, then reduce the heat to maintain a steady simmer, skimming any foam or scum that rises to the surface, for 1 hour. Do not let it boil or you'll end up with a cloudy stock.

3. Carefully transfer the whole chicken to a large bowl. Reserve for another use or eat it right away (yum!). Strain the broth through a fine-mesh sieve, pressing on the solids to extract as much liquid as possible. Discard the solids. Use the stock immediately, refrigerate for up to 3 days, or freeze for up to 3 months.

Vegetable Stock

Proceed as above, but omit the chicken and double the vegetables. You can also throw in vegetable scraps you may have around, such as asparagus peels, tomato cores, and squash rinds. Other chopped vegetables, such as parsnips, garlic, and potatoes make nice additions, too. For real depth of flavor, stir in 3 tablespoons white miso once the stock starts to simmer.

❧ Starting with Soup

Yes, soup's the best way to start a meal. It's also a great way to start cooking if you're not a regular in your own kitchen. When I was at a healthy eating expo in Las Vegas with Alere Health, I met Patricia, a woman who stopped cooking at home when her son grew up and moved out of the house. She told me, "It's just me now, so I figured I'd eat out." As the years passed, Patricia found herself gaining weight and generally developing an unhealthy eating lifestyle.

I brought Patricia right up on the cooking demo stage with me to teach her how to whip up pea soup, the perfect simple dinner for one. With the whole cooking class cheering her on, Patricia helped me chop onions, simmer the broth, stir in the peas, and blend the whole thing into a creamy, tastes-like-spring soup. When she slurped that first spoonful, she broke into one of the biggest smiles I've ever seen. She said, "I made that! And it's delicious!"

Patricia shared with me that she was surprised at how easy it is to make something healthy from scratch. And when she saw how effortless it is to make a big batch and freeze single portions, she decided then and there to start cooking for herself. I was— and am—so happy for her and for everyone else in the class who was inspired by her to start cooking at home, too. Eventually, I hope they'll move on to other dishes, as well, but homemade soup's an ideal place to begin. Nourishing and comforting, it's a meal to curl up with and be proud of, one that'll make you feel like a great cook.

Groundnut Stew

Serves 4

From West Africa to the American South, this satisfying dish is a mainstay in the black community. That's one of the reasons I did it for one of my *Top Chef* challenges. The other is that it's so yummy. I've simplified my *Top Chef* version, but kept the same flavors and silky texture. I don't like thick, cloying versions, and struck a balance between luscious and light here.

I use hot habanero chile in this stew and start with just a little. After you've simmered the soup but before you put the sweet potatoes in, taste to see if the spice level is where you want it. If you want more heat, just add more chile.

You can enjoy this right away, but if you want even more depth of flavor, just let it sit for an hour at room temperature before reheating it and serving. And this is definitely one of those soups that's better after it sits in the fridge overnight.

1 tablespoon extra virgin olive oil
1 large yellow onion, chopped
½ teaspoon cumin seeds
2 teaspoons kosher salt
1 large red bell pepper, stemmed, seeded, and chopped
1 jalapeño chile, stemmed, seeded, and finely diced
2 garlic cloves, minced
2½ teaspoons grated peeled fresh ginger
One 14.5-ounce can diced fire-roasted tomatoes
1 quart Chicken Stock (page 54) or store-bought unsalted
    chicken broth
1 fresh or dried bay leaf
¼ habanero chile, stemmed, seeded, and minced, plus more
    if you like
1 large sweet potato, peeled and cut into ½-inch dice
One 15-ounce can small red beans, rinsed and drained
3 tablespoons creamy natural peanut butter
¼ teaspoon freshly ground black pepper
½ cup roasted, salted peanuts, chopped
2 tablespoons chopped fresh flat-leaf parsley leaves
1 tablespoon chopped fresh mint leaves
1 lime, cut into wedges

1. Heat a large, deep skillet over medium heat. Add the oil and swirl to coat the bottom of the pan. Add the onion, cumin, and 1 teaspoon salt. Cook, stirring occasionally, until the onion has lightly browned and caramelized a little, about 3 minutes.

2. Add the bell pepper, jalapeño, garlic, and ginger. Cook, stirring, for 1 minute. Don't let the mix burn!

3. Add the tomatoes, stock, bay leaf, ½ teaspoon salt, and the habanero. Bring to a boil over high heat, then reduce the heat to low and simmer for 30 minutes.

4. Stir in the sweet potato and raise the heat to medium. Cook until tender, about 15 minutes, then stir in the beans.

5. Transfer ½ cup liquid from the pan to a small bowl. Stir in the peanut butter until smooth and stir back into the pan. Resist the urge to just throw the peanut butter into the soup; it doesn't work! Stir in the pepper and ½ teaspoon salt or more to taste. At this point, the soup can be refrigerated for up to 3 days.

6. Return the soup to a simmer. Remove and discard the bay leaf. When ready to serve, garnish with the peanuts, parsley, and mint. Serve with the lime wedges.

Oyster Stew

Serves 8

This stew won me a car on *Top Chef,* so, yeah, it's good. Toot! Toot! That's right. I'm tootin' my own horn—and the horn of my new car—over this one. Not because I think I'm so great, but because I learned a really valuable life lesson making this dish.

When we found out that the winner would get a car for this challenge, we really got into the competition. Even though I needed a new car, I still took the time to help anyone who needed help. Lending a tool here, stirring for someone over there. I love my fellow contestants and I wanted to support them. But doing that didn't leave me much time for my own dish. They all promised me they'd help me if I needed anything.

You know where this is going, right? I got my soup simmering and had to shuck the oysters to finish it off. I'll be honest: I didn't know how to open an oyster. At least not quickly. Finally, a kind soul showed me how to do it fast: You hold it firmly with a kitchen towel, slide an oyster knife between the shells at the hinge, then push the knife down while twisting it to pop open the hinge. Once open, you slide the knife around the perimeter of the shell to loosen the top from the bottom, then scrape the knife against the shells to loosen the oyster. It's not too hard, but I had a ton to open for that challenge and no one would help me.

I was really startin' to sweat. I knew I had to go and be fabulous in front of millions of viewers, but that day, I just had to get the job done. And I did. And won a car. So there. But I didn't begrudge my fellow contestants—then or now. I experienced the same pressure they were feeling, so I get it. You don't want to stop to shuck oysters for someone else. But I also don't regret helping them and I'm not just saying that because I won the challenge. I really and sincerely believe in teamwork and helping others, in the kitchen and in life. I'm not just about cooking with love; I'm about living with love. There's a joy and satisfaction in doing unto others and sometimes that's even better than a new car.

And maybe even as good as this oyster stew. It's my take on a Southern classic, using a fumet (the fancy French name for fish stock) as its base. If you don't have the time to make the fish fumet, you can use clam juice instead. Just be careful when seasoning, because clam juice can be very salty. And you don't actually have to shuck oysters yourself, though it can be fun once you master it. Fish counters often sell freshly shucked oysters or the fishmongers will do it for you. (You also need to ask them for the fish bones you'll need for the fumet.) Ask for select oysters and smell them before you take them home. They should smell fresh and sweet, not fishy.

FISH FUMET

2 tablespoons unsalted butter
1 large yellow onion, cut into ½-inch dice
1 carrot, cut in half lengthwise then into ¼-inch-thick half-moons
2 celery ribs, cut into ½-inch-thick slices
1 cup dry white wine
5 pounds fish bones from mild white fish (such as halibut,
    sea bass, or flounder), rinsed well
4 sprigs fresh parsley
2 teaspoons dried thyme leaves
1 fresh or dried bay leaf
1 teaspoon whole white peppercorns

STEW

1 lemon
4 strips bacon, finely chopped
2 celery ribs, finely diced (1 cup)
1 small yellow onion, finely diced (1 cup)
1 medium leek (white and pale green parts only), trimmed,
    finely diced, and thoroughly rinsed (1 cup)
4 sprigs fresh thyme
Kosher salt and freshly ground white pepper
24 oysters, shucked, liquor reserved
1 quart whole milk
2 fresh or dried bay leaves
3 tablespoons unsalted butter
¾ cup all-purpose flour
⅛ teaspoon freshly grated nutmeg
2 teaspoons canola oil (optional)
1 small Yukon gold potato, peeled and finely diced (½ cup)
¼ small celery root, peeled and finely diced (½ cup)
4 scallions (green onions), trimmed and thinly sliced (½ cup)
½ cup heavy cream

1. To make the fumet: In a large saucepot, melt the butter over medium heat. Add the onion, carrot, and celery and cook, stirring occasionally, until the onions are translucent, about 7 minutes. Add the wine and bring to a simmer. Scatter the fish bones on top and add enough cold water to cover by 1 inch. Bring to a simmer and add the parsley, thyme,

bay leaf, and peppercorns. Simmer for 45 minutes, skimming away any scum that accumulates at the surface.

2. Strain the fumet through a fish-mesh sieve; discard the solids. Transfer 1 quart of the strained fumet into a large saucepan. If you have any remaining, refrigerate in an airtight container for another use. Bring to a boil, then adjust the heat to maintain a simmer.

3. To make the stew: With a vegetable peeler, remove strips of lemon peel and reserve. Reserve the lemon for another use.

4. In a large skillet, cook the bacon over medium heat, stirring occasionally, until browned and crisp, about 6 minutes. Use a slotted spoon to transfer the bacon to paper towels to drain. Reserve the bacon fat in a small bowl. (No need to wash the skillet.)

5. In a large saucepot, heat 1 tablespoon bacon fat over medium heat. Add the celery, onion, and leek. Cook, stirring occasionally, until the onion is translucent, about 5 minutes. Add the thyme and lemon peel and cook, stirring occasionally, for 3 minutes. Season with salt and pepper.

6. Add a few oysters to the simmering fish fumet and poach for 2 minutes. Use a slotted spoon to transfer the cooked oysters to a half sheet pan. Repeat with the remaining oysters.

7. Strain the poaching liquid and the reserved oyster liquor through a fine-mesh sieve into the saucepot with the veggies. Add the milk and bay leaves.

8. In the same skillet you used to cook the bacon, melt the butter over medium heat. Whisk in the flour. Continue whisking while slowly adding 1½ cups of the liquid from the saucepot. When fully incorporated, stir the flour mixture back into the saucepot. Stir in the nutmeg. Bring to a simmer and cook, stirring occasionally, until thickened. Season to taste with salt and pepper.

9. In a clean skillet, heat 2 teaspoons bacon fat over medium-high heat. If you don't have enough bacon fat, use canola oil instead. Add the potato and celery root and cook, stirring occasionally, until tender, about 10 minutes. Lower the heat if the vegetables brown too quickly. Remove from the heat and toss in the scallions and reserved bacon.

10. Remove and discard the thyme sprigs, lemon peel, and bay leaves from the stew. Stir the cream into the stew, then stir in the poached oysters. Divide among serving bowls and top with the potato mixture. Serve immediately.

Watermelon Gazpacho with Cucumber, Jicama, Sweet Peppers, and Basil

Serves 6

Over the years, I've done countless versions of this. But for a cooking class full of young lawyers, I streamlined it so that they could throw the soup together after a long day at the office. Because I use every last drop of the accumulated juices from the melon and vegetables, I've made this into a super refreshing soup. The proportions below are what I like, but what I told the students—and what I do myself—is taste and adjust the seasonings at the end. As we all know from picking and eating watermelons, you never quite know what you're gonna get until you open it up.

> One 3-pound seedless watermelon, flesh coarsely chopped,
>   rind discarded
> 1 large cucumber, peeled, seeded, and coarsely chopped
> 1 small red onion, cut into ¼-inch dice
> 1 teaspoon freshly grated lime zest
> 2 tablespoons fresh basil leaves, very thinly sliced, plus ¼ cup,
>   finely chopped
> Kosher salt
> 1 slice sourdough bread, crust discarded, bread torn into small pieces
> 1 medium jicama, peeled and coarsely chopped
> 1 medium yellow bell pepper, stemmed, seeded, and coarsely chopped
> 1 celery rib (preferably an inner pale green one), coarsely chopped
> 2 jalapeño chiles, stemmed, seeded, and coarsely chopped
> 2 garlic cloves, peeled and cut into quarters
> ¾ cup extra virgin olive oil
> 3 tablespoons fresh lime juice
> 2 tablespoons sherry vinegar
> ¼ cup fresh flat-leaf parsley leaves, finely chopped

1. In a small bowl, combine ½ cup each of the watermelon and cucumber and ¼ cup of the onion. Gently toss with the lime zest, sliced basil, and ½ teaspoon salt. Let stand for 1 hour.

2. Strain the mixture through a fine-mesh sieve, reserving the solids and liquid separately. Cover and refrigerate the solids to serve as the garnish.

3. In a medium bowl, combine the strained liquid and the bread. Soak for about 1 minute.

4. In a large bowl, toss the jicama, bell pepper, celery, jalapeños, garlic, the remaining watermelon, cucumber, and onion, and 1½ teaspoons salt until well combined. Add the soaked bread and its liquid to the bowl. Transfer half of the mixture to a stand blender and process for 30 seconds. With the blender running, slowly drizzle in ¼ cup of the oil and continue to blend until completely smooth, about 2 minutes.

5. Strain the puree through a fine-mesh sieve into another large bowl, pressing on the solids to extract as much liquid as possible. Puree and strain the remaining vegetable mixture with the remaining ½ cup olive oil.

6. Stir in the lime juice, vinegar, parsley, and chopped basil. Cover and refrigerate the soup for at least 2 hours and up to overnight. It should be very cold and the flavors should have developed.

7. Divide the gazpacho among six serving bowls. Top with the reserved garnish and serve immediately.

Peacock! Pureed Soups

When I shout, "Peacock!" you know that everything is right with the world. It's how I feel when something I've worked on turns out beautifully—with the effortless drama of a peacock opening his rainbow of feathers. That's what pureed soups are like. You slice and dice, sauté, simmer, blend, strain, and the silky soup at the end tastes and looks gorgeous. Peacock!

Here are a few of my tricks for making pureed soups even easier:

- When you're adding sprigs of fresh herbs in the beginning, be sure to count how many you throw in there. That way, when it's time to take the sprigs out, you know how many to dig around for.

- To get the soups really, really smooth in a stand blender, I turn the speed to high. I keep the machine going until the top of the mixture is a spinning vortex and the rest is silky smooth with no tiny bits left.

- To pour the pureed soup back into the saucepan, I pour it along the curved back of a large spoon to prevent splatters.

- If you're ladling soup into a bowl, dip the bottom of the ladle back into the soup in the pot after scooping to prevent drips.

Summer Vegetables in Green Chile Broth

Serves 6

When it gets warm out, I'm torn between wanting a hot soup and a cold soup. So I've brought the two temperatures together in this light but intense vegetable blend. The base is totally vegetarian, and I give it a depth of flavor by roasting the chiles and garlic and toasting the spices. That piping hot broth goes over a just-cooked medley of green beans, zucchini, corn, and hominy, then a chilled basil-parsley puree finishes it off. It's great getting a hit of hot and cold in each bite!

GREEN CHILE BROTH

2 tablespoons canola or other neutral oil

2 medium yellow onions, cut into ½-inch dice

2 medium leeks (white and pale green parts only), trimmed,
cut in half lengthwise then into ½-inch-thick half-moons,
and thoroughly rinsed

3 celery ribs, cut into ½-inch-thick slices

6 jalapeño chiles, roasted, peeled, stemmed, and seeded (see Notes)

4 garlic cloves, thinly sliced

1 head garlic, roasted, garlic cloves squeezed out of peels,
peels discarded (see Notes)

3 ears corn, husks and silk removed, kernels cut off and reserved,
cobs reserved

2 teaspoons coriander seeds, toasted and ground (page 296)

2 teaspoons cumin seeds, toasted and ground (page 296)

2 fresh or dried bay leaves

2 quarts Vegetable Stock (page 55) or store-bought unsalted
vegetable broth

2 teaspoons kosher salt

1 teaspoon freshly ground black pepper

GREEN PUREE

One 10-ounce package fresh baby spinach

Leaves from 1 bunch fresh basil

Leaves from 1 bunch fresh flat-leaf parsley

2 garlic cloves, sliced

1 tablespoon freshly grated lemon zest

2 tablespoons fresh lemon juice
Kosher salt and freshly ground black pepper

GARNISH
Kosher salt
½ pound green beans, trimmed and cut into
    ¼-inch-thick coins
1 medium zucchini
Canola or other neutral oil
One 28 ounce can hominy, rinsed and drained
Fresh flat-leaf parsley leaves, torn

1. To make the broth: Heat the oil in a large saucepot over medium heat. Add the onions, leeks, celery, jalapeños, and sliced garlic. Cook, stirring occasionally, until the onions are translucent, about 10 minutes.

2. Add the roasted garlic, corn cobs, coriander, cumin, bay leaves, stock, salt, and pepper. Bring to a boil, then cover and reduce the heat to maintain a steady simmer. Simmer for 45 minutes.

3. Remove and discard the corn cobs and bay leaves. Using an immersion blender or stand blender (working in batches if necessary), puree the broth and vegetables until very smooth. Strain through a fine-mesh sieve and discard the solids. Transfer 1 quart of the broth to a container and refrigerate until very cold. To chill it quickly, set the container in a larger bowl filled with ice and water. Keep the remaining broth covered over low heat to keep it hot.

4. To make the puree: Use an immersion blender or stand blender (working in batches if necessary) to puree the spinach, basil, parsley, garlic, lemon zest and juice, and cold broth until very smooth. Strain through a fine-mesh sieve and season with salt and pepper. Refrigerate to keep cold.

5. To make the garnish: Fill a bowl with ice and water. Bring a medium saucepan of water to a boil. Add 2 teaspoons salt, then the green beans. Cook, stirring occasionally, just until crisp-tender and bright green, about 4 minutes. Drain well and transfer the beans to the ice water. When cool, drain again and transfer to a small bowl.

6. Trim the zucchini and cut lengthwise in quarters. Cut out and discard the seeds, then cut into ¼-inch dice. Transfer to a medium bowl and toss in just enough oil to lightly coat.

Season with salt. Heat a large skillet over medium-high heat until hot. Add the zucchini and cook, tossing, until bright green and crisp-tender, about 1 minute. Transfer to a plate. Heat and toss the reserved corn kernels until crisp-tender, then fold in the hominy and heat through.

7. Divide the green beans, zucchini, and corn mixture among six serving bowls. Ladle the hot broth over, then top with the cold puree. Garnish with parsley and serve immediately.

NOTES

To roast jalapeños, place on a hot grill or set directly on the burner grate of a gas stove over an open flame and cook, turning, until blackened and blistered.

To roast a head of garlic, trim off the top ¼ inch. You should be able to see the tops of the cloves. Place the garlic in a small baking dish, cut side up. Drizzle with oil and sprinkle with salt and pepper. Cover tightly with foil, then bake in a 350°F oven until the cloves are tender, about 45 minutes.

Seersucker in Summer Corn Chowder with Tomatoes

Serves 6

Over the past few years, I've been lucky enough to travel the country to cook for charities that I support. Different cities inspire me with their cultures and cuisine and Chicago was no exception when I was there for the TrueChild benefit. I stopped by a farmers' market and couldn't resist scooping up sunny yellow corn, teeny tiny tomatoes, and stunning chanterelles for my take on corn chowder. I like to keep it light, to give it the feel of a seersucker suit in summer. Classy, fun, and never too heavy.

Feel free to use chanterelles here if you want to splurge, but I think it's just as tasty with the less-cost-prohibitive shiitakes. Also, this can easily transform into a heartier main dish. The flavorful, satisfying broth is a great backdrop for fish or shrimp. Simply add chunks of white fish or shrimp to the broth during the last minute or so of simmering to lightly poach them.

CHOWDER

4 ears corn, husks and silks removed
2 tablespoons extra virgin olive oil
1 medium leek (white and pale green parts only), trimmed, cut into ¼-inch slices, and thoroughly rinsed
1 garlic clove, minced
3 sprigs fresh thyme
Kosher salt
1 quart Chicken Stock (page 54) or store-bought unsalted chicken broth
2 cups water
2 large red-skinned potatoes, peeled and cut into ½-inch dice
Freshly ground black pepper

GARNISH

1 cup grape tomatoes, cut into quarters lengthwise
1 teaspoon minced fresh flat-leaf parsley stems

3 tablespoons minced fresh flat-leaf parsley leaves
1 teaspoon unsalted butter
1 sprig fresh thyme
1 garlic clove, crushed
2 tablespoons extra virgin olive oil
16 small shiitake mushroom caps, cut into
      ¼-inch dice
Kosher salt
1 celery rib, thinly sliced

1. To make the chowder: Hold an ear of corn flat on a cutting board, resting on its kernels, not upright. Using a sharp chef's knife, slice the kernels off the cob, cutting about halfway through the kernels. Continue rotating the cob and slicing until all the kernels are cut off. Hold the same ear of corn over a dish. Using the blunt back of the blade, scrape the pulp and milk from the cob. Repeat with the remaining ears; reserve the cobs. You can cover and refrigerate the kernels, corn pulp and milk, and cobs separately up to 1 day ahead.

2. Heat the oil in an 8-quart saucepot over low heat. Add the leek, garlic, thyme, and 1 teaspoon salt. Cook, stirring occasionally, until the leek is tender, about 3 minutes. You don't want any color on the leek, but you also don't want a raw leek flavor in the soup.

3. Add the stock and water. Add the cobs and corn pulp to the pot. Bring to a boil, then reduce the heat to maintain a steady simmer. Simmer for 30 minutes.

4. Remove and discard the corn cobs and thyme sprigs. Stir in the potatoes. Simmer until the potatoes are tender, about 30 minutes.

5. To make the garnish: In a small bowl, toss the tomatoes with the parsley stems and 1 tablespoon of the parsley leaves.

6. Heat a large nonstick skillet over medium-high heat. Add the butter, thyme, garlic, and 1 tablespoon of the oil and swirl to coat the bottom of the pan. Add the mushrooms in a single layer and cook, without stirring, until browned, about 5 minutes. Cook, stirring, for 1 minute more, then stir in the reserved corn kernels and a pinch of salt. Cook, stirring occasionally, until the corn's yellow becomes a little brighter, about 1 minute. You want to do the corn at the very end (what I call ticky boo!) because you don't want the

kernels to get tough. Discard the thyme sprig and garlic. Stir the mushrooms and corn into the chowder.

7. Wipe out the skillet and heat over medium-high. Heat the remaining tablespoon of oil. Add the celery and a pinch of salt and cook, stirring, until just bright green, about 1 minute. Add to the chowder.

8. Stir ¼ teaspoon salt and the remaining 2 tablespoons parsley into the chowder. Season to taste with salt and pepper. Divide the soup among 6 serving bowls. Top with the tomatoes and serve immediately.

Spicy Carrot-Ginger Soup

Serves 6

As a kid, I was a big fan of carrots. Oh, wait, I still am. I love 'em roasted, glazed, as a snack. But nothing beats a silky carrot soup. To bring out carrots' subtle sweetness, I've boosted the flavor in the broth by steeping an herbal tea bag in it and stirring in coconut water. But I balance the sweetness, too, with ginger and chile, then give the whole thing richness by stirring in coconut milk and silken tofu at the end. The result is *mmm-mmm* creamy but with really clean flavors.

I could just eat bowlfuls of this alone, but I originally created it as the base for a fish dish. At the Pebble Beach Food and Wine Festival, I stayed up until three in the morning to puree twenty gallons of this soup so that I could poach bluefish in it. It was a huge hit! Simply reheat the pureed soup until barely simmering, stir in more coconut milk to thin it, and gently poach any oily fish in it. The combination of sweet, heat, and spice in the soup pairs perfectly with rich, fatty fish.

2 tablespoons extra virgin olive oil
1 medium leek (white and pale green parts only), trimmed,
cut in half lengthwise then into ¼-inch-thick half-moons,
and thoroughly rinsed
1 medium yellow onion, coarsely chopped
2 celery ribs, coarsely chopped
5 medium carrots, cut into ½-inch-thick rounds
Kosher salt
One 2-inch piece fresh ginger, cut in half lengthwise, then cut into
¼-inch-thick slices
1 jalapeño chile, stemmed, cut in half lengthwise, and seeded
2 garlic cloves, chopped
½ teaspoon crushed red chile flakes
1 quart Vegetable Stock (page 55) or Chicken Stock (page 54) or store-bought
unsalted broth
2 cups coconut water
1 high-quality lemon-ginger tea bag, paper tag removed
⅔ cup silken tofu
⅔ cup light coconut milk
Freshly ground black pepper
¼ cup unsweetened flaked coconut, toasted (see Note)

1. Heat a large saucepan over medium-high heat. Add 1 tablespoon oil and heat until it dimples and squiggles. Add the leek, onion, and celery and stir until well coated with the oil. Add the carrots and ¾ teaspoon salt. Cook, stirring occasionally, until the onion is just translucent but not soft, about 5 minutes.

2. Add the ginger, jalapeño, garlic, and chile flakes. Cook, stirring, until the vegetables are caramelized, about 4 minutes. You really want to bring out the brown richness of the veggies here.

3. Stir in the stock and coconut water. Bring to a boil, reduce the heat to maintain a simmer, and add the tea bag. Simmer until the carrots can be mashed easily with a wooden spoon, about 30 minutes.

4. Remove and discard the tea bag. Stir in the tofu and coconut milk. Using an immersion blender or stand blender (working in batches if necessary), puree until very smooth. Strain through a fine-mesh sieve. Season to taste with salt and pepper.

5. Reheat to serve the soup hot or chill it to serve cold. Garnish with coconut flakes just before serving.

NOTE

To toast coconut, spread the flakes in a layer on a half sheet pan and bake at 325°F until golden brown and crisp, stirring occasionally. Don't let 'em burn! Cool completely before using.

Tomato–Sweet Potato Bisque

Serves 6

Last Thanksgiving my nephew had dental surgery just before the feast. I felt so bad that he couldn't chew, I told him I'd make him tomato soup. "Um, no!" was his teenage response. I know he's a picky eater, but I made it anyway. He tore this soup up! There wasn't a drop left in his bowl and he kept coming back for more. Just goes to show you should feed picky eaters what they think they don't like. You never know. I didn't like tomatoes when I was growing up because I thought they were too acidic. That's why I pair them with sweet potatoes here; their starchy earthiness tempers the tomato's acid. The result is creamy, naturally sweet, and deeply satisfying.

2 tablespoons extra virgin olive oil
2 medium carrots, coarsely chopped
1 celery rib, coarsely chopped
1 jumbo sweet onion, coarsely chopped
Kosher salt
1 jalapeño chile, stemmed, seeded, and chopped
4 garlic cloves, chopped
2 sprigs fresh thyme
4 fresh basil leaves
One 14.5-ounce can diced fire-roasted tomatoes
1 quart Vegetable Stock (page 55) or store-bought unsalted
    vegetable broth, plus more if desired
1 medium sweet potato, peeled and chopped
¼ cup heavy cream
Freshly ground black pepper

1. Heat a large saucepan over medium-high heat. Add the oil and heat until just hot. Add the carrot, celery, onion, and ½ teaspoon salt. Cook, stirring occasionally, until the onions just turn translucent, about 5 minutes.

2. Add the jalapeño, garlic, thyme, and basil. Cook, stirring occasionally, until the vegetables are nice and brown, about 7 minutes.

3. Stir in the tomatoes with their juices, then stir in the stock and sweet potato. Bring to a boil, then reduce the heat to maintain a steady simmer. Simmer until the sweet potato is

very, very tender, about 1 hour. The sweet potatoes should be soft enough to mash easily with the back of a spoon.

4. Remove and discard the thyme sprigs. Using an immersion blender or stand blender (working in batches if necessary), puree until silky smooth. Reheat the soup over low heat. Stir in the cream. For a thinner soup, stir in more stock. Season to taste with salt and pepper and serve hot.

Catering Like Carla

🍴 Strain through a fine-mesh sieve for a more refined soup.

🍴 Use silken tofu, blended until smooth, in place of the cream to make this a dairy-free soup.

🐚 *My Journey*

Believe it or not, I didn't really start cooking until I was almost thirty. In my first post-college apartment, I threw a small dinner party for a couple of friends—or at least I tried to. I was working as a CPA in Florida and had never cooked a real meal before, so I decided I couldn't mess up vegetable soup. Let's just say I was *so* wrong. I don't know how many cans of tomato paste I used for that one pot of soup, but my friend Rhonda gasped, "Ugh, I'm sorry, but what *is* this?" When I explained that it was vegetable soup, not a concentrated tomato sauce, she replied, "You know what? How about we go out to eat?" Only later did my friends admit how bad that red stuff really was. I still love those friends dearly, and Rhonda and I now laugh about that night, but the love definitely didn't come through my food that day.

But it wasn't that tomato paste disaster that got me cooking for real; it was an audit. While taking an inventory of I-beams for my job in central Florida in the middle of what felt like a 200-degree day, I was burning hot under the sun reflecting off those long pieces of steel, like an ant under a magnifying glass. I just stood there, sweating, and watched the middle-aged auditor with whom I was working fold and line up the corners of a receipt for one whole minute. I thought to myself with horror, "This can't be me." I was gripped by a fear of being forty and hating my job. So I quit the "good" job I supposedly went to college for, packed my bags, gave my CPA certificate to my mother, and moved to France armed with one telephone number, a hotel reservation, and ten French words. I was going to be a model in the fashion industry, not to learn about food—but I started really eating and tasting and teaching myself to cook there.

One of my most memorable meals was with my cousin, who happened to be attending school in France. We found one of those uniquely Parisian restaurants, where you can sit at a table forever without being shooed out the door. I can't even remember my main course, a salad maybe, but *dessert*. Oh. My. God. It was *the* best blueberry pie I'd ever had. Inside the flaky crust were these tiny wild blueberries bound by a smooth sauce. With just the right hit of lemon, it had this perfectly balanced sweetness. I was in heaven. Pie in Paris may not be as romantic as macarons, but it was just what I wanted at that simple meal. It reminded me of home and all the love at the dinner table that I missed while living so far away. It took a slice of blueberry pie across the Atlantic for me to recognize just how much I cherished my home and the food I ate growing up.

When I was in high school, I was convinced that I had to get out of the South if I ever wanted to make it. I was an aspiring actor and my teacher, a native New Yorker with dark green tinted glasses and a deep raspy voice, was my she-ro. I admired and adored her.

She instructed me, "You have to get rid of that Southern accent if you want to be an actor who actually gets work." After I left for college, I kept going farther away, in every sense of the word. And yet, when I was in France, the food that brought me the most comfort was a pie that reminded me of the berry cobbler Granny used to make. Food memories are so powerful!

The same was true in Italy. During a trip to Milan for the runway shows, a fellow model and I went searching for some lunch. We stopped by a pizza place where the guy behind the counter took out a pair of scissors to cut the huge slice we had decided to share. I thought that was the craziest thing—until I took a bite of the pizza. Ooh, now *that* was crazy good, the best pizza I'd ever eaten, with this crisp-bottomed, perfectly doughy crust. On top was a light smear of tomato sauce with a little cheese and basil. We just kept saying, almost in a chant, "Oh, my god, this is so good. This is so good." (Yes, models do love to eat!) That pizza brought back memories of home, too, but tasted a million times better than anything I'd ever had. For the first time, I realized that familiar foods could taste different from the versions I already knew and still bring comfort.

So when I started to teach myself to cook in Europe, I wanted to make the dishes I loved from home and explore the endless possibilities of making them even better. When I returned to the United States, I turned those self-taught dishes into a lunch business. From there, I attended culinary school and worked as a chef in several high-end restaurant kitchens before starting my own catering company. Even as I expanded my cooking skills, I always stayed focused on trying to create in my food that comfort that only home can bring, and I'm a better chef for it. At each stage, I learned great culinary techniques to achieve just that.

Remember that tomato thing? Well, now I make an amazing tomato and sweet potato bisque, if I do say so myself. When I was homesick in France, I decided to make chicken pot pie. The local market didn't have celery, but it had this other pale green thing that looked celery-ish. Well, not really, but I needed something, so I used that instead. It was all wrong in my chicken pie—it cooked up soft and sweet instead of savory and crunchy—but it was a great discovery. That was the first time I'd ever seen or tasted a leek and it soon became one of my favorite ingredients. I use it now to flavor my cod en papillote and in my mushroom tart.

In every stage of my career, I find myself returning time and again to the Southern food I grew up eating, but that hasn't stopped me from embracing dishes that I fell for in France and Italy. What really ties my food and my life together is the love and comfort that I get from cooking for others. I can't, and don't want to, say that I only make one type of food, and you shouldn't, either. Cooking is all about discovering new tastes from around the world, then finding your way home again in the kitchen.

Creamy Potato and Garlic Soup with Pumpernickel Croutons

Serves 6

Growing up, I would never have imagined that I'd like, let alone make, a garlic soup. But chef Robert Thompson at the Henley Park Hotel in Washington, D.C., a wonderful mentor and the first chef I worked under, proved me wrong. He taught me so many classic French techniques and one is the way in which sharp garlic mellows into a complex sweetness when slowly cooked. In fact, all alliums do. That's why I like to combine four here—garlic, onion, leek, and shallot—to bring a rich depth of flavor to a classic potato soup. Creamy, sweet, and super satisfying. You could skip the croutons, but I don't recommend it. A salty, crunchy bite in each creamy spoonful takes this over the top.

2 large heads garlic
2 tablespoons unsalted butter
1 tablespoon canola or other neutral oil
1 medium yellow onion, thinly sliced
2 medium leeks (white and pale green parts only), trimmed,
*   thinly sliced, and thoroughly rinsed*
2 shallots, very thinly sliced
4 sprigs fresh thyme
Kosher salt
3 large russet potatoes, peeled and cut into ⅓-inch dice
2 cups whole milk
1 fresh or dried bay leaf
1 quart Chicken Stock (page 54) or store-bought unsalted
*   chicken broth*
3 slices pumpernickel bread, cut into ¼-inch dice
1 tablespoon extra virgin olive oil
¼ cup heavy cream
⅛ teaspoon freshly grated nutmeg
Freshly ground black pepper

1. Cut the base off the heads of garlic to separate the cloves. Immerse the cloves in a bowl of cold water and let stand for 5 minutes. The water will help the garlic cloves slip right out of their skins. You should have ½ cup cloves.

2. Heat a large, wide saucepan over low heat. Add the butter and canola oil and heat until the butter melts. Add the garlic cloves, onion, leeks, shallots, thyme, and 1 teaspoon salt. Cook, stirring occasionally, until the onion is translucent but not browned, about 7 minutes.

3. Stir in the potatoes, milk, bay leaf, and 2 cups of the stock. Bring to a boil, then reduce the heat to maintain a steady simmer. Simmer until the potatoes are very tender, about 1 hour.

4. While the soup simmers, preheat the oven to 300°F. On a half sheet pan, toss the bread with the olive oil and ¼ teaspoon salt. Spread in a single layer and bake until browned and crisp, about 20 minutes.

5. Remove the thyme sprigs and bay leaf from the soup. Using an immersion blender or stand blender (working in batches if necessary), puree the potatoes and liquid until just smooth. Return the soup to the saucepan (if using a stand blender) and stir in the cream, the remaining 2 cups chicken stock, and 1 teaspoon salt. Heat through over low heat and stir in the nutmeg. Season to taste with salt and pepper. Serve hot with the croutons.

Fennel and Celery Root Soup

Serves 8

For a clean taste of fall, start here. Fennel has a fresh anise flavor and celery root is like a more flavorful and less starchy potato. Together, they blend into a creamy soup that toes the line between end-of-summer freshness and chilly-days-ahead warmth. It's important to begin this recipe by cutting the onion and fennel into paper-thin slices, because you want them to melt down together. You should use a mandoline if you have one or cut the vegetables with a very sharp knife.

> 2½ tablespoons extra virgin olive oil
> 1 medium yellow onion, very thinly sliced
> 3 small heads fennel, stalks discarded, fronds reserved,
>   bulbs very thinly sliced
> Kosher salt
> 1 tablespoon unsalted butter
> 1 large leek (white and pale green parts only), trimmed,
>   thinly sliced, and thoroughly rinsed
> Freshly grated zest of 1 lemon
> 2 medium celery roots, peeled and coarsely chopped
> 1½ quarts Chicken Stock (page 54) or store-bought
>   unsalted chicken broth, plus more if desired
> 1 teaspoon fennel seeds, toasted (page 296)
> 2 fresh or dried bay leaves
> Freshly ground black pepper
> 2 tablespoons heavy cream
> 1 ripe Bosc pear, peeled, cored, and cut into
>   ¼-inch dice

1. Heat an 8-quart saucepot over medium-high heat. Add the olive oil and heat until it dimples. Add the onion, sliced fennel, and 1 teaspoon salt and stir well until everything is evenly coated with the oil. Cook, stirring frequently, until very soft but not browned, about 5 minutes. You really want the onion and fennel to get nice and sweet here.

2. Reduce the heat to medium and add the butter, leek, and half of the lemon zest. Cook, stirring occasionally, until softened, about 4 minutes.

3. Add the celery roots, chicken stock, fennel seeds, bay leaves, and a pinch of pepper. Bring to a boil, then reduce the heat to maintain a steady simmer. Simmer until the celery root is very tender, about 1 hour.

4. Remove and discard the bay leaves. Using an immersion blender or stand blender (working in batches if necessary), puree the mixture until smooth. Strain through a fine-mesh sieve. Return the soup to the saucepan and heat on low. Stir in the cream. For a thinner soup, stir in more stock.

5. Finely chop ¼ cup of the reserved fennel fronds; discard the rest. Stir 1 tablespoon fronds into the soup. In a small bowl, toss the remaining fronds with the pear and the remaining lemon zest.

6. Divide the soup among eight serving bowls. Top with the pears. Serve immediately.

Side Dishes

Veggies are the most important food group. Really, they are. Sure, they're good for you, but I love them because they taste so good. Instead of starting my menus with meat, I think first about vegetables, then build out my meals from there. Every season, there are so many options to choose from, sweet roots to bitter greens to a rainbow of freshness. And the techniques are simple: oven- or pan-roasting them to heighten flavor in their browning, sautéing greens just to wilt and brighten them. Seasoning simply—with ingredients like olive oil, garlic, thyme, and chiles—brings out their freshness and makes any meal really delicious.

Country Greens

Serves 8

No Southern meal is complete without greens. Traditionally, they're simmered long and slow until melty and soft. I love 'em that way, but actually prefer a little bite to them—both in their mustardy flavor and hearty leafy texture.

Growing up in the South, I learned that the greens were sometimes besides the point. The pot likker, the leftover cooking broth, is what really matters, at least as much as the greens themselves. Traditionally, salt pork simmers alongside the greens to flavor the likker. I use smoked turkey wings to get a broth that's just as tasty but has even more complex gamey, savory flavors. Be sure to serve this with Skillet Cornbread (page 111) for sopping. And save any leftover likker to make soup.

> *2 pounds smoked turkey wings*
> *1 teaspoon minced garlic*
> *1 teaspoon crushed red chile flakes*
> *2 quarts water*
> *2 pounds collard greens, rinsed and dried*
> *2 pounds kale, rinsed and dried*
> *Kosher salt and freshly ground black pepper*

1. In a large pot, combine the turkey, garlic, chile flakes, and water. Bring to a boil over high heat, then reduce the heat to simmer for 30 minutes.

2. Meanwhile, prepare the greens: Working in batches, hold the stems of the collards with one hand and the leaves with the other, folding up the leaves together like the wings on a butterfly. Pull the leaves down, leaving the stems clean. If the leaves are really large, cut them down the center. Stack a few leaves, then roll them like a cigar. Slice the roll into thin shreds. Repeat with the remaining collard leaves, then with the kale.

3. Add the sliced greens to the pot and simmer until tender, about 20 minutes. Season to taste with salt and pepper.

4. Remove the wings and let cool until you can handle them. Pull the meat from the wings, discard the bones, and return the meat to the pot. Serve hot.

Sautéed Collard Greens with Brussels Sprout Leaves and Gremolata

Serves 8

I cooked professionally for a long time before I returned to my Southern roots. It took me even longer to realize that I didn't have to make comfort food exactly like Granny. I love her more than anyone; she's always been my guiding light and inspiration. When I started playing with the soul food flavors I grew up savoring at Granny's table, I came to appreciate her influence even more.

Case in point: collard greens. I had only ever known them braised. On a whim, I sautéed thin ribbons. Um, why hadn't I done it before? I love the leaves just tender, and decided to add an Italian twist by adding gremolata at the end. The bright lemon-parsley-garlic combo just heightens the flavors and makes them go *ding*! This dish is super simple, but it'll make you feel like a pro with its bright blend of fresh fall greens.

GREMOLATA

Freshly grated zest of 1 lemon
1 garlic clove, minced
¼ cup fresh flat-leaf parsley leaves, chopped
1 teaspoon extra virgin olive oil
½ teaspoon kosher salt
¼ teaspoon freshly ground black pepper

GREENS

3 bunches collard greens (3 pounds), rinsed and dried
Kosher salt
12 Brussels sprouts, trimmed, leaves separated, rinsed, and dried
3 tablespoons extra virgin olive oil
2 garlic cloves, peeled
1 teaspoon crushed red chile flakes
¼ cup Chicken Stock (page 54) or Vegetable Stock (page 55)
     or store-bought unsalted broth
Freshly ground black pepper

1. To make the gremolata: In a small bowl, combine the lemon zest, garlic, parsley, oil, salt, and pepper. Stir until well mixed.

2. To make the greens: Thinly slice the collard greens using the technique for Country Greens (page 87).

3. Fill a bowl with ice and water. Bring a small saucepan of water to a boil. Add 1 teaspoon salt, then add the Brussels sprout leaves. Cook, stirring occasionally, just until crisp-tender and bright green, about 20 seconds. Drain well and transfer to the ice water. When cool, drain again.

4. Heat a large saucepot over medium-high heat. Heat the oil, then add half the collard greens. Cook, stirring, until wilted, about 1 minute. Add the remaining collards and cook, stirring, until wilted, about 1 minute longer. Season with salt and stir well.

5. Add the garlic and chile flakes, then stir in the stock. Bring to a boil, then reduce the heat to maintain a steady simmer. Cook, stirring occasionally, until the greens are tender and wilted down and the liquid evaporates, about 10 minutes. Discard the garlic.

6. Stir in the Brussels sprout leaves and gremolata until well mixed. Season to taste with salt and pepper. Serve immediately.

Catering Like Carla

❧Separating Brussels sprouts into individual leaves seems painstaking, right? Yeah, it sorta is. The easiest way to do it is to trim the bottoms then cut them in half from top to stem. Then pick the leaves off, one by one.

🫕 *Home Again*

I've become known for my Southern food, but the truth is I didn't always love cooking comfort food. In fact, when I began cooking professionally and refining my French techniques, I shied away from comfort classics. I wanted to print on my business card: "Catering by Carla—I don't do meatballs or fried chicken." But over time, I learned that I could bring the same techniques, obsession with quality ingredients, sophisticated seasonings and presentation, and passion for authenticity to any type of cuisine. In other words, I can cook any cuisine with love. And so can you.

One day, I decided to take the plunge and make fried chicken for a group of longstanding and loyal catering clients. Child, you would've thought I had made them *foie gras,* they were so surprised and excited. That was a good day. It's fun to see your customers get excited by your food, and it was a turning point in helping me return to my culinary past. I had become confident in my exploration of Mediterranean, Asian, and other global dishes—I could turn out a mean red pepper risotto and Persian grilled lamb—and I was ready to embrace the down-home dishes I grew up loving. I was even ready to add my own global, elegant updates to them, as I do in my duck ragù over butternut squash grits.

My soulful food instincts were reaffirmed again—on national television. On *Top Chef,* I put out great French dishes like a deconstructed bouillabaisse, which I've since turned into a bouillabaisse sauce with roasted red snapper, but the fans were telling me to embrace my native Southern food. In that high-stakes environment, I listened to the fans and turned to what I know best: Granny's Southern cooking and baking (not to forget Grandma Hall and my dad). And I started to have fun making my food! (Easier said than done on TV, trust me.) When Jacques Pépin challenged me to create what he would want for his "last supper"—squab and peas—I conjured the spirit of Granny's Sunday suppers and my love of green peas. I was so happy to be working with one of my favorite ingredients, and so was Chef Pépin. In fact, he said he could "die happy" after eating that dish. Teehee. That's right.

Hugging Jacques Pépin with my Granny's food—I guess that kind of sums up what my cooking is all about. A joyful and sophisticated marriage of French techniques, global flavors, and Southern soul.

Hoppin' John Black-Eyed Pea Confit

Serves 6

Every New Year's Eve of my childhood, I ate bowls and bowls of black-eyed peas. They were simply simmered and super satisfying. Best of all, they brought good luck for the year ahead.

To make a good thing even better, I cook my black-eyed peas in olive oil. (*Confit* is a classic French technique for slowly cooking, then preserving, food in fat, and is most commonly associated with duck.) The peas impart an earthiness to the fruity oil and get plumped with richness. Don't be afraid of the amount of oil here! You're not eating it all in one go. Enjoy some with the peas, then strain the rest to make your next batch of peas or to drizzle over a salad, meat, fish, bread, or just about anything you can think of. All the flavor's in that fat and you want to get it any way you can.

> *½ pound dried black-eyed peas (scant 1¼ cups),*
> *picked over, rinsed, and shaken well until dry*
> *1½ cups extra virgin olive oil*
> *3 strips thick-cut bacon, cut in half crosswise*
> *6 garlic cloves, smashed and peeled*
> *7 sprigs fresh thyme*
> *½ teaspoon crushed red chile flakes*
> *¼ teaspoon kosher salt*

1. Place the black-eyed peas in a large saucepot and add enough cold water to cover by about 2 inches. (When your fingertip touches the peas, the water should come to your second knuckle.) Bring to a boil over high heat, then reduce the heat to maintain a steady simmer. Cook, stirring occasionally, until the peas are just tender but still intact, about 30 minutes. You don't want them to fall apart. Drain well and spread on a half sheet pan to cool.

2. Meanwhile, preheat the oven to 300°F.

3. In a large ovenproof saucepan, combine the oil, bacon, garlic, thyme, chile flakes, and salt. Heat over medium heat until bubbles begin to form on the surface. Carefully stir in the peas, then transfer to the oven.

4. Bake uncovered until the garlic is very soft, about 45 minutes.

5. Serve warm as is with Skillet Cornbread (page 111) and Country Greens (page 87), turn into Hoppin' John Salad (page 47), serve just the beans with rice and reserve the oil for future uses, spread the garlic on toast, or do whatever you want with it. The possibilities are endless! However you serve it, enjoy!

"Creamed" Corn

Serves 6

I'm all about the side dishes on a Southern spread. When I go to a soul food restaurant, I order only sides. I can never decide which ones I want, so I pass on the meat. It takes the place of two sides! And creamed corn has always been one of my favorites. When I was a kid, I even liked (okay, luuuuuved) the canned stuff. But the homemade version my aunt made was so much better. Any Southerner worth her salt knows how to make creamed corn and knows that from-scratch is best. The reason? The "cream" comes from the corn itself. When you scrape all the juicy milk from the cob, you get its natural sweet starchiness, which lends a silky mouthfeel and an extra boost of corny-ness to this simple side. When I have a bowl of this goodness, I can just call it a day.

> 6 ears corn, husks and silk removed
> 2 tablespoons unsalted butter
> 1 shallot, minced
> 2 sprigs fresh thyme
> 1 teaspoon sugar
> Kosher salt and freshly ground black pepper

1. Hold an ear of corn flat on a cutting board, resting on its kernels, not upright. Using a sharp chef's knife, slice the kernels off the cob, cutting about halfway through the kernels. Continue rotating the cob and slicing until all the kernels are cut off. Hold the same ear of corn over a dish. Using the blunt back of the blade, scrape the pulp and milk from the cob. Repeat with the remaining ears. Discard the cobs. You can cover and refrigerate the kernels and the corn pulp and milk separately up to 1 day ahead.

2. Heat a medium skillet over low heat. Add the butter and melt. Add the shallot and thyme and cook, stirring occasionally, until the shallot is translucent, about 2 minutes.

3. Raise the heat to medium. Add the corn kernels and sugar. Cook, stirring continuously, until the corn is crisp-tender and deep yellow, about 10 minutes. Stir in the corn pulp and cook just until heated through, stirring. Season to taste with salt and pepper. Serve warm.

Smashed Herbed Potatoes

Serves 4

Don't be fooled. These aren't mashed potatoes. They're potatoes that get smashed, just a little, to open them up so that they can soak up buttery, herby goodness. Sweet caramelized red onion clings to the crags in the little potatoes. When I first made these, I fried the potatoes after smashing them. They're awesome that way, too, but this way, you get more pure potato—and fewer calories! That's why I love making them with the freshest new spring potatoes I can find at farmers' markets. This is great with a Sunday roast, or for a light lunch with a nice salad.

> 2 tablespoons extra virgin olive oil
> 1 small red onion, thinly sliced
> Kosher salt and freshly ground black pepper
> 1 pound new baby potatoes, scrubbed
> 2½ cups Chicken Stock (page 54) or store-bought
>   unsalted chicken broth
> 1 tablespoon unsalted butter
> 2 tablespoons mixed fresh herbs (preferably a combination
>   of thyme, flat-leaf parsley, rosemary, and sage), finely chopped

1. Heat a large saucepan over medium heat. Add the oil and heat, then add the onion, season lightly with salt and pepper, and cook, stirring occasionally, until just tender and lightly browned, about 2 minutes.

2. Add the potatoes and toss until well coated. Pour the stock over the potatoes, add 1 teaspoon salt, cover, and bring to a boil. Adjust the heat to maintain a steady simmer and cook, turning the potatoes every 5 minutes, until the potatoes are tender, about 15 minutes.

3. Uncover and raise the heat to medium-high. Cook until the stock has reduced by half and thickened enough to coat the potatoes, about 7 minutes. The pan will be almost dry and the stock the consistency of a thin batter.

4. Remove the pan from the heat. With a slotted spoon, transfer the potatoes to a large dish and let stand until cool enough to handle, about 5 minutes. Using the bottom of a cup, gently smash the potatoes just until they break open.

5. Return the potatoes to the saucepan and toss gently with the onions. Reheat over medium-low heat until warmed through. Add the butter, herbs, and a pinch of salt. Toss gently until the butter melts. Season to taste with salt and pepper.

Root Vegetable Ragout

Serves 6

For the fall, I like to combine all my favorite root veggies in a single dish. I used to turn them into a tasty gratin, but boy, that's fattening and time-consuming. This is a nice, light alternative that brings out the best in the natural earthy sweetness of the roots. You've got to try this with Pork Tenderloin Medallions (page 169). It's also great with roasted duck.

2 medium carrots
2 medium parsnips
1 small rutabaga
1 medium turnip
1 medium Yukon gold potato
2½ tablespoons extra virgin olive oil
Kosher salt
1 small yellow onion, cut into ¼-inch dice
1 tablespoon unsalted butter
½ cup Chicken Stock (page 54) or store-bought unsalted chicken broth
Freshly ground black pepper
2 tablespoons fresh flat-leaf parsley leaves, chopped
2 tablespoons fresh thyme leaves, chopped
Freshly grated zest of 1 lemon

1. Preheat the oven to 425°F.

2. Peel the carrots, parsnips, rutabaga, turnip, and potato and cut them into ½-inch dice. Combine them on a half sheet pan, toss with 2 tablespoons of the olive oil, and season with salt. Spread the vegetables in a single layer.

3. Roast, stirring and rotating the pan occasionally, until tender and golden, about 25 minutes.

4. Meanwhile, heat a large skillet over medium heat. Heat the remaining ½ tablespoon oil. Add the onion and cook, stirring frequently, until tender, about 3 minutes.

5. Stir in the butter until it melts, then stir in the roasted vegetables. Add the chicken stock and season with salt and pepper. Simmer until the stock thickens and coats the vegetables, about 3 minutes. Stir in the parsley, thyme, and lemon zest. Serve hot or warm.

Roasted Baby Carrots

Serves 8

I'm not talking about the baby carrots sold as snacks. Those tiny torpedos don't have much flavor and they cook up weird. I'm talking about gorgeous young carrots, about 5 inches long and tapered, with pert green tops, available at farmers' markets. They're extra tender because they're young, and have a vegetal, green sweetness. Be sure to use a duller peeler on them and turn them carefully so that you only remove a single strip of peel all around. Otherwise you'll end up peeling them into pencils. If you can't find baby carrots, just peel big ones and cut them into 5-inch lengths, ½ inch in diameter.

When these babies come out of the oven, they're beautifully caramelized even before they're glazed with a touch of honey syrup. They're so simple and satisfying, they can be stars on their own, but taste great with everything.

2 pounds baby carrots, trimmed and peeled
2 tablespoons extra virgin olive oil
½ teaspoon kosher salt
5 garlic cloves, peeled
8 sprigs fresh thyme
¼ cup cider vinegar
2 teaspoons honey

1. Preheat the oven to 475°F.

2. On a half sheet pan, toss together the carrots, oil, salt, 4 of the garlic cloves, and 7 of the thyme sprigs until well coated.

3. Roast until the carrots are browned and tender, about 25 minutes. Discard the garlic and thyme.

4. Meanwhile, in a small saucepan, combine the vinegar, the remaining garlic clove, and the remaining thyme sprig. Bring to a boil and reduce the liquid to 1 tablespoon, about 7 minutes. Remove from the heat and stir in the honey. Discard the garlic and thyme.

5. Pour the honey sauce over the hot carrots and turn until well coated. Serve hot or at room temperature.

Spicy Sweet Potato Puree

Serves 4

For a few winters, I cooked for a family on a breathtakingly beautiful island in the Bahamas. Surrounded by blue water, I was inspired to create this dish. There's nothing more satisfying than the earthy sweetness of these orange potatoes paired with tangy citrus and fiery chile and spices. This simple side is as tasty with tofu as it is with pork.

3 medium sweet potatoes
½ cup Chicken Stock (page 54) or store-bought unsalted
chicken broth
½ cup heavy cream
Two 3-inch strips lime zest, removed with a vegetable
peeler
1 tablespoon fresh lime juice
1 garlic clove, minced
½ teaspoon finely chopped jalapeño
1 teaspoon yellow mustard seeds, toasted (page 296)
1 teaspoon whole coriander seeds, toasted (page 296)
Kosher salt and freshly ground black pepper
1 tablespoon unsalted butter

1. Preheat the oven to 375°F. Line a half sheet pan with parchment paper.

2. Put the sweet potatoes on the pan and roast until soft enough for a knife to pierce through easily, about 40 minutes. Let cool slightly.

3. In a medium saucepan, combine the stock, cream, lime zest and juice, garlic, jalapeño, mustard, and coriander. Bring to a boil and season to taste with salt and pepper. Adjust the heat to maintain a steady simmer and cook until reduced by a third. Strain through a fine-mesh sieve into a bowl and discard the solids.

4. When the potatoes are still warm but not hot, carefully peel them. Place them in a food processor. With the machine running, add enough of the strained cream to create a smooth puree. Add the butter and continue processing until melted and fully incorporated. Season to taste with salt and pepper.

Creamy Goat Cheese Grits

Serves 6

I wanted to take a Southern classic and add a surprising twist. My mind went all the way to Italy, where I first tasted polenta and said to myself, "This is like grits, but with olive oil and parm!" I began playing with grits, stirring in ultracreamy mascarpone, then shifting to fresh goat cheese for its distinctive tang.

> 2½ cups whole milk
> 2½ cups Vegetable Stock (page 55) or
>   store-bought unsalted vegetable broth,
>   plus more as needed
> Kosher salt
> 1½ cups stone-ground grits
> 3 tablespoons unsalted butter
> ½ cup crumbled goat cheese

1. In a large saucepan, combine the milk and stock and generously season with salt. Whisk the grits into the cold liquid, then continue whisking while bringing to a boil over medium heat. As soon as it comes to a boil, reduce the heat to maintain a light simmer.

2. Continue cooking, whisking frequently, until the grits are soft and creamy and most of the liquid has been absorbed, about 40 minutes. If the mixture becomes dry before the grits soften, add more stock.

3. Stir in the butter and goat cheese until they melt and are fully incorporated into the grits. Season to taste with salt. Serve immediately.

Super Squashy Butternut Squash Grits

Serves 10

I hate, hate, hate wasting food. I try to avoid throwing anything out, even vegetable trimmings. Here, I've turned all the scraps from squash—the rind, seeds, and strings—into a broth layered with flavor. Because squash has natural sugary overtones, I add lots of hot chiles to cut through the sweetness. I then use that broth to cook grits that I top with sautéed squash. The squash makes a world of difference in the grits. So much so that this could actually be an impressive vegetarian main dish. When I'm not eating it on its own, I usually serve it under my hearty autumn Duck Ragù (page 217).

BUTTERNUT SQUASH BROTH

One 2-pound butternut squash
1 leek, trimmed, coarsely chopped, and
thoroughly rinsed
2 yellow onions, coarsely chopped
3 carrots, coarsely chopped
2 celery ribs, coarsely chopped
2 serrano chiles, coarsely chopped
6 garlic cloves, smashed
1 tablespoon whole black peppercorns
2 sprigs fresh thyme
1 sprig fresh rosemary
2 fresh or dried bay leaves
1 quart Vegetable Stock (page 55) or Chicken Stock
(page 54) or store-bought unsalted broth

CREAMY SQUASH GRITS

1¼ cups whole milk
Kosher salt
1 cup stone-ground grits
2 teaspoons extra virgin olive oil, plus more if needed
1½ tablespoons unsalted butter
2 tablespoons heavy cream
2 tablespoons chopped fresh herb leaves (preferably
a mixture of parsley, rosemary, and thyme)

1. To make the broth: Trim and peel the squash, then cut in half lengthwise and scoop out the seeds, reserving the peel, seeds, and strings. Cut enough of the flesh into ¼-inch dice to measure 1½ cups. Reserve. Coarsely chop the remaining flesh.

2. In a very large saucepan, combine the coarsely chopped squash, squash peel, seeds, and strings, and the leek, onions, carrots, celery, chiles, garlic, peppercorns, thyme, rosemary, bay leaves, and stock. Add enough water to cover the vegetables by 3 inches, about 3 quarts liquid total. Bring to a boil, then reduce the heat to maintain a steady simmer. Simmer uncovered for 1½ hours.

3. Strain through a fine-mesh sieve, pressing on the solids to extract as much liquid as possible. Reserve 1¼ cups for the grits and refrigerate the remaining broth for up to 3 days or freeze for up to 3 months.

4. To make the grits: In a large saucepan, combine the milk and squash broth and generously season with salt. Whisk the grits into the cold liquid, then continue whisking while bringing to a boil over medium-high heat. As soon as the mixture comes to a boil, reduce the heat to maintain a light simmer.

5. Continue cooking, whisking frequently, until the grits are soft and creamy and most of the liquid has been absorbed, about 30 minutes. If the mixture becomes dry before the grits soften, add more squash broth.

6. While the grits are cooking, in a large bowl, toss the diced squash with the oil until evenly coated. Season with salt. Heat a large skillet over medium heat. When the pan is hot, add a single layer of the squash and cook, tossing occasionally, until browned and tender, about 4 minutes. Add a little more oil to the pan if the squash is sticking. Transfer to a half sheet pan. Repeat with the remaining squash.

7. Stir the butter, cream, and herbs into the grits until the butter melts. Divide among 6 serving dishes and top with the squash. Serve immediately.

Fresh Corn Grits Cakes

Makes 18 cakes

Here's the problem with grits: If you don't eat them hot as soon as they're done, they start to thicken and clump. Not very appetizing. I wanted to serve grits with my Swamp Thing: Braised Pork Shoulder in Smoked Pork–Corn Broth (page 176) for a critical *Top Chef* challenge, but I knew I'd lose points if I served cold grits. I couldn't guarantee the grits would get to the judges hot. I decided to go ahead and let the grits cool all the way into a firm block, then I cut them into pretty little cakes and fried them. They're amazing this way! In fact, they remind me of the cornbread patties my granny used to make. You get this crunchy crust and then a warm, soft center. With fresh corn mingling with the cornmeal, you're amping up corn's sweetness all around. When the harvest begins and the kernels are still young and fresh and juicy, this dish is just out of this world.

> 3 cups Chicken Stock (page 54) or Vegetable Stock (page 55)
>   or store-bought unsalted broth, plus more if needed
> 1 cup whole milk
> 3 ears corn, husks and silk removed, kernels cut off
>   and reserved, cobs reserved
> 1 fresh or dried bay leaf
> 1½ cups stone-ground grits
> Kosher salt and freshly ground black pepper
> 2 tablespoons unsalted butter
> All-purpose flour, for dusting
> Canola or other neutral oil, for frying

1. Line a 13 by 9-inch baking pan with parchment paper, leaving an overhang on two sides.

2. In a large saucepan, combine the stock, milk, corn cobs, and bay leaf. Bring to a boil, then reduce the heat to maintain a steady simmer. Simmer for 30 minutes. Remove and discard the cobs and bay leaf.

3. Whisk the grits, 1½ teaspoons salt, and ½ teaspoon pepper into the simmering broth. Adjust the heat to maintain a light simmer. Continue cooking, whisking frequently, until the grits are soft and creamy and most of the liquid has been absorbed, about 30 minutes. If the mixture becomes dry before the grits soften, add more stock.

4. Stir in the butter and corn kernels until the butter melts. Season to taste with salt and pepper.

5. Pour the grits into the pan and spread into an even layer, smoothing the top. Refrigerate until chilled and firm.

6. Lift the grits out of the pan using the parchment paper overhang. Trim the edges of the large rectangle of grits, then cut the grits into 3 by 2¼-inch rectangles. Lightly dust the grits cakes with flour.

7. Heat a large nonstick skillet over medium-high heat. Add enough oil to coat the bottom of the pan. Add a few grits cakes and cook, turning once, until golden brown, about 2 minutes per side. Transfer to serving plates. Repeat with the remaining grits. Serve hot or warm.

Turkey Sausage and Cornbread Dressing

Serves 8

My very first food business, The Lunch Basket (later The Lunch Bunch), catered to the black community in my neighborhood. Part of my mission was to give them really yummy meals that didn't include beef or pork. I wanted to show them that healthy eating could be satisfying and tasty. So instead of ham biscuits for lunch, I stuffed the sandwiches with roast turkey. Oh, man, they ate it up! All of it! I could barely keep up with demand, cooking out of my little apartment.

When the holidays rolled around, I used turkey sausage in a classic cornbread dressing and got rave reviews. It was a good test-drive for my family's feast because my sister, Kim, and her husband don't eat pork. They couldn't get enough of this dressing and it's become a staple on the table each year.

> *4 teaspoons canola or other neutral oil, plus more as needed*
> *2 medium yellow onions, cut into ¼-inch dice*
> *2 celery ribs, cut into ¼-inch dice*
> *1 teaspoon poultry seasoning*
> *Kosher salt*
> *1 pound fresh turkey sausage, casing removed*
> *Skillet Cornbread (page 111), cut into ½-inch dice*
> *2 large eggs, slightly beaten*
> *½ cup heavy cream*
> *1 cup Chicken Stock (page 54) or store-bought*
> *   unsalted broth*

1. Preheat the oven to 375°F.

2. Heat a large nonstick skillet over medium heat. Heat 2 teaspoons of the oil, then add the onions and celery and cook, stirring occasionally, until soft and golden, about 10 minutes. Stir in the poultry seasoning and season with salt. Transfer to a large bowl.

3. Raise the heat to medium-high. Cook the sausage in the same skillet, stirring and breaking up into crumbles with a wooden spoon, until browned and cooked through, about 5 minutes. Transfer to the bowl with the vegetables. Add the cornbread and toss until well mixed.

4. In a medium bowl, whisk the eggs, cream, and stock until well combined. Pour over the cornbread and stir until well mixed. Form the mixture into 2-inch-diameter patties, each 1-inch thick.

5. Wipe out the skillet. Heat over medium heat. Add enough of the remaining oil to coat the bottom of the pan. Add a few of the patties and cook, turning once, until browned, about 2 minutes per side. Transfer to a half sheet pan. Repeat with the remaining patties, replenishing the oil and heating it with each batch. Transfer to the oven and bake until heated through, about 15 minutes.

Skillet Cornbread

Makes one 9-inch round

Almost everything is sweeter in the South—the tea, the lemonade, the desserts. But cornbread is the exception. Cornbread from the North is actually sweeter, closer to a muffin. Southern cornbread is a starch, not a sweet, and is used for soaking up all the yummy juices on the plate. This version is perfect for doing just that.

> 2 cups stone-ground yellow cornmeal
> 2 tablespoons sugar
> 4 teaspoons baking powder
> ½ teaspoon table salt
> 3 large eggs
> 1 cup sour cream
> 1 cup "Creamed" Corn (page 95) or canned
>   cream-style corn
> ½ cup plus 2 tablespoons canola or other
>   neutral oil

> SPECIAL EQUIPMENT
> *9-inch cast-iron skillet*

1. Preheat the oven to 425°F. Heat a 9-inch cast-iron skillet in the oven until very hot.

2. In a large bowl, combine the cornmeal, sugar, baking powder, and salt. In a medium bowl, whisk together the eggs, sour cream, creamed corn, and ½ cup oil. Pour the wet ingredients into the dry ingredients and mix until smooth.

3. Pour the remaining 2 tablespoons oil into the hot skillet, and then pour in the batter. The batter will begin sizzling right away.

4. Bake until golden and a cake tester inserted in the center comes out clean, about 25 minutes. Serve hot or warm.

Flaky Buttermilk Biscuits

Makes about 3½ dozen 1½-inch biscuits

Biscuits are all about feel: how good they make you feel when you inhale one warm and how you need to get a feel for the dough to perfect them. As a caterer, I relied on my mixers and other appliances to turn out huge batches of food. But biscuits I always did by hand, the way Granny taught me. To cut the shortening and butter into the flour, you should use your fingers. I add the fats separately because you want to mash the shortening in to evenly distribute through the flour, but the butter should be just flattened into flour-coated paper-thin disks. The shortening makes the dough tender throughout and the butter creates the flaky layers. Once you add the buttermilk, you have to work the dough gently so that it doesn't get tough.

If you follow those steps, your first batch of biscuits will be great. If you keep making biscuits, you'll start to master the motions and the dough and they'll get better each time. I can't imagine this will be a one-time project for anyone because biscuit making is just so fun. I love the feeling of sticky dough all over my hands. Almost as much as I love the feeling of splitting a biscuit's perfectly crusty sides to release the steam from the tender, buttery center before popping both halves in my mouth.

> *2½ cups all-purpose flour, plus more for shaping*
> *the dough*
> *1 tablespoon baking powder*
> *1 teaspoon sugar*
> *1 teaspoon table salt*
> *½ teaspoon baking soda*
> *2 tablespoons vegetable shortening*
> *8 tablespoons (1 stick) cold unsalted butter,*
> *cut into ½-inch dice, plus 2 tablespoons, melted*
> *1½ cups cold low-fat buttermilk*
> *Nonstick cooking spray*

1. Line a half sheet pan with parchment paper.

2. In a large bowl, whisk together the flour, baking powder, sugar, salt, and baking soda. Add the shortening and use your fingertips to pinch it into the flour to form small, pea-size pieces.

3. Drop the cold butter into the flour-shortening mixture and toss until all of the cubes are coated. With your fingertips, press the cubes to completely flatten them. Freeze the mixture in the bowl for 15 minutes.

4. Reserve 1 tablespoon buttermilk in a small bowl and add the remaining to the flour mixture. Mix until the dough forms a shaggy ball and there are no dry bits of flour left. The dough should be slightly sticky.

5. Lightly coat your work surface with nonstick cooking spray, then flour. (The spray keeps the flour in place.) Transfer the dough to the work surface and lightly dust the top with flour. Lightly coat your hands with flour and gently press the dough with the heels of your hands to form it into a smooth ball. With a lightly floured rolling pin, roll the dough to ½-inch thickness. With a floured 1½-inch biscuit cutter, cut out dough rounds. Flip the rounds over so that the smooth sides that were against the work surface face up and place on the pan, spacing the rounds 1 inch apart. Gently gather the scraps and roll and cut again. Refrigerate the rounds until cold, about 15 minutes.

6. While the rounds are chilling, preheat the oven to 450°F.

7. Stir the melted butter into the reserved buttermilk and brush onto the tops of the biscuits. Bake, without opening the door, until the tops are golden brown and crisp, about 15 minutes. Check on them occasionally in case your oven runs hot.

8. Transfer the pan to a wire rack and let sit for 5 minutes before serving the biscuits hot.

Catering Like Carla

🍴 I make my biscuits small because that's the proportion of crust to center that I like. Also, I feel like I can eat more of them that way! Of course, you can cut your biscuits larger if you'd like. Just bake them a little longer.

🍴 You must, must serve biscuits hot or warm. Depending on your entertaining schedule, you can either make them through step 3 or through step 5 up to a day ahead.

Golden Raisin Scones

Makes 4 dozen

When I was in culinary school and interning at the Henley Park Hotel, I happened to be in the kitchen when the staff went into a frenzy. They needed more scones for their daily tea service. The sous chef spun around and asked me, "Have you ever made scones before?" I answered honestly, "Um, no, but I made biscuits every day for five years for my Lunch Bunch business." He didn't hear a word after "biscuits," he just sent me to bake up a batch, muttering, "Same thing." Turns out, they are. Checking my scones before they went out to the diners, the chef exclaimed, "Whoa! You make really great scones!"

Why, thank you. I do. Over the years, I've tweaked that Henley Park version to make it my own. I like classic raisin scones and I follow a few simple rules to make them delicious: I make sure my butter is really cold before starting and throw the cubes in the freezer if they're not cold enough. I don't knead scone dough, I just bring it together and then gently pat it. And when I'm pressing the dough into rounds, the bottom of the dough gets pinched with the cutter. I flip my rounds and place them on the baking sheet, bottoms up, so that the pinched side will rise. Child, you don't want to keep a good scone down! Let it rise!

Lightly sweet and infused with a creamy flavor, these scones are nice with clotted cream or even whipped cream, but they're also great on their own. All you need is a hot cuppa Earl Grey or English Breakfast tea with a little cream swirled in.

4 cups all-purpose flour, plus more for shaping
    the dough
2 tablespoons baking powder
1 tablespoon sugar
1 tablespoon cream of tartar
1 teaspoon table salt
½ pound (2 sticks) cold unsalted butter,
    cut into ¼-inch-thick slices
1½ cups golden raisins
½ cup heavy cream
2 large eggs
½ cup plus 1 tablespoon whole milk
Nonstick cooking spray
1 large egg yolk

1. Preheat the oven to 400°F. Line two half sheet pans with parchment paper.

2. Into a large bowl, sift together the flour, baking powder, sugar, cream of tartar, and salt. Drop in the butter slices and toss until all of the pieces are coated. With your fingertips, press the slices to flatten, then toss again with the flour.

3. Stir in the raisins. In a medium bowl, whisk together the cream, eggs, and ½ cup of the milk until well blended. Pour into the flour mixture and mix until just combined. There shouldn't be any bits of flour left, but avoid overmixing.

4. Lightly coat your work surface with nonstick cooking spray, then flour. (The spray keeps the flour in place.) Transfer the dough to the work surface and gently pat to ¾-inch thickness. If the dough starts to stick to your hands, lightly flour your hands. With a floured 1½-inch biscuit cutter, cut out dough rounds. Flip the rounds over so that the smooth sides that were against the work surface face up, and place on the pan, spacing the rounds 2 inches apart. Gently gather the scraps, stack, pat to ¾ inch, and cut again.

5. In a small bowl, beat the egg yolk with the remaining tablespoon milk until blended and brush onto the tops of the scones. Bake until golden brown, about 25 minutes.

6. Transfer the pan to a wire rack and let cool for 5 to 10 minutes. Serve warm.

Catering Like Carla

❧To make these ahead, prepare them through step 4, then cover tightly with plastic wrap and freeze. Uncover, brush with the milk–egg yolk mixture, and bake straight from the freezer. They'll take just a few minutes longer in the oven.

Parker House Rolls

Makes 2 dozen

Here's a bit of real estate advice: When you show your home to prospective buyers, pop a pan of buttery yeast rolls in the oven. Those folks'll drop all their dough (ha!) on your house. There isn't a better smell in the world. That's what I love about baking yeast breads—I just know something yummy's comin'. My first boyfriend's grandmother made the best rolls and I sometimes wonder if it's why I fell for him. That smell in their home!

If you've never attempted to bake yeast rolls, you should start with this recipe. My recipe is very user friendly because the dough is so soft and pliable and will definitely rise. Plus, the mixer does all the work for you. Kneading dough is very satisfying and you can do it here if you'd like, but the machine handles it well, too. Either way, these rolls come out sweet and tender, with a thin buttery crust. If you can find White Lily flour, a Southern brand that has a lower gluten content than most flours, use it here for even more tender, delicate rolls.

The technique below for shaping the dough into balls comes from an amazing chef in Virginia. When I met her in her kitchen, I was sure she was well into her nineties. But she stood at the counter, solid as a rock, squeezing round after round of dough. I was so fascinated by her technique—and so impressed by her rolls—that I asked her to teach me her cool trick. My first dozen came out all misshapen (her rolls were perfect!), but I soon got the swing of it—and you will, too.

> 1¼ cups whole milk
> 2 tablespoons sugar
> 1 packet active dry yeast (2¼ teaspoons)
> 1 large egg, beaten, at room temperature
> 4 cups all-purpose flour, plus more for rolling and
>   cutting (optional)
> 1 tablespoon table salt
> 8 tablespoons (1 stick) unsalted butter cut into 1-inch pieces,
>   at room temperature, plus more for your hands,
>   plus 6 tablespoons (¾ stick), melted
> Canola or other neutral oil, for the bowl

1. In a small saucepan, heat the milk and sugar, stirring to dissolve the sugar, until lukewarm (90° to 110°F). Remove from the heat and whisk in the yeast and egg. Let stand until foamy, about 5 minutes.

2. In the bowl of an electric mixer fitted with a paddle, beat the flour and salt on low speed until blended. With the machine on low, add the dissolved yeast in a steady stream. Mix until just moistened, about 1 minute. With the machine still on low, add the room temperature butter, one piece at a time, beating until each piece is incorporated before adding the next. The dough may look broken. Stop and scrape down the sides and bottom of the bowl occasionally. Beat on medium speed until the dough is well combined and looks scrappy, about 2 minutes.

3. Swap the paddle for the dough hook and knead the dough on medium-low speed until nice and smooth, about 5 minutes, occasionally stopping to scrape the dough off the hook and from the sides and bottom of the bowl. Transfer the dough to a very lightly oiled metal bowl. Turn the dough to coat in the oil, then cover with plastic wrap. Let rise in a warm place until doubled in size, about 1 hour.

4. Uncover the dough and gently press down with your hands. The dough should be sticky without actually sticking to your fingers. Cover with plastic wrap again and let rest for 5 minutes.

5. Coat your hands with soft butter, as if you're washing your hands in the butter. Pinch off a golf ball–size piece of dough, then squeeze it through your thumb and index finger of one hand into a tight ball. The motion is similar to when you squirt water at someone in the swimming pool. Remember that from camp? You need a bigger opening between your fingers for dough than for water, but it's the same squirting-squeezing motion. Place the ball on a pan, with the pinched side against the pan. Repeat with the remaining dough, spacing the balls 2 inches apart.

6. Alternatively, you can also make the classic Parker House shape: Roll out the dough on a lightly floured surface with a lightly floured rolling pin to ½-inch thickness. With a floured 3-inch biscuit cutter, cut out rounds. Brush the rounds lightly with melted butter, then fold in half, gently pressing the two sides together. Space on the pans 2 inches apart.

7. Cover the pans lightly with plastic wrap if it's drafty in your kitchen. Let rise in a warm place until doubled in size, about 1 hour.

8. While the rolls are rising, preheat the oven to 400°F.

9. Uncover the rolls and lightly brush the tops with melted butter. Bake until golden brown and cooked through, about 20 minutes. Serve hot or warm.

❧To make these ahead of time, cover and refrigerate the shaped rolls for up to 1 day before they rise for a second time. Take them out of the fridge and let stand in a warm place for at least an hour before baking.

❧For fun flavor twists on these rolls, don't brush the tops with butter. Instead, brush the tops with 1 large egg beaten with 1 teaspoon water, then sprinkle on poppy seeds, sesame seeds, flaky sea salt, or a flavored salt.

❧To make a variety of shapes for a pretty basket of bread on the table, you can try both shaping methods above and you can also bake rounds of the dough in buttered small fluted tins. To make clover rolls, form the dough into little balls and place 3 balls together in a buttered muffin tin before buttering the tops with melted butter.

❧Here's a Granny tip: She used to save the wax paper wrappers from her sticks of butter. She used them to drape over her dough or her shaped rolls before lightly covering the bowl with a tea towel. She never wasted a thing and that was a great way of getting more buttery flavor onto her bread.

Basil Bacon Bread

Makes 2 loaves

Yeast breads in the South tend to be sweet, and sometimes I want my bread savory. But I still love the almost-fluffy texture of Southern-style loaves. Those two bread slices that come on every barbecue plate are perfect for sponging up sauces and making sandwiches. I took a few of my salty favorites—bacon and sun-dried tomatoes—and brightened them with basil in this slicin' loaf. I've kept a little sweetness in my loaf, but laced it with both crumbled bacon bits and rendered fat. The crumb is tight here—not at all holey—but the texture is quite light. This will make any sandwich special, but has enough flavor to be enjoyed on its own, too.

> *3 strips bacon*
> *3 tablespoons unsalted butter, melted*
> *4 envelopes active dry yeast (3 tablespoons)*
> *¾ cup warm water (90° to 110°F)*
> *3 tablespoons plus 1 teaspoon sugar*
> *1½ cups whole milk*
> *1 teaspoon dried basil leaves*
> *2 sun-dried tomatoes packed in oil, minced*
> *1 tablespoon table salt*
> *2 large eggs, 1 beaten, 1 left whole for the egg wash*
> *6 to 7 cups all-purpose flour, plus more for shaping dough*
> *Canola or other neutral oil, for the bowl*
> *2 teaspoons water*

1. In a medium skillet, cook the bacon over medium heat, turning occasionally, until browned and crisp, about 10 minutes. Drain on paper towels. When the bacon is cool and crisp, crumble into fine pieces and reserve. In a small bowl, stir 1 tablespoon of the rendered fat into the butter.

2. In another small bowl, stir together the yeast, water, and 1 teaspoon sugar. Let stand until foamy, about 5 minutes.

3. In the bowl of an electric mixer fitted with a paddle, mix the milk, basil, sun-dried tomatoes, salt, fat mixture, and the remaining 3 tablespoons sugar on low speed until well combined. With the machine running, beat in the dissolved yeast. Beat in the beaten egg

until incorporated. Add the flour, 1 cup at a time, beating well after each addition, until a soft dough is formed. The amount of flour you add will depend on the humidity of your kitchen. The dough should be sticky but stiff; your mixer will sound like it's laboring to mix it when it's ready.

4. Swap the paddle for the dough hook and knead the dough on medium-low speed until nice and smooth, about 7 minutes, occasionally stopping to scrape the dough off the hook and the sides and bottom of the bowl. The dough is ready when it springs back when you poke it with your index finger.

5. Transfer the dough to a lightly oiled metal bowl. Turn the dough to coat in the oil, then cover with plastic wrap or a damp kitchen towel. Let rise in a warm place until doubled in size, about 1 hour.

6. Transfer the dough to a lightly floured work surface. With lightly floured hands, pat the dough into a 2-inch-thick round. Sprinkle the reserved bacon on top of the dough. Fold the dough in half and start kneading by pressing the dough against the work surface with the heel of your hand. Rotate the dough a quarter turn, fold it in half, and press forward again. Keep going until the bacon is evenly distributed and you can feel bacon bits on the outside of the dough.

7. Form the dough into a ball, turning and pulling the sides of the dough under to make the ball smooth. Transfer to a lightly oiled metal bowl. Turn the dough to coat in the oil, then cover with plastic wrap or a damp kitchen towel. Let rise in a warm place until doubled in size, about 1 hour.

8. Meanwhile, preheat the oven to 325°F. Line a half sheet pan with parchment paper.

9. Uncover the dough and cut in half. Transfer each half to the pan and very gently shape into an oblong loaf about 9 inches long and 5 inches wide. There's no need to punch down the dough here; pat it lightly to get it into the free-form shape. Use a sharp knife to cut 4 diagonal slashes across the top of each loaf. In a small bowl, beat the remaining egg with the water. Brush the egg wash over both loaves.

10. Bake until golden brown and a thermometer inserted into the center of the loaf (stick it in from the bottom so you don't see the hole on top) registers 200°F, about 40 minutes. When you turn a loaf over and tap the bottom, it should sound hollow. Transfer the loaves to a wire rack and let cool completely.

Catering Like Carla

❧ If your dried basil is a little old, crush it with your fingers to refresh its scent before adding it. If, when you're crushing it, it still doesn't smell like anything, toss it out and run out to the store for a new bottle.

❧ The cooled baked loaves can be wrapped tightly in plastic wrap and frozen for up to 2 weeks.

Vegetarian Dishes

You don't have to be a vegetarian to enjoy meatless meals. I love creating dishes with just vegetables, grains, eggs, and dairy and experimenting with all the flavors and textures. Because I spent much of my career as a caterer, I had a lot of opportunities to come up with vegetarian options for clients. The key is to make the main meal feel special and substantial, but to remember that sometimes, a giant platter of well-cooked and well-dressed vegetables can do just that. The other thing to remember is that meat-free dishes are well worth trying, regardless of how carnivorous you are. You don't want to miss out on the deep deliciousness here just 'cause you're lookin' for meat!

4. Add the macaroni to the boiling water and cook until barely al dente, about 2 minutes. Drain well, then immediately add to the cheese sauce. Fold until well mixed, then pour into a 2½-quart casserole and spread in an even layer. Sprinkle the remaining cheese all over the top.

5. Bake until bubbling and the top is browned, about 30 minutes.

6. Remove from the oven and let rest for 5 minutes. Serve hot.

🍴 *Remembering My Roots*

Early on in culinary school, I learned that not every technique applies to every dish. My French curriculum at L'Academie de Cuisine in Gaithersburg, Maryland, turned out to be a big departure from Granny's cooking. When you go to culinary school, you think you can do so much better than what you grew up with. So I had the audacity to tell Granny, a seasoned cook for over seventy years who was footing the bill for my education, that I learned that her béchamel sauce was wrong because it was "broken" (a highfalutin cooking term I learned in class). Granny was so offended! She set me straight Southern-style: "Just because you went to that fancy school, doesn't mean you know everything. I will wash your mouth out with soap if you talk to me like that again." Uh, oops! She had a right to be mad; her béchamel was perfect for *her* baked mac and cheese.

If you ever learn a new technique from a cookbook or cooking show, including mine, and your grandmother taught you differently, you should stick to grandma's way. (The caveat here is that if grandma's way doesn't actually work or taste good, you should tweak it until it does.) I'm doing my best to preserve my family's recipes by teaching my niece how to make the dishes, and you should do the same, learning from the generations before and passing what you know to the generations that follow. Along the way, you'll pick up new dishes and add them to the family repertoire. It's a beautiful thing, keeping recipes in the family and making the treasury bigger over the years.

Grilled Cheese Trio:
Broccoli Pesto and Cheddar;
Sun-Dried Tomato Pesto and Mozzarella;
Arugula-Artichoke Pesto and Havarti

Makes as many as you want!

Folks often want to know what I eat when I'm not eating for work. Well, this is it. I have grilled cheese at home a lot. It's what I throw together after a long day and really savor when I can finally put my feet up. The crisp bread and melty, gooey inside is one big long *mmm-mmm* sigh for me.

But I don't just throw any ol' sliced bread and cheese together. My basic formula is:

artisanal bakery–bought or homemade bread + flavorful pesto + good cheese

I keep all of them on hand in my fridge or freezer so my end-of-day treat tastes and feels really special with little effort.

I'm not gonna give you a super specific recipe for the sandwich. That will totally depend on your mood. Sometimes, you want it cheesier, sometimes, pesto-ier. But I'm giving you the building blocks and the fundamental techniques. That's all you need to craft a yummy sandwich.

BROCCOLI PESTO
2 cups broccoli florets, boiled to just crisp-tender and drained well
2 garlic cloves, coarsely chopped
¼ cup pine nuts, toasted (page 296)
½ cup packed fresh flat-leaf parsley leaves
¼ cup freshly grated Parmigiano-Reggiano cheese
Freshly grated zest and juice of ½ lemon
Kosher salt
¼ cup extra virgin olive oil

SUN-DRIED TOMATO PESTO
½ cup sun-dried tomatoes packed in oil, drained and chopped
2 garlic cloves, coarsely chopped
¼ cup pine nuts, toasted (page 296)

1 tablespoon fresh basil leaves
½ cup freshly grated Parmigiano-Reggiano cheese
2 teaspoons fresh lemon juice
½ teaspoon smoked sweet paprika
Kosher salt
½ cup extra virgin olive oil

ARUGULA-ARTICHOKE PESTO

2 cups packed baby arugula
1 cup chopped drained marinated artichokes
2 garlic cloves, coarsely chopped
¼ cup pine nuts, toasted (page 296)
½ cup packed fresh flat-leaf parsley leaves
¼ cup freshly grated Parmigiano-Reggiano cheese
Freshly grated zest and juice of ½ lemon
Kosher salt
¼ cup extra virgin olive oil

SANDWICHES

Basil Bacon Bread (page 121) or other really good loaf
    of bread, cut into ⅓-inch-thick slices
Sharp or extra sharp aged cheddar or Havarti cheese,
    thinly sliced; or fresh mozzarella, patted dry and
    cut into ¼-inch-thick slices
Unsalted butter, at room temperature

1. To make the pestos, follow this formula for each of the variations: In a food processor, combine the vegetable(s), garlic, pine nuts, herbs, cheese, lemon, spice (if any), and a pinch of salt. Pulse until it forms a chunky paste, stopping to scrape the sides and bottom of the workbowl occasionally. With the machine running, add the oil in a steady stream. Keep processing to your taste, pulsing less for a coarse pesto, more for a smooth one. Season to taste with salt. You can keep the pesto in an airtight container in the fridge for 1 week or in the freezer for up to 3 months.

2. To make the sandwiches: Spread pesto on one side of each of two slices of bread. Arrange a layer of cheese over the pesto on one slice of bread: cheddar for the broccoli, mozzarella for the sun-dried tomato, Havarti for the arugula. Sandwich with the other slice of bread, pesto side down. Spread a generous layer of butter on both outsides of the sandwich.

3. Place the sandwich in a nonstick skillet and turn the heat to medium-low. Cook, turning occasionally, until the bread is nice and toasty and golden brown and the cheese is really melty and the sandwich is hot all the way through. Go slow! Too often in a grilled cheese, the bread is brown and the cheese cold. Um, no. Don't want that. Turn the heat down if you see that happening.

4. Eat the sandwich as soon as it comes out of the pan, standing up if you have to. You've got to enjoy it hot. Otherwise, it's not so enjoyable. (But don't burn your tongue on the hot cheese. That's not so enjoyable, either.) If you're making this for other people, too, your kids or friends or whatnot, hand 'em their sandwiches and tell them to chow down. This is casual fun food, meant for eating in a nice warm kitchen that smells all good and grilled-cheesy.

Goat Cheese and Leek Tart with Pink Peppercorn Crust

Serves 8

Leeks suspended in a creamy custard is one of life's great pleasures. To offset the natural sweetness of tender leeks, I combine tangy crème fraîche and even tangier goat cheese with savory parm. Instead of baking the mix in a plain buttery crust, I season the dough, too, with more salty parm and pink peppercorns. This special spice, which you can find in gourmet markets or even some supermarkets, has this amazing heady floral note that adds zing to cheese and cuts through its richness.

PINK PEPPERCORN CRUST

½ teaspoon table salt
2 tablespoons water
1 cup all-purpose flour, plus more for rolling
2 tablespoons finely grated Parmigiano-Reggiano cheese
½ teaspoon pink peppercorns, crushed
¼ pound (1 stick) cold unsalted butter, cut into
    ½-inch-thick slices
Dried beans, to use as pie weights

FILLING

2 tablespoons unsalted butter
2 sprigs fresh thyme
2 garlic cloves, smashed
1 medium leek (white and pale green parts only),
    trimmed, cut in half lengthwise then into thin
    half-moons, and thoroughly rinsed
Kosher salt
1 large egg
6 ounces goat cheese (¾ cup), softened
⅔ cup finely grated Parmigiano-Reggiano cheese
½ cup crème fraîche
½ cup whole milk
1 tablespoon minced chives
2 tablespoons fresh flat-leaf parsley, minced

1 teaspoon freshly grated lemon zest
Freshly ground white pepper

1. To make the crust: Chill the bowl and paddle of an electric mixer until cold. Dissolve the salt in the water and chill until cold.

2. In the chilled bowl, combine the flour, cheese, and peppercorns and mix until well blended. Toss in the butter until well coated. Mix on medium speed until the butter forms pea-size pieces. Add the cold water all at once and beat just until the dough comes together. Form the dough into a disk, wrap tightly in plastic wrap, and refrigerate for 30 minutes.

3. While the dough chills, preheat the oven to 350°F.

4. On a lightly floured surface, with a lightly floured rolling pin, roll the disk into a ¼-inch-thick round, about 12 inches across. Carefully transfer the round to a 10-inch tart pan with a removable bottom, gently pressing it against the bottom and up the sides. Trim the top flush with the rim of the pan. Line the dough with parchment paper and fill with dried beans. Bake until the crust starts to brown slightly, about 30 minutes. Transfer to a wire rack to cool and carefully remove the parchment paper with the beans. Raise the oven temperature to 400°F.

5. To make the filling: In a medium skillet, combine the butter, thyme, and garlic. Heat over medium-low heat until the butter melts. Add the leek, season with salt, and cook, stirring occasionally, until translucent and tender, about 10 minutes. Remove from the heat and discard the thyme and garlic. Let the leek cool.

6. In a medium bowl, whisk the egg until well mixed. Add the goat cheese and parmesan a little at a time, whisking after each addition until fully incorporated. Whisk in the crème fraîche and milk until smooth. Stir in the chives, parsley, lemon zest, 1½ teaspoons salt, and a pinch of pepper. Scatter the leek evenly over the crust. Slowly pour the cheese custard over the leek. Carefully transfer to the oven. Bake until the custard has set, about 20 minutes.

7. Transfer the pan to a wire rack and let cool. Push the tart up from the bottom and transfer it to a serving platter. Serve warm or at room temperature.

Catering Like Carla

You can make this tart smaller for parties. A 4-inch tartlet is nice for an individual lunch serving. Just bake it for less time at the end.

Rustic Mushroom Tart

Serves 6

I'm all about the recovery when I'm cooking. Sometimes, I even try to anticipate disasters. This simple tart is a solution to a problem that may not even exist. Don't have a tart pan with a removable bottom? Just put the dough on a baking sheet and fold it up over the filling! (Only works with dry fillings, of course.) And this garlicky, earthy mushroom base is perfect for a casual tart. It just begs to look all French country, so you can nonchalantly tell your guests, "Oh, I just threw this together." The mushrooms practically melt into the rosemary-ricotta layer and make this one of those truly satisfying meatless main dishes.

> ¾ cup Homemade Ricotta (page 19) or store-bought
>   whole milk ricotta
> ½ cup crumbled goat cheese, at room temperature
> ¼ cup finely grated Parmigiano-Reggiano cheese
> 2 teaspoons chopped fresh rosemary leaves
> Freshly ground black pepper
> 1 tablespoon unsalted butter
> 1 tablespoon extra virgin olive oil, plus more for drizzling
> ¾ pound mixed mushrooms (such as cremini and shiitake),
>   sliced (4 cups)
> 1 medium leek (white and pale green parts only), trimmed,
>   cut in half lengthwise then into thin half-moons,
>   and thoroughly rinsed
> 3 garlic cloves, finely chopped
> Kosher salt
> ¼ cup dry white wine
> 1 disk Flaky Butter Crust (page 257)
> ½ lemon

1. Preheat the oven to 400°F.

2. In a large bowl, stir together the ricotta, goat cheese, parmesan, rosemary, and ¼ teaspoon pepper until well mixed.

3. In a large skillet, heat the butter and oil over medium-high heat until the butter melts. Add the mushrooms, leek, garlic, and ½ teaspoon salt. Cook, stirring occasionally, until

the mushroom juices release and evaporate and the mushrooms start to brown, about 5 minutes. Add the wine, bring to a boil, and simmer until it evaporates. Season to taste with salt and pepper.

4. On a large sheet of parchment paper, roll the dough into a 12-inch round. Slide the parchment paper with the dough on it onto a half sheet pan.

5. Spread the ricotta mixture evenly over the dough, leaving a 2-inch border. Spoon the mushrooms in an even layer over the cheese. Fold the border of the dough over the mushrooms, pleating the dough every 2 inches. Immediately transfer to the oven.

6. Bake until the crust is golden brown, about 25 minutes. Grate the lemon zest directly over the mushroom filling and drizzle with a little olive oil. Cut into wedges and serve immediately.

Garlicky Spinach Soufflé

Serves 6

Growing up, I was a real tomboy. So my friends and I were in awe of this girl Allison Parker (wc called her Parker). She would walk around with her little purse in the crook of her arm just so, and we'd call out, "Parker! You're such a lady!" Honestly, it was a term of endearment. I wouldn't have known what to do with a handbag.

Years later, when my catering business was in full swing, I often thought of Parker. I had to do a lot of ladies' lunches and to plan the menu, I'd ask myself, "What would Parker want?" I needed a wow factor, something special and classy. Spinach soufflé turned out to be the ideal main dish, with a pretty salad on the side. With a tall top speckled green, this soufflé is at once airy and substantial. Savory parmesan and Dijon mustard add oomph to the eggy mixture.

If you've ever felt intimidated by a soufflé, you should go ahead and give this a try. The key is to beat the egg whites until they're stiff and white before gently folding them into the batter. You'll know you haven't beaten the whites enough if they look like spit. Oh, excuse me. There's that tomboy in me again . . .

> 4 tablespoons (½ stick) unsalted butter, plus more
>   for the ramekins
> ½ pound bulk spinach, heavy stems removed,
>   rinsed but not dried
> ⅓ cup all-purpose flour
> 1 garlic clove, minced
> 1½ cups whole milk
> 1 tablespoon Dijon mustard
> 1 teaspoon kosher salt
> ¼ teaspoon freshly ground black pepper
> ¼ teaspoon freshly grated nutmeg
> ⅔ cup freshly grated Parmigiano-Reggiano cheese
> 4 large eggs, separated

1. Preheat the oven to 400°F. Butter six 6-ounce (¾ cup) ramekins. Place them on a half sheet pan.

2. Heat a large skillet over medium heat. Add the spinach and cook, stirring, until it just wilts, about 1 minute. Transfer to a colander and squeeze out as much liquid as possible. Coarsely chop the spinach.

3. In a medium saucepan, melt the butter over medium heat. Whisk in the flour, adding a little at a time, then whisk in the garlic. Bring to a bubble and simmer, whisking constantly, for 1 minute. The mixture will turn tan; keep whisking it to prevent it from burning.

4. Whisk in the milk, adding a little at a time until fully incorporated, then whisk in the mustard, salt, pepper, and nutmeg. Whisk in ½ cup of the cheese. Remove from the heat.

5. In a large bowl, whisk the egg yolks until lightly mixed. Whisk in the cheese sauce, adding a little at a time, until well combined. Stir in the spinach.

6. Beat the egg whites in a large bowl until they form stiff peaks. Add a quarter of the egg whites to the spinach mixture and whisk well. You want to just loosen it up. Add half of the remaining egg whites and gently fold them in, turning the bowl as you run a spatula along the sides and into the center. Repeat with the remaining egg whites.

7. Carefully divide the batter among the ramekins. Don't let any of it get on the rims. If it does, wipe it off with a paper towel. Sprinkle the remaining parmesan on top of each. Again, don't get any on the rims. The soufflés won't rise as nicely if the ramekin rims are dirty.

8. Place the ramekins, still on the pan, in the oven. Bake until puffed and golden brown, about 25 minutes. Serve immediately! You don't want your soufflés to deflate. That wouldn't be very ladylike at all.

Catering Like Carla

❧ You can make the soufflés ahead of time, all the way to getting the batter into the ramekins and topping with cheese. Cover tightly with plastic wrap and refrigerate up to overnight. Uncover and bake directly from the refrigerator. They won't rise nearly as high or be as airy in texture, but they'll still taste good.

❧ You can use frozen chopped spinach if you don't want to wilt fresh spinach, but the soufflés won't taste quite as fresh and light. Use 1 cup thawed frozen chopped spinach (from a 10-ounce package) and squeeze out as much water as possible.

Spring Pea Flan

Serves 8

Have I mentioned how much I like peas? Maybe too many times, but I just can't say enough about them. In this simple flan, you get a nice dose of peas' creamy sweet texture in a crème fraîche–cream–milk trio. Lemon thyme, an herb worth growing in your garden or finding at a specialty store, adds a brightness that makes this dish scream spring.

*4 tablespoons (½ stick) unsalted butter, plus more
    for the ramekins*
Kosher salt
1 pound shelled fresh peas or thawed frozen (3¼ cups)
1 teaspoon canola or other neutral oil
*2 medium leeks (white and pale green parts only),
    trimmed, cut in half lengthwise then into thin
    half-moons, and thoroughly rinsed*
2 tablespoons water
¼ teaspoon freshly ground black pepper
1 teaspoon freshly grated lemon zest
1 teaspoon fresh lemon thyme leaves
1 cup crème fraîche
3 tablespoons all-purpose flour
1 cup whole milk
1 cup heavy cream
2 cups finely grated Parmigiano-Reggiano cheese
3 large eggs

1. Preheat the oven to 325°F. Butter eight 6-ounce (¾ cup) ramekins. Place them in a large, deep roasting pan.

2. If using fresh peas, fill a bowl with ice and water. Bring a medium saucepan of water to a boil. Add 2 teaspoons salt, then add the peas. Cook, stirring occasionally, until crisp-tender and bright green, about 8 minutes. Drain well and transfer to the ice water. When cool, drain again and transfer to a small bowl.

3. Heat the oil and 1 tablespoon of the butter in a medium saucepan over medium-low heat until the butter melts. Add the leeks, 2 tablespoons water, ½ teaspoon salt, and the

pepper. Cook, stirring occasionally, until melted and tender, about 6 minutes. Transfer to a stand blender along with the lemon zest, thyme, crème fraîche, and peas. Puree until smooth, stopping to scrape down the sides of the bowl occasionally.

4. In a medium saucepan, melt the remaining 3 tablespoons butter over medium heat. Whisk in the flour, adding a little at a time. Bring it to a bubble and simmer, whisking constantly, for 30 seconds. You want it to stay pale; keep whisking to prevent it from browning.

5. Whisk in the milk and cream, adding a little at a time. Bring to a simmer, whisking frequently. Whisk in the cheese and bring the sauce to a simmer again, whisking frequently.

6. In a large bowl, whisk the eggs until blended. Whisk in the sauce, adding a little at a time, until well combined. Stir in the pea puree. Whisk in 1½ teaspoons salt. Strain through a fine-mesh sieve, then divide the custard among the ramekins.

7. Pour enough hot water into the roasting pan to come halfway up the sides of the ramekins, being careful to not get any water in the ramekins. Carefully transfer the pan to the oven. Bake until set but still a little jiggly, about 35 minutes.

8. Let the flans cool in the ramekins in the water until warm. Transfer to a wire rack to cool to room temperature. Serve at room temperature or cover tightly and refrigerate up to overnight to serve this cold.

Catering Like Carla

To prevent the ramekins from sliding in the roasting pan, you can line the bottom of the pan with a thin kitchen towel.

You can also make this as one giant flan. Pour the custard into a 2-quart casserole and bake for 1 hour and 15 minutes. To serve, spoon it out.

Mustard-Marinated Grilled Veggies

Serves 4

There's something funny about our eating culture. We don't tend to think that we can have just vegetables as a main course. Well, we can! I think the secret to making vegetables—just vegetables—feel satisfying enough as an entrée is to make them really flavorful. That's why I marinate them in wine and mustard before giving them a charry depth on the grill. You then serve the vegetables with the marinade, which has picked up great flavor from the veggies. And there are a few other tricks here, too. For example, you have to get rid of the seeds in summer squash. When cooked, the seeds get watery and don't hold the savory flavors of the marinade. Finally, arrange the vegetables beautifully on the plate. They're already stunning on their own. All you need to do is make them shine.

> 2 garlic cloves, unpeeled
> 3 tablespoons finely minced scallions (green onions)
> ½ cup Dijon mustard
> ¼ cup dry white wine
> 2 tablespoons extra virgin olive oil
> 1 teaspoon sugar
> ½ teaspoon kosher salt
> ¼ teaspoon freshly ground black pepper
> 1 pint grape tomatoes
> 1 red bell pepper, stemmed, seeded, and cut into
>   1-inch-wide strips
> 1 yellow bell pepper, stemmed, seeded, and cut into
>   1-inch-wide strips
> 1 zucchini, cut in quarters lengthwise, seeded,
>   then cut in thirds crosswise
> 1 yellow squash, cut in quarters lengthwise, seeded,
>   then cut in thirds crosswise
> 1 medium red onion, cut into ½-inch-thick rounds

SPECIAL EQUIPMENT
Three 8-inch bamboo or metal skewers

1. If you want to use bamboo skewers, soak them in cold water for at least 30 minutes.

2. In a small skillet, cook the garlic over medium heat until browned in spots. Remove from the heat. When cool enough to handle, peel and mince. Transfer to a medium bowl and whisk in the scallions, mustard, wine, oil, sugar, salt, and pepper to make the marinade.

3. Skewer the tomatoes. Put the tomatoes, bell peppers, zucchini, squash, and onion in a 13 by 9-inch baking pan. It's fine if they're stacked up. Drizzle the marinade over the vegetables and toss well to evenly coat. Marinate at room temperature for at least 30 minutes and up to 2 hours.

4. Heat an outdoor grill to high.

5. Wipe off excess marinade from the vegetables, reserving the marinade, and arrange the vegetables in a single layer on the grill grate. Cook for 2 minutes, then flip and cook for 2 minutes more. The tomatoes should blacken in spots and pop, and the peppers and squash should brown but still be crisp-tender.

6. Transfer the tomatoes, peppers, and squash to a dish. Move the onions to a cooler part of the grill or turn the heat down to medium. Continue cooking the onions until evenly browned and cooked through, about 7 minutes more.

7. Serve the vegetables with the reserved marinade.

Catering Like Carla

❧ If you'd like to serve these in a party spread, divide the vegetables among lots of small bowls. You can split them up by type or mix them up. Arrange some of the vegetable bowls on a large platter. When a bowl starts running low, simply replace it with one of the other bowls. That way, the platter will never look empty or messy.

Oat and Lentil Salad

Serves 6

On a hot day, I feel a little squeamish trying a creamy mayo-based salad at a picnic. That type of salad has to be kept cold, which isn't easy. That's why I love this salad: It can be served at room temperature and still taste great. It's chock full of protein and so filling that it makes a great main course, too. If you've never tried oats in a savory dish before, get ready to be pleasantly surprised. They add a nutty chew to the salad and fiber, to boot. Be sure to use small unhulled lentils here, not the bigger, flatter kind. The small ones have an awesome little bite and don't get mushy.

> 1½ quarts Vegetable Stock (page 55) or store-bought
>   unsalted vegetable broth
> 3 fresh or dried bay leaves
> 1 cup small brown lentils, picked over and rinsed
> 1 cup small French Le Puy lentils, picked over and rinsed
> 1 cup old-fashioned rolled oats
> 1 orange
> 1 lemon
> 2 limes
> ½ small red onion, cut into ¼-inch dice
> 2 garlic cloves, minced
> 1 teaspoon minced peeled fresh ginger
> 3 tablespoons canola or other neutral oil
> Kosher salt and freshly ground black pepper
> ½ pound snow peas, strings removed, thinly sliced at an angle
> ½ red, yellow, or orange bell pepper, stemmed, seeded,
>   and finely diced (½ cup)
> 2 scallions (green onions), trimmed and thinly sliced
> ¾ cup pecans, toasted and chopped (page 296)
> 2 teaspoons fresh thyme leaves
> 2 teaspoons chopped fresh flat-leaf parsley leaves
> 1 teaspoon chopped fresh oregano leaves

1. In a large saucepan, combine 1 quart of the stock and 2 of the bay leaves. Bring to a rolling boil. Add all the lentils and reduce the heat to maintain a steady simmer. Simmer, stirring occasionally and skimming any foam that rises to the surface, until just tender,

about 25 minutes. You still want the lentils to have a bite. Drain through a sieve set over a large bowl. Reserve the stock for another use; remove and discard the bay leaves. Transfer the lentils to a half sheet pan and spread out to cool and stop cooking.

2. Meanwhile, in a medium saucepan, combine the remaining 2 cups stock and 1 bay leaf. Bring to a rolling bowl and stir in the oats. Reduce the heat to maintain a steady simmer. Simmer, stirring occasionally, just until tender, about 3 minutes. Drain through a sieve set over a large bowl. Reserve the stock for another use; remove and discard the bay leaf. Transfer the oats to the pan with the lentils and spread out to cool and stop cooking.

3. Into a medium bowl, finely grate 1 tablespoon orange zest and squeeze ¼ cup orange juice, 1 teaspoon lemon zest and 3 tablespoons lemon juice, and 1 teaspoon lime zest and 3 tablespoons lime juice. Stir in the onion, garlic, ginger, oil, ½ teaspoon salt, and ¼ teaspoon pepper. Let the dressing stand for 10 minutes.

4. Fill a bowl with ice and water. Bring a medium saucepan of water to a boil. Add 1 teaspoon salt, then the snow peas. Cook, stirring occasionally, just until crisp-tender and bright green, about 15 seconds. Drain well and transfer to the ice water. When cool, drain again.

5. In a large bowl, combine the bell pepper, scallions, pecans, thyme, parsley, oregano, lentils, oats, and snow peas. Toss until well mixed. Pour the dressing over and toss until evenly coated. Season to taste with salt and pepper. Serve immediately.

Catering Like Carla

The only reason you have to serve this immediately is because the snow peas will begin to discolor when the acid hits them. And the pecans get a little soggy. You can make the whole salad and keep refrigerated up to 3 days ahead of time, leaving the snow peas and pecans out. When ready to serve, toss them in.

Pecan and Oat–Crusted Tofu

Serves 4

During a *Top Chef* Quickfire challenge, I had to come up with a creative dish using oatmeal. When I think oatmeal, I immediately think healthy, so I decided to do a tofu dish. Tofu is bland, and you have to squeeze all the water out of it, then get flavor into it by submerging it in a marinade. If you don't take the time to press the water out of the tofu first, the marinade won't soak in. To give the springy tofu texture, I coat it in crunchy pecans and oats and fry it until crisp. This is super tasty on its own, but also great over Oat and Lentil Salad (page 145).

1 pound firm tofu
¼ cup soy sauce
1 garlic clove, minced
2 teaspoons sriracha or other chili-garlic sauce
1 teaspoon freshly grated lime zest
2 tablespoons fresh lime juice
2 tablespoons fresh orange juice
2 tablespoons fresh lemon juice
1 tablespoon plus ½ teaspoon freshly grated orange zest
1½ teaspoons freshly grated lemon zest
¼ cup water
½ cup old-fashioned rolled oats
¼ cup pecans, lightly toasted (page 296)
2 large eggs
Canola or other neutral oil, for frying

1. Cut the tofu into quarters crosswise, then cut in half lengthwise to form rectangles. Line a half sheet pan with a double layer of paper towels. Arrange the tofu in a single layer on the paper towels. Cover with a double layer of paper towels, then place another half sheet pan on top. Weigh the top pan down with a cast-iron skillet or heavy cans. Let stand for 30 minutes.

2. In a large resealable plastic bag, combine the soy sauce, garlic, sriracha, lime zest and juice, orange juice, lemon juice, 1 tablespoon of the orange zest, 1 teaspoon of the lemon zest, and the water. Add the tofu, seal the bag, and let stand for 30 minutes.

3. Bring a small saucepan of water to a boil. Add the oats and cook, stirring, until just tender, about 3 minutes. Drain and spread out on a large plate to cool and stop cooking. When cool, transfer to a food processor along with the pecans, and the remaining ½ teaspoon orange zest and ½ teaspoon lemon zest. Pulse until finely chopped. Transfer to a large dish.

4. In a large shallow dish, beat the eggs until well blended. Pour enough oil into a large nonstick skillet to come ¼ inch up the side. Heat over medium-low heat until hot. The oil should dimple and have wavy lines.

5. Remove the tofu from the marinade and pat dry with paper towels. Dip 1 piece in the egg to lightly coat, then press into the pecan crust to coat both sides. Repeat with 3 more pieces. Transfer the coated pieces to the hot oil and cook until lightly browned on all sides, carefully turning over with a spatula, about 2 minutes per side. Transfer to a wire rack. Repeat with the remaining tofu, egg, and pecan crust, replenishing and reheating the oil between batches.

Black Bean Patties with Mango Relish and Tropical Vinaigrette

Serves 6

My time in the Bahamas, both as a private chef and as a finalist on *Top Chef All-Stars,* is so significant that I keep returning to its local flavors. I can't get enough of tropical fruits and love playing with ways to use them in savory dishes. I found that mango tastes great with beans, so I did a tangy fruit sauce and relish to go over crisp bean patties. I'm not a fan of mushy beans, so I've kept some beans whole and added red bell pepper and corn for their sweet crunch. These patties are filling enough to stand alone on a plate, but they'd also be yummy with fried plantains.

TROPICAL VINAIGRETTE

⅓ cup finely diced fresh mango (from 1 mango)
¼ cup mango juice
¼ cup rice vinegar
1½ tablespoons fresh lime juice
1 tablespoon fresh orange juice
½ teaspoon honey
¼ teaspoon kosher salt
2 tablespoons extra virgin olive oil

TROPICAL RELISH

¾ cup finely diced fresh mango
½ teaspoon freshly grated lime zest
1 teaspoon fresh lime juice
1 teaspoon chopped fresh cilantro leaves
¼ teaspoon kosher salt

FRITTERS

1 cup cooked or canned black beans
½ cup stone-ground yellow cornmeal
½ cup all-purpose flour
1½ teaspoons baking powder
½ teaspoon table salt
1 teaspoon chili powder

1 teaspoon ground cumin
½ teaspoon cayenne pepper
½ cup whole milk
1 large egg
1 cup grated sharp cheddar cheese
1 small red bell pepper, stemmed, seeded,
    and finely diced (¾ cup)
½ cup fresh corn kernels (cut from 1 ear)
2 tablespoons fresh cilantro leaves, chopped
Peanut oil, for frying

1. To make the vinaigrette: In a stand blender, puree the mango and mango juice until smooth. Add the vinegar, lime juice, orange juice, honey, and salt and blend until smooth. With the machine running, add the oil in a steady stream. Blend until emulsified.

2. To make the relish: In a bowl, combine the mango, lime zest and juice, cilantro, and salt.

3. To make the fritters: Mash half of the beans until smooth. In a large bowl, combine the cornmeal, flour, baking powder, salt, chili powder, cumin, and cayenne. In another bowl, whisk together the milk and egg until smooth. Pour into the cornmeal and mix well. Stir in the cheese, bell pepper, corn, cilantro, mashed beans, and whole beans until well combined. Pat a ¼ cup of the mixture into a 3-inch-diameter patty and place on wax paper. Repeat with the remaining mixture.

4. Pour enough oil into a large nonstick skillet to come ½ inch up the side. Heat over medium heat until hot. The oil should dimple and have wavy lines. Add a few patties (don't crowd the pan!) and cook, turning once, until golden brown and heated through, about 3 minutes per side. Transfer to a wire rack. Repeat with the remaining patties.

5. Divide the patties among serving plates and top with the relish. Drizzle the vinaigrette all over and serve immediately.

Roasted Red Pepper Risotto

Serves 6

The great chef Roberto Donna demonstrated how to make wild mushroom risotto in my cooking school class, and I was hooked. I had never tasted anything so decadent, creamy, and fragrant. I had always loved rice, so I began to experiment with my own risottos. After years of tweaking, I came up with a secret trick to boost flavor. I stir in a very thin soup or flavored broth at the very end, just before serving. The red pepper soup here adds a rich intensity, so the recipe for it makes more than you need just for this risotto. You can slurp it straight or freeze it for up to one month to use however else you like.

Both the soup and the roasted tomatoes take a couple hours, but they're both well worth the effort. I first created it for a warm weather event, when all the ratatouille vegetables were at their peak, and now I make it every summer.

RATATOUILLE

8 small plum tomatoes
Kosher salt
Extra virgin olive oil
1 small eggplant, finely diced
1 medium zucchini, seeded and finely diced
1 medium yellow squash, seeded and finely diced
1 large shallot or small yellow onion, finely diced
2 garlic cloves, minced
1 sprig fresh thyme
Freshly ground black pepper

ROASTED RED PEPPER SOUP

2 tablespoons extra virgin olive oil
2 large leeks (white and pale green parts) or yellow onions,
*   finely diced (1½ cups)*
2 medium carrots, finely diced (¾ cup)
2 stalks celery, finely diced (½ cup)
Kosher salt and freshly ground black pepper
2 large roasted red bell peppers, finely diced (1 cup)
3 garlic cloves, crushed
3 cups Vegetable Stock (page 55) or store-bought unsalted
*   vegetable broth*

2 fresh or dried bay leaves
4 sprigs fresh thyme
4 sprigs fresh flat-leaf parsley
1 teaspoon whole black peppercorns

RISOTTO

3 tablespoons extra virgin olive oil
1 medium yellow onion, finely diced
2 cups Arborio or medium-grain rice
½ cup dry white wine
Kosher salt and freshly ground black pepper
5 cups Vegetable Stock (page 55) or store-bought
    unsalted vegetable broth, at room temperature
½ cup finely grated Parmigiano-Reggiano or
    Asiago cheese, plus extra for serving

1. To make the ratatouille: Preheat the oven to 250°F.

2. Cut the tomatoes in half lengthwise and place on a half sheet pan, cut side up. Sprinkle with salt and drizzle with oil. Bake until shriveled and dark red, about 2 hours.

3. Transfer the pan to a wire rack and raise the oven temperature to 425°F. Let the tomatoes cool completely, then peel off the skins. Reserve the oil in the pan. Coarsely chop the tomatoes. (The tomatoes and reserved oil can be made up to 2 days ahead, covered separately, and refrigerated.)

4. In a large bowl, sprinkle the eggplant with salt, toss well, and let stand for 15 minutes. Pat dry with paper towels, then toss with the oil from the roasted tomatoes. Spread in a single layer on a half sheet pan. Roast until browned and slightly dry, about 18 minutes.

5. Heat a large skillet over high heat. Toss the zucchini and squash with olive oil to coat. Add to the hot pan and cook, tossing, just until tender, about 2 minutes. Do not crowd the pan as you want to sear the vegetables; cook in batches if necessary. Transfer to a plate. Wipe out the skillet.

6. Heat more oil in the same skillet over medium heat. Add the shallot and cook, stirring occasionally, until tender, about 3 minutes. Add the garlic, then stir in the thyme and the roasted tomatoes. Season with salt and pepper. Cook for 5 minutes, then stir in the eggplant, squash, and zucchini. Season to taste with salt and pepper and reserve.

7. To make the soup: Heat the oil in a large saucepan over medium-high heat. Add the leeks, carrots, and celery and cook, stirring occasionally, until soft, about 7 minutes. Season with salt, then add the roasted pepper and garlic. Cook, stirring occasionally, until the vegetables are tender, about 15 minutes.

8. Stir in the stock. Make a bouquet garni by wrapping the bay leaves, thyme, parsley, and peppercorns in cheesecloth and tying with kitchen twine. Add to the pot and bring to a boil. Season again with salt and pepper and adjust the heat to maintain a steady simmer. Simmer until the flavors have fully developed, about 45 minutes.

9. Remove the bouquet garni and transfer the soup to a stand blender (working in batches if necessary). Puree until smooth. The soup should be very thin. Season to taste with salt and pepper. The soup can be refrigerated for up to 1 week or frozen for up to 3 months.

10. To make the risotto: Heat the oil in a 12-inch heavy pot over medium heat. Add the onion and cook, stirring occasionally, until soft, about 5 minutes. Add the rice, stirring until well mixed. Add the wine, bring to a boil, then reduce the heat to maintain a steady simmer. Simmer until the mixture is almost dry, stirring occasionally. Season with salt and pepper.

11. Add 3 cups stock and bring to a boil, stirring occasionally. Reduce the heat to maintain a simmer and cook, stirring occasionally, until the bottom of the pot is dry when the rice is pulled back with a spoon, about 10 minutes.

12. Continue adding ½ cup stock at a time, stirring continuously until each addition is absorbed before adding the next. Cook until the rice is creamy but still somewhat firm in the center. If you're not serving immediately, spread the rice into an even layer on a half sheet pan to stop the cooking process.

13. Heat 1 cup of the soup in a large pot over medium heat. Stir the rice into the soup and reheat for about 10 minutes. Add more soup if needed to thin the risotto. Stir in the cheese. Garnish with the ratatouille (discard the thyme) and serve with additional cheese.

Meat

For some reason, people often mistake me for a vegetarian. I do love veggies—and consider them my favorite part of any meal—but I still enjoy nice meaty dishes, too. There's nothing quite like a beautiful piece of meat. For weeknight meals, I quickly fry it in a pan. On weekends, I heat up the grill in the spring and summer and crank up the oven in the fall and winter for big cuts of meat. Whole roasts are great for entertaining—succulent *and* impressive!

Beer-Braised Pulled Barbecued Brisket

Serves 16

In the South, you can get pulled pork in Memphis and sliced brisket in Texas. Me, I like to pull brisket. This was always a huge hit when I was catering. I'd get calls from all my regulars, asking, "Hey, Carla? Can I get twenty pounds of beef?" It's great for entertaining because you can just leave it alone for a few hours and then you end up with an amazing dish. Be sure to use a beer that you like the taste of here because it ends up being the sauce, too.

BARBECUE DRY RUB

2 tablespoons chili powder
1 tablespoon kosher salt
1 tablespoon freshly ground black pepper
1 tablespoon packed brown sugar
1 tablespoon sweet paprika
1 teaspoon garlic powder
1 teaspoon onion powder
1 teaspoon ground cumin
1 teaspoon dried thyme leaves
1 teaspoon cayenne pepper

1 whole beef brisket (6 to 7 pounds)
1 cup apple wood chips for smoking
One 12-ounce bottle lager or other strong beer
1 cup ketchup
½ cup cider vinegar

1. In a medium bowl, combine the chili powder, salt, pepper, brown sugar, paprika, garlic powder, onion powder, cumin, thyme, and cayenne. The rub can be kept in an airtight container at room temperature for up to 1 week.

2. Reserve 3 tablespoons dry rub. Rub the remaining dry rub all over the brisket. Place in a large resealable plastic bag or in a pan large enough to hold the brisket snugly and cover tightly with plastic wrap. Refrigerate for at least 6 hours or up to overnight.

3. Let the beef stand at room temperature for 1 hour before you start cooking. Soak the wood chips in cold water for at least 30 minutes. Heat one side of an outdoor grill to high

by turning on half the burners on a gas grill or by banking charcoal to one side of the grill. Line an aluminum pan large enough to hold the brisket with two layers of aluminum foil, overhanging the sides enough to cover the pan later.

4. Lightly oil the grill grate. Place the brisket on the hot part of the grill and grill, turning once, until lightly browned, about 8 minutes per side. Don't let the dry rub burn.

5. Place the aluminum pan on the unheated part of the grill and place the brisket in it. Pour the beer around the beef and loosely close the foil over the brisket. Place the wood chips in the smoking box in a gas grill or scatter over the charcoal. If you don't have a smoking box in your gas grill, you can fashion your own: Fill an aluminum pan with the soaked chips, cover with foil, and poke holes in the foil. Set near the heating element. Cover the grill and cook for 2½ to 3 hours or until the meat is fork tender, replenishing the charcoal each hour. Try to maintain a grill temperature of 350°F.

6. Carefully transfer the brisket to a cutting board and let stand for 15 minutes. Meanwhile, carefully pour all the pan juices into a fat separator. Pour the juices into a small saucepan; discard the fat remaining in the separator. You should have 1 to 1½ cups of pan drippings. Stir in the ketchup, vinegar, and reserved dry rub. Bring to a boil over high heat, then reduce the heat to maintain a simmer. Cook, stirring occasionally, until the sauce is just thick enough to coat the back of a spoon, about 10 minutes.

7. While the sauce cooks, slice the brisket against the grain into 2-inch-thick pieces. With your fingers, pull the meat into bite-size pieces. Transfer to a large bowl and toss in just enough of the sauce to coat the meat. Serve with the remaining sauce on the side.

Catering Like Carla

❧ The key to success here is getting the right cut of brisket. You want ¼-inch-thick layer of fat all around the meat so that it can absorb the rub and stay moist and juicy while it's cooking. The flesh itself should be well marbled with fat. As with all beef, choose USDA Choice.

❧ You can make the brisket up to an hour ahead of time. Just keep it in the cooking juices so that it stays moist. Make the sauce and slice the meat just before serving.

Roasted Filet of Beef

Serves 12

Talk about a classic. Every home cook should know how to do a good piece of meat. Mustard's my effortless way of adding a depth of flavor, while the herbs and salt together bring a fresh tanginess. I know it sounds like a lot, but you really want to be liberal with your salt here. Tenderloin needs it and only half of it goes directly on the meat. That nice shower of salt that goes on the meat right before searing gives it a great crust and highlights all the richness of the marinade and beef.

1 whole beef tenderloin (5 to 6 pounds)
½ cup Dijon mustard
¼ cup extra virgin olive oil
4 garlic cloves, minced
1 tablespoon chopped fresh flat-leaf parsley leaves
1 tablespoon chopped fresh thyme leaves
1 teaspoon chopped fresh rosemary leaves
1½ teaspoons freshly ground black pepper
2 tablespoons kosher salt
4 tablespoons canola or other neutral oil

1. Remove the excess fat, chain (the tough narrow muscle running alongside the tenderloin), and silverskin (the silvery white thin membrane on the meat) from the beef tenderloin, then cut the beef in half crosswise to form two shorter roasts. Tie both pieces at 1-inch intervals with kitchen twine.

2. In a medium bowl, stir together the mustard, olive oil, garlic, parsley, thyme, rosemary, and pepper until smooth. Sprinkle half of the salt over the beef, then slather the mustard mixture all over both pieces. Place the beef in large resealable plastic bags or in a pan large enough to hold it snugly and cover tightly with plastic wrap. Refrigerate for at least 3 hours or up to overnight.

3. Let the beef stand at room temperature for 1 hour before you start cooking. Preheat the oven to 450°F. Fit a rack into a roasting pan.

4. Wipe off any excess marinade from the beef and discard. Sprinkle the remaining salt all over the beef.

5. Heat 2 tablespoons of the canola oil in a large skillet over medium-high heat. Add one of the beef pieces and cook, turning to sear all sides, until well browned, about 5 minutes per side. Transfer to the roasting pan. Wipe out the skillet and add the remaining canola oil. Heat until hot, then sear the other piece of beef.

6. Transfer to the roasting pan with the other piece of beef and place in the oven. Roast until the internal temperature of the beef registers 125°F with a meat thermometer for medium-rare, about 20 minutes, checking the meat with a meat thermometer at 15 minutes, just in case.

7. Remove the meat from the oven and transfer to a cutting board. Let it rest for 15 minutes before slicing.

Catering Like Carla

❧ I love doing this for big parties, but you can halve the amounts for a smaller dinner. Just use half a tenderloin, but sear and cook it for the same time.

❧ I recommend buying a whole beef tenderloin untrimmed and then trimming and tying it yourself at home because you can save a lot of money that way. As a bonus, you get the extra scraps of meat, which are great for stir-fries. You can always ask your butcher to do this step for you or buy tenderloins already trimmed and tied.

Marinated Flank Steak
with Roasted Red Pepper Tapenade

Serves 6

Here's the secret to really tasty weeknight dinners: keep a stash of savory toppings and sauces in the fridge. Make them on the weekends and serve them any night of the week. I love this roasted red pepper tapenade with chicken and fish, too, but it's especially good with steak. And flank in particular. This budget-friendly cut packs a lot of meaty flavor and has a great chew. It holds up to marinating overnight so you can just throw the steaks on the grill when you get home from work. Of course, you can also serve this at a casual summer dinner party.

STEAK

3 tablespoons soy sauce
2 tablespoons red wine vinegar
1 tablespoon canola or other neutral oil
1 tablespoon fresh lemon juice
2 teaspoons Worcestershire sauce
1½ teaspoons Dijon mustard
1 garlic clove, minced
¼ teaspoon freshly ground black pepper
1 whole flank steak (1½ pounds)

ROASTED RED PEPPER TAPENADE

2 red bell peppers
2 tablespoons capers, rinsed and coarsely chopped
2 garlic cloves, minced
2 tablespoons fresh flat-leaf parsley leaves, chopped
1 teaspoon fresh thyme leaves, chopped
1 teaspoon freshly grated lemon zest
½ teaspoon smoked sweet paprika
2 tablespoons extra virgin olive oil
Kosher salt and freshly ground black pepper

1. To make the steak: In a small bowl, combine the soy sauce, vinegar, oil, lemon juice, Worcestershire, mustard, garlic, and pepper. Place the steak in a large resealable plastic

bag and pour the marinade over. Seal the bag tightly and refrigerate for at least 6 hours or up to overnight.

2. To make the tapenade: Heat an outdoor grill or grill pan to high. Grill the peppers until charred and blackened all over. Transfer the peppers to a bowl and cover with plastic wrap. Keep the grill on.

3. When the peppers are cool enough to handle, peel off the skin, remove and discard the stems and seeds, and cut the flesh into a ¼-inch dice. In a medium bowl, combine the diced peppers, capers, garlic, parsley, thyme, lemon zest, paprika, and oil. Season to taste with salt and pepper.

4. Remove the steak from the marinade and discard the marinade. Grill the steak, turning occasionally, to your desired doneness, about 12 minutes for medium-rare.

5. Transfer the steak to a cutting board and let rest for 5 minutes before slicing. Serve with the tapenade.

Mama's Hamburger Help-Me Meal

Serves 6

My mama's the woman who made me who I am, the one who really made me a cook. Because she didn't cook. She doesn't like doing it and she never did. To feed us, she'd buy seasoning mixes for ground beef. When I saw her pull the box out of the pantry, I'd run two doors down to my friend Karen's house. In the summer, I'd jump right into her pool because I knew exactly how much time I had left to play before Mama would stretch out the kitchen window and yell toward Karen's house, "Carla! Come in for dinner! Dinner's ready!"

Because I knew Mama didn't like cooking, this meal was a special one in our weeknight rotation. Something about its heartiness made me feel like we were going back to our roots, the way our forefathers ate. This simple, hug-like food brings so much comfort, it catapults me back in time. It makes me want to dig into a bowlful on my soft couch, watching an old movie like *It's a Wonderful Life* or a Shirley Temple flick. It reminds me of harder times when you needed to stretch meat with a whole pound of inexpensive pasta. In flush times, it's what you want to serve at a raucous football party. You fill up your biggest skillet to the rim with this mix and serve it sloppy and hot.

As a professional chef, I'm not too proud to do my own take on the boxed dinner of my childhood. And I definitely don't want to make it too cheffy. Fresh ingredients, of course, but with the soul of a pantry dinner. My husband, Matthew, insists that it be done with macaroni and I have to agree. Go ahead and use good sharp cheddar here and be sure to let it melt into the sauce to get all gooey. Maybe finishing with fresh parsley seems fancy, but it adds a refreshing note. It brings all the comfort of the past to the fresh and new present.

1 teaspoon extra virgin olive oil
1 medium yellow onion, finely diced
Kosher salt
1 garlic clove, minced
1½ pounds ground beef chuck
1 teaspoon dried oregano leaves
¼ teaspoon cayenne pepper
Freshly ground black pepper
2 tablespoons all-purpose flour
2 cups drained canned diced tomatoes
¾ cup Chicken Stock (page 54) or store-bought
*   unsalted chicken broth, plus more if needed*

1 pound elbow macaroni
½ pound sharp cheddar cheese, grated (2 cups)
¼ cup fresh flat-leaf parsley leaves, chopped

1. Bring a large pot of water to a boil.

2. Heat a large skillet over medium heat. Heat the oil, then add the onion and season with salt. Cook, stirring occasionally, until tender, about 5 minutes. Add the garlic and cook, stirring, for 1 minute.

3. Add the beef, oregano, and cayenne and season generously with salt and pepper. You need to season the beef well at this point because the seasonings won't get in there if you add them later. Cook, stirring to break the meat up into little pieces, until cooked through, about 7 minutes. Drain the fat out of the pan and discard.

4. Sprinkle the flour over the beef and stir until well mixed. Stir in the tomatoes and stock. Raise the heat to medium-high and bring to a boil. Simmer hard over medium heat for 10 minutes.

5. While the beef simmers, add the macaroni and 1 teaspoon salt to the boiling water. Cook a minute less than the label directs and drain well.

6. Stir into the beef. Stir in half of the cheese. If the mixture is too thick and stiff, stir in more stock to loosen it up.

7. Divide among serving bowls and top with the parsley and remaining cheese. Serve immediately.

Catering Like Carla

Yes, this is explicitly a weeknight family meal, but you can still serve it to guests at a casual party. You can keep the meat sauce warm over low heat and stir in the macaroni and cheese just before serving.

Granny's Slow-Cooked Sunday Smothered Pork Chops

Serves 4

Smothered pork chops are a time-honored tradition in the South. A lot of versions call for cooking the chops and making the sauce with lard or butter or both, but my Granny always did this dish with oil. Decades before everyone became more aware of health and nutrition, Granny was at the forefront. She spent her days as a hospital dietitian, but her life's work was as a loving wife, mother, and grandmother. When my grandfather began to suffer from heart problems, she immediately took her family's classic Southern recipes and made them more nutritious. And those are the recipes she passed down to me. You really don't miss the extra fat here because there's still plenty of delicious porkyness in bone-in chops—a must-have cut for juicy, flavorful meat. And this onion gravy tastes plenty rich and is all the more satisfying without extra saturated fat.

> 4 bone-in pork loin chops (each 1½ inches thick)
> 2 teaspoons kosher salt
> 1 teaspoon freshly ground black pepper
> ⅓ cup all-purpose flour
> ⅓ cup canola or other neutral oil
> 2 yellow onions, thinly sliced
> 3 tablespoons finely chopped garlic
> 1 cup Chicken Stock (page 54) or store-bought
>   unsalted chicken broth
> 1 cup water
> 2 tablespoons Worcestershire sauce
> 1 tablespoon white vinegar or cider vinegar
> 1 teaspoon Dijon mustard
> 1 teaspoon molasses
> 1 teaspoon ground allspice

1. Rinse the pork chops and pat dry with paper towels. Sprinkle the salt and pepper all over the chops, then dredge in flour to lightly coat. Reserve the remaining flour.

2. In a large, deep skillet, heat the oil over medium heat. Add two of the pork chops and cook, turning once, until well browned, about 5 minutes per side. Transfer the chops to a plate. Repeat with the remaining chops.

3. Add the onions and garlic to the fat in the pan and cook, stirring, for 1 minute. Reduce the heat to low and add the reserved flour. Cook, stirring, until it begins to brown, about 8 minutes.

4. In a small bowl, combine the stock, water, Worcestershire, vinegar, mustard, molasses, and allspice. Add to the pan and stir until well incorporated. Bring to a boil, then reduce the heat to maintain a simmer. Return the pork chops and their accumulated juices to the pan.

5. Cover and simmer until the chops are very tender, about 45 minutes, turning the chops halfway through cooking. Serve hot.

Pork Tenderloin Medallions with Root Vegetable Ragout

Serves 6

When I'm teaching a new technique to home cooks, the food is sometimes just the by-product of the demo. I've created plenty of tasty dishes that way, including this one. I wanted to show how a simple marinade can turn a plain Jane cut of meat into a special dish. To get the most out of the citrus sweetness in this marinade, I cut the whole tenderloin into medallions. Not only are they cuter that way, they also get a deeper flavor because more surface area soaks up the marinade and browns in the hot pan. Plus, cutting this lean meat into medallions helps it cook very quickly. This pork is ideal for Root Vegetable Ragout (page 99), but also works with any type of bittersweet fall vegetable.

> *2 whole pork tenderloins*
> *   (each about ¾ pound)*
> *½ cup fresh orange juice*
> *2 garlic cloves, minced*
> *1 tablespoon spicy brown mustard*
> *1 tablespoon honey*
> *Dash of Worcestershire sauce*
> *2 tablespoons canola or other*
> *   neutral oil*
> *Root Vegetable Ragout (page 99)*

1. If the pork still has silverskin (the thin silvery white membrane on the meat), trim it off. Rinse the pork well, then pat dry with paper towels. Cut each tenderloin crosswise into 2-inch-thick medallions.

2. In a large resealable plastic bag, combine the juice, garlic, mustard, honey, and Worcestershire. Add the pork, seal the bag, and turn to coat well. Seal and refrigerate for at least 2 hours or up to overnight.

3. Preheat the oven to 350°F. Remove the pork from the marinade and wipe off any excess; discard the marinade.

4. Heat a large skillet over medium-high heat. Heat half of the oil. Add half the pork and cook, turning once, until well browned, about 2 minutes per side. Transfer to a half sheet pan. Repeat with the remaining oil and pork.

5. Transfer the pan to the oven and bake until the pork is medium in the center, 140°F, about 13 minutes. Serve over the Root Vegetable Ragout and drizzle with the pan juices.

🍳 *Safety First!*

When I started cooking, I wanted to make a special dinner for my boyfriend at the time. I marinated some chicken, then grilled it, then spooned the chicken marinade over the chicken as a sauce. Just poured it right over that chicken. Didn't heat it or anything.

I didn't know that you shouldn't do that—and besides, it tasted good. Later that night, my boyfriend got stuck-in-the-bathroom sick. I tried to be compassionate to his "sensitive stomach," but honestly, I was thinking, "What's wrong with you? Why are you such a wuss?" We broke up soon after that.

Years later in cooking school, my instructor started out his marinating lesson with a scary-stern face. He shouted, "Never ever serve a marinade that has touched raw meat without cooking it first. Never! You could kill someone." Oh, oops. Lesson learned.

In my recipes, I try to use just enough marinade to coat the meat so that you don't have any leftover. In the cases when you do have enough leftover to justify not tossing it down the drain, bring the marinade to a hard boil and boil for at least 5 minutes. You can then use it as a sauce or refrigerate it to use as a marinade again.

Cuban Pork Loin with Marinated Red Onions and Queso Blanco in Grilled Tortillas

Serves 18

In my current hometown of Washington, D.C., I participate in a luncheon that Farm Food Voices hosts on Capitol Hill. The organization supports small farmers, who donate their produce, meat, and dairy for the meal to show Congress members and lobbyists how great their work is. As chefs, we take those beautiful products and transform them into a huge feast. One year, I decided to create these little tortilla cornets filled with thinly sliced local pork. I wanted to give it an international spin by taking the seasonings of traditional Cuban roast pork and using them on the loin roast. The garlicky citrus brine keeps this lean cut of meat moist and perfectly balances the crunchy tart onions. I encourage you to seek out local farmers for sustainably raised meat when picking out your roast for this unbeatable dish.

BRINED PORK

1½ cups sugar
1 cup kosher salt
3 quarts cold water
2 cups fresh orange juice
2 heads garlic, cloves separated and crushed
3 fresh or dried bay leaves
One 4-pound boneless pork loin roast

GARLIC-ORANGE RUB

6 garlic cloves, coarsely chopped
1 tablespoon ground cumin
1 tablespoon dried oregano leaves
1 teaspoon crushed red chile flakes
1 teaspoon freshly grated orange zest
1 teaspoon kosher salt
1 teaspoon freshly ground black pepper
3 tablespoons fresh orange juice
1 tablespoon white vinegar
1 tablespoon olive oil

MARINATED RED ONIONS AND PEPPERS

1 medium red onion, thinly sliced
1 red bell pepper, stemmed, seeded,
    and thinly sliced
½ habanero chile, stemmed, seeded,
    and finely chopped
2 fresh or dried bay leaves, torn into a few pieces
2 tablespoons white vinegar
½ teaspoon kosher salt
¼ teaspoon freshly ground black pepper

2 tablespoons canola or other neutral oil
24 flour tortillas (6-inch round)
4 ounces queso blanco or fresco, crumbled
    (about 1 cup)
Fresh cilantro sprigs, for garnish

1. To brine the pork: In a very large bowl or pot, combine the sugar, salt, and water, stirring until the sugar and salt dissolve. Stir in the juice, garlic, and bay leaves, then add the pork. The meat should be completely submerged in the brine. Cover tightly and refrigerate for at least 6 hours and up to 12 hours.

2. To make the rub: In a food processor, pulse the garlic, cumin, oregano, chile flakes, orange zest, salt, and pepper until a coarse paste forms. With the machine running, add the juice, vinegar, and oil.

3. Remove the pork from the brine; discard the brine and solids. Rinse the pork thoroughly, then pat dry with paper towels. Rub the garlic paste all over the pork and place in a large resealable plastic bag. Refrigerate for at least 3 hours or up to overnight.

4. To make the marinated onions: In a medium bowl, combine the onion, bell pepper, chile, bay leaves, vinegar, salt, and pepper. Let sit until the onion turns pink and soft, at least 1 hour and up to overnight. (Cover and refrigerate if marinating overnight.)

5. Preheat the oven to 375°F.

6. Heat a large cast-iron skillet over high heat. Add the oil and sear the garlic-rubbed pork until browned on all sides, about 15 minutes total. Transfer the pan to the oven and roast until the pork registers 140°F, about 25 minutes.

7. Transfer the pork to a cutting board and let rest for at least 15 minutes before cutting into very thin slices.

8. Heat a grill pan or cast iron skillet over medium-high heat. Warm the tortillas, one at a time, turning occasionally, until lightly browned and softened.

9. Arrange a few slices of meat in each warm tortilla, top with some marinated onions, cheese, and cilantro. Serve immediately.

Catering Like Carla

❧ If you don't want to assemble each tortilla yourself, you can set up a make-your-own buffet line. As you warm each tortilla, put it in a foil packet, stacking the warm tortillas on top of one another. Those go on the table first, then dishes of the pork, onions, cheese, and cilantro.

Swamp Thing:
Braised Pork Shoulder
in Smoked Pork–Corn Broth

Serves 8

During my *Top Chef* challenge on Ellis Island in New York, I had to make a dish that symbolized my family and heritage. I loved every part of that challenge, but the best part was when they surprised me by bringing my husband, Matthew, to help me plan the meal and partake in it. We used the tomatoes and corn in season and paired them with pork, both fresh and cured. I am Southern, after all. I refined a classic stew by creating a complex broth that eats like a sauce. That went over hunks of succulent pork and a medley of collard greens, sweet potatoes, and corn. I was so happy with how this comforting bowl of love came out, I didn't even care if I went home on this dish. I knew it was very special. When I was cooking, I told my ancestors, "This food is for you." And when everyone at the table took a bite, they tasted that honoring of the past, too. Matthew told me there was a long silent pause when everyone started eating because the dish was so good. That's just what I want as a cook: for everyone to soak up the love I pour in.

> One 3½-pound boneless pork butt, untrimmed,
>   cut into 1½-inch chunks
> Kosher salt and freshly ground black pepper
> 1 tablespoon canola or other neutral oil
> One 6-ounce piece boneless naturally cured ham hock,
>   sliced, or 4 strips thick-cut bacon
> 3 carrots, coarsely chopped
> 2 celery ribs, coarsely chopped
> 1 medium leek (white and pale green parts only), trimmed,
>   coarsely chopped, and thoroughly rinsed
> 1 large yellow onion, coarsely chopped
> 1 pound vine-ripened tomatoes, cored and cut into quarters
> 2 dried chiles de arbol, stemmed and coarsely chopped
> 1 cup dry red wine
> 3 ears corn, husks and silk removed, kernels cut off
>   and reserved, cobs reserved

5 cups Chicken Stock (page 54) or store-bought
unsalted chicken broth
2 fresh or dried bay leaves
1 bunch collard greens, rinsed and dried
1 large sweet potato, peeled and finely diced
4 teaspoons extra virgin olive oil

1. Preheat the oven to 350°F.

2. Pat the pork pieces dry with paper towels and generously season with salt and pepper. Heat a large Dutch oven or roasting pan over high heat, then heat the canola oil until it dimples. You want to make sure the oil is hot. Add half of the pork in a single layer, spacing the pieces apart. As soon as the meat hits the pan, you should hear a sizzle. If you don't hear anything, you're about to boil meat. Let the pork sit until it's browned, then turn to another side and brown. Keep browning and turning until the pork is browned on all sides, about 6 minutes. Transfer to a half sheet pan and repeat with the remaining pork. If the pork is getting too dark too fast and seems like it might burn, turn the heat down a little.

3. Add the ham hock and cook, stirring, until the fat renders and the meat is browned, about 2 minutes. If you're on a diet, look the other way.

4. Add the carrots, celery, leek, onion, tomatoes, and chiles. Cook, stirring and scraping up those tasty browned bits in the pan, until the onion is just starting to become translucent and the other vegetables are lightly seared, about 4 minutes. The goal is not to cook the vegetables now; it's mainly to get those browned bits up.

5. Return the pork with any accumulated juices to the pan, arranging the pork pieces to sit in a single layer on top of the vegetables. Add the wine, bring to a boil, and cook until you can't smell the alcohol, about 5 minutes.

6. Add the corn cobs, stock, and bay leaves. Bring to a boil, then transfer to the oven. Cook until the meat is fork-tender, about 2 hours. Don't overcook or the meat will get dry.

7. When the pork is almost done, prepare the collards: Working in batches, hold the stems of the collards with one hand and the leaves with the other, folding up the leaves together like the wings on a butterfly. Pull the leaves down, leaving the stems clean. If the leaves are really large, cut them down the center. Stack a few leaves, then roll them like a cigar. Slice the roll into thin shreds. Repeat with the remaining collard leaves.

8. When the pork chunks are done, remove them and reserve. Strain the broth through a fine-mesh sieve, pressing on the solids to extract as much liquid as possible. Discard the solids. Keep the pork and liquid warm.

9. In a large bowl, toss the sweet potato with 2 teaspoons of the olive oil and a pinch of salt until well coated. Heat a large nonstick skillet over high heat until really hot. Add half of the sweet potato in a single layer. Cook, shaking and tossing the pan occasionally, until browned, about 3 minutes. The sweet potato should be tender, but neither mushy nor crunchy. Transfer to a half sheet pan. Repeat with the remaining sweet potato.

10. In the same skillet, heat 1 teaspoon olive oil until hot. Add the corn kernels and cook, tossing, until just browned, about 1 minute. Reserve in the pan with the sweet potato.

11. In the same skillet, heat the remaining 1 teaspoon olive oil. Add the collards, season with salt, and cook, stirring, until bright green and just wilted, about 30 seconds. Remove from the heat and stir in the sweet potato and corn.

12. Divide the vegetable mixture among eight serving bowls. Top with pork and spoon the strained broth all over. Serve immediately.

Osso Buco

Serves 8

Winter is meant for fall-off-the-bone stews. And this classic Italian one is among my favorites. I like to keep it simple and traditional because you want the delicate yet hearty meat to shine here. Instead of simply spooning the stew over pasta or polenta, I finish the stew with a traditional blend of parsley, lemon, and garlic. That zing totally brightens the warming, meaty sauce and reminds you that spring is coming soon.

8 pieces veal osso buco (each 2 inches thick)
Kosher salt and freshly ground black pepper
2 tablespoons extra virgin olive oil
2 large yellow onions, diced (4 cups)
2 large carrots, diced (2 cups)
2 medium ribs celery, diced (1 cup)
6 sprigs fresh thyme
4 garlic cloves, chopped
1 cup dry white wine
2 cups canned diced fire-roasted tomatoes with their juices
1 quart veal stock (see Note) or Chicken Stock (page 54)
Creamy Goat Cheese Grits (page 103) or cooked pasta
*   or polenta, for serving*
Gremolata (page 88)

1. Let the veal stand at room temperature for 1 hour before cooking. Preheat the oven to 300°F.

2. Generously season each piece of veal on both sides with salt and pepper. Heat a very large (10-quart) Dutch oven over medium-high heat. Add the olive oil, heat, then add half the veal pieces, flat side down. Cook, turning over once, until nicely browned, about 5 minutes per side. You really want good color. Transfer to a plate. Repeat with the remaining veal.

3. Reduce the heat to medium and add the onions, carrots, celery, and thyme to the pot. Cook, stirring occasionally, until the onions are translucent, about 5 minutes. Add the garlic and cook, stirring and scraping the bottom and sides of the pot, until the garlic is golden, about 2 minutes. Make sure you scrape up the *fond,* the super flavorful browned bits of meat stuck to the bottom of the pan. It adds goodness to the dish!

4. Pour in the wine and continue stirring and scraping the pan. Raise the heat to medium-high and cook until the wine has reduced by half. Stir in the tomatoes, then return the meat to the pan, nestling the pieces in a single layer. Add any accumulated juices to the pan, then pour in the stock.

5. Bring to a boil, and then reduce the heat to maintain a simmer. Cover the pan and transfer to the oven. Bake until the meat is fork-tender, about 3 hours. Season with salt and pepper to taste.

6. Serve the osso buco over the grits or hot pasta or polenta. Top with gremolata.

NOTE
ε You can find good veal stock in specialty markets.

Persian Marinated Lamb Roast with Cucumber-Yogurt Sauce on Grilled Pita

Serves 6

Persian flavors are among my favorites—warm spices like cinnamon and allspice paired with sharp garlic and parsley. In re-creating the flavors of lamb with pita, I decided to try using a loin roast. This cut of meat is incredibly tender and tasty and looks so pretty when rolled. You can ask your butcher to tie your lamb for you or do it yourself. Just roll it up and tie it with kitchen twine every inch or so. It should be securely tied, but not too tight. After it's done cooking, you can snip through the twine and cut it into perfect, juicy slices to nestle in simply seasoned grilled pitas and top with creamy cucumber sauce.

MARINATED LAMB

¼ cup extra virgin olive oil
2 tablespoons minced garlic
2 tablespoons minced fresh mint leaves
2 tablespoons minced fresh flat-leaf parsley leaves
1 teaspoon kosher salt
½ teaspoon ground cinnamon
½ teaspoon ground allspice
¼ teaspoon cayenne pepper
¼ teaspoon freshly ground black pepper
1 boneless lamb loin roast (1½ pounds),
*   rolled and tied*

ZAATAR PITAS

1 tablespoon dried thyme leaves
1½ teaspoons ground red sumac (optional)
1 teaspoon white sesame seeds, toasted (page 296)
¼ teaspoon kosher salt
6 pocketless pita breads
Extra virgin olive oil

Cucumber-Yogurt Sauce (recipe follows)
2 plum tomatoes, cored, seeded, and diced

1. To make the lamb: In a large resealable plastic bag, combine the oil, garlic, mint, parsley, salt, cinnamon, allspice, cayenne, and pepper. Add the lamb, seal the bag, and turn to coat well. Seal and refrigerate for at least 6 hours or up to overnight.

2. Heat an outdoor grill to high. Meanwhile, let the lamb stand at room temperature for 30 minutes.

3. Remove the lamb from the marinade, wiping off any excess with paper towels. Discard the marinade. Place the lamb on the grill, cover, and cook for 5 minutes. Turn to another side, cover, and cook for 5 minutes longer. Continue turning and cooking until evenly browned on all sides and a meat thermometer inserted into the thickest part of the meat registers 130°F for medium-rare, about 20 minutes total. Transfer to a cutting board and let rest for 15 minutes. Keep the grill on high.

4. While the lamb rests, make the pitas: In a small bowl, combine the thyme, sumac, sesame seeds, and salt. Brush the pitas with olive oil and sprinkle the thyme mixture on both sides of each pita. Place on the hot grill grate and grill until just browned, about 30 seconds. Flip carefully and grill until the other side is browned, about 30 seconds.

5. Thinly slice the lamb against the grain and serve with the pitas, cucumber sauce, and tomatoes.

Cucumber-Yogurt Sauce

Makes about 1½ cups

> ½ seedless cucumber, finely diced
> ½ cup plain whole-milk yogurt
> ½ cup sour cream
> 1 garlic clove, minced
> 1 teaspoon ground cumin
> 1 teaspoon freshly grated lime zest
> Kosher salt and freshly ground black pepper

In a medium bowl, combine the cucumber, yogurt, sour cream, garlic, cumin, and lime zest. Season to taste with salt and pepper. Let stand for at least 1 hour or cover and refrigerate for up to 1 day.

Poultry

I just love, love, love chicken. (I got that from Mama!) It's so versatile and can be easily transformed based on the flavors that go into the dish. Game birds, like duck, are also delicious and easier to handle than most people think. There's something ultimately satisfying about poultry, especially when you start with whole birds. For fast, simple meals, I rely on the boneless cuts from the supermarket. When I have more time, I prefer to start with bone-in whole birds or pieces, which are cheaper and impart a lot more flavor.

Chicken Pot Pie (with Crust on the Bottom!)

Serves 8

This was one of my favorites as a kid, one of the first meals I made on my own, and one that I'm constantly reinventing to make even better. It triggers so many happy food memories! The key to my version is having crust on the top and bottom—and getting that bottom crust browned and crisp before it gets soaked with sauce. I bake the crust alone, then spoon the hot filling over one piece and top with another. I love the way the crust stays flaky (yum) and doesn't have that gooey raw dough layer (blech). Plus, it makes it great for entertaining. You can bake the crust early, keep the filling simmering, and just combine them when you're ready to serve.

PIE CRUST

Flaky Butter Crust (page 257)
1 large egg
1 teaspoon water

FILLING

3 tablespoons canola or other neutral oil
4 medium yellow onions, diced
1 pound carrots, cut in half lengthwise then into
  ½-inch-thick half-moons
6 celery ribs, cut in half lengthwise then into
  ½-inch-thick slices at an angle
6 fresh sage leaves
4 sprigs fresh thyme
2 sprigs fresh rosemary
2 fresh or dried bay leaves
Kosher salt and freshly ground black pepper
2 quarts Chicken Stock (page 54) or store-bought
  unsalted chicken broth
Two 2½-pound chickens, each cut into 8 pieces
  (2 wings, 2 legs, 2 breasts, 2 thighs)
4 tablespoons (½ stick) unsalted butter
¾ cup all-purpose flour
¼ cup heavy cream
One 10-ounce package frozen baby peas (2 cups)

1. To make the pie crust: Divide the dough into 8 pieces, flatten each piece into a disk, and wrap each tightly in plastic wrap. Chill for 30 minutes.

2. Place one oven rack near the top of the oven and one near the bottom. Preheat the oven to 400°F.

3. Roll each disk into an ⅛-inch-thick round. Transfer to parchment paper–lined half sheet pans. In a small bowl, beat the egg with the water. Brush the egg wash over all the dough rounds.

4. Bake until golden, about 20 minutes, switching the positions of the pans halfway through baking. Transfer the pans to wire racks and let cool completely.

5. To make the filling: In an extra large Dutch oven or a stockpot, heat the oil over medium heat. Add the onions, carrots, celery, sage, thyme, rosemary, and bay leaves. Season with salt and pepper, then cook, stirring occasionally, until just tender, about 15 minutes. Add the chicken stock and bring to a boil.

6. Add all the chicken pieces, return to a boil, then lower to heat to maintain a bare simmer. Cover and cook until the chicken is just cooked through, about 30 minutes. Begin checking the chicken after 15 minutes; pull pieces out and transfer to a large platter as they're finished. Smaller pieces, like the wings, will be done first.

7. Strain the stock through a sieve, reserving the vegetables and stock separately, but removing and discarding the herbs. Keep the broth hot.

8. When the chicken is cool enough to handle, remove and discard the skin and bones and pull the meat into bite-size pieces.

9. In a very large saucepan, melt the butter over medium-low heat. Whisk in the flour until smooth. Whisk in the hot stock and bring to a boil, whisking occasionally. Continue cooking until the sauce has the consistency of heavy cream, then stir in the heavy cream. Bring to a boil again, then stir in the chicken pieces and vegetables until well coated. When the filling is hot, stir in the peas. Season to taste with salt and pepper.

10. Break each pastry round to form two half-moons and place one in the bottom of each serving dish. Divide the chicken filling among the dishes and top with the other half of pastry. Serve immediately.

❧To make these pies extra special, I turn the dough into cloches, the pretty French domes set over hot dishes. Simply ball up a sheet of aluminum foil the same diameter as the bowl of your serving dish, but no larger than 4 inches in diameter. Make eight balls. Arrange the balls on a half sheet pan, pressing them down slightly so they don't roll around. Press a small sheet of parchment paper on top of each ball to cover. Line another half sheet pan with parchment paper.

Working with one disk of dough at a time, roll the dough into an ⅛-inch-thick round. With a knife or large biscuit cutter, cut out a round 2 inches larger than your foil ball. Use some of the trimmings to form a marble-size ball. Reserve the remaining trimmings; these will go under the chicken filling as the bottom crust. Drape the dough round over a parchment-covered foil ball.

Gently press the small dough ball onto the top of the round. Repeat with the remaining dough and foil balls. Transfer the dough trimmings to the second parchment paper–lined pan. Brush all the dough with the egg wash. Bake both pans as above, then carefully remove the domes when they're completely cooled. Place the baked dough trimmings on the bottom of the serving dishes and top with the chicken filling, then with the cloches.

❧ For special occasions, I like to top the pies with pea salt. I get dehydrated peas, Just Peas, from a company called Just Tomatoes. In a spice grinder, I process ½ cup dehydrated peas with 1 tablespoon kosher salt until the mixture is finely ground and well blended. Sprinkle the pea salt all over the top crust and filling just before serving.

❧ Crazy for Chicken Pot Pie

It was not an easy road to the finals of *Top Chef All-Stars*. As the competition went on, I began to worry that my simple soulful style wouldn't be enough for the judges and began considering moving away from what I know best to think of newfangled dishes to impress. Then we got a new challenge: cook a birthday lunch for comedian and late-night talk show host Jimmy Fallon. We would each make one of his favorite dishes—and they were all yummy comfort foods!

When I found out that I'd get to cook chicken pot pie for him, I giggled like a schoolgirl and jumped for joy. Literally. On national TV. Because that's how much I love chicken pot pie. I felt like I had won the lottery! I craved it, I saw it, I picked it on the cell phone shootout. Aagh, nice! On that *Top Chef* episode, I nailed the dish, topping the buttery bottom crust with my light, creamy sauce and brightening it all with my homemade pea salt. Everyone who ate it could feel and *taste* the love. They tasted my memories of that soulful dish—and their own memories of pot pies past—and got a big hug from me with that pretty little pie. That's what I mean when I say I make food that hugs you.

A big lesson learned that day, though. When you really want to impress at the table, just make something you yourself really love. It may be something fancy pants with a million ingredients and even more steps, or it may be a simple, homey dish. Whatever it is, as long as you're excited by it, whoever's eating it will be, too.

Creamed Chicken with Broccoli and Mushrooms

Serves 4

My sister, Kim, made this dish all the time when we lived together in college. After classes, she'd come home and throw canned soup and frozen broccoli in the pan. And she kept making it when her kids were little to get them to eat their veggies. She told them the broccoli was a little tree and they ate it up! In honor of my big sis, I'm remaking this dish with fresh ingredients and adding sautéed mushrooms, one of my favorite flavors.

Kosher salt
2 large heads broccoli, stalks peeled and thinly sliced
*   at an angle, florets cut into 1-inch pieces*
1 tablespoon canola or other neutral oil
Freshly ground black pepper
1¼ pounds boneless, skin-on chicken thighs
1 large shallot, finely diced
1 garlic clove, finely chopped
3 sprigs fresh thyme or tarragon
1¾ pounds cremini mushrooms, very thinly sliced
*   (8 cups)*
1 tablespoon unsalted butter
2 tablespoons all-purpose flour
2 tablespoons dry (fino) sherry
1½ cups Chicken Stock (page 54) or store-bought
*   unsalted chicken broth*
1 cup whole milk
¼ teaspoon freshly grated nutmeg
¼ teaspoon cayenne pepper
2 tablespoons heavy cream
2 ounces sharp cheddar cheese, shredded (½ cup)

1. Bring a large saucepan of water to a boil and salt generously. Add the broccoli stalks and cook for 1 minute, then add the florets. Cook them together for 3 minutes more. Drain and reserve.

2. Heat the oil in a large, deep skillet over high heat. Sprinkle ½ teaspoon each salt and pepper all over the chicken. Add to the skillet in a single layer, skin side down, and sear, turning the pieces over once, until golden on both sides, about 5 minutes. Transfer to a plate.

3. Reduce the heat to medium and add the shallot, garlic, and thyme. Cook, stirring, until the shallots are transparent, about 2 minutes. Add the mushrooms, butter, and ¼ teaspoon each salt and pepper. Raise the heat to medium-high and cook, stirring, until the mushrooms wilt, release their juices, and their juices evaporate, about 8 minutes.

4. Sprinkle the flour over the mushrooms and stir until well mixed. Stir in the sherry and cook for 1 minute, then stir in the stock. Continue stirring and add the milk, ½ cup at a time. Stir in the nutmeg and cayenne and bring to a boil.

5. Reduce the heat to medium and return the chicken with their juices to the pan. Cover and simmer until the chicken is cooked through, about 10 minutes. Stir in the cream, then the broccoli, reserving some florets for garnish. Discard the thyme.

6. Sprinkle the cheese on top and garnish with the reserved florets. Season with more salt to taste.

Catering Like Carla

If you're making this for vegetarians, you can use seitan or extra firm tofu in place of the chicken. For the seitan, simply use it the way you'd use chicken. For the tofu, place the cut-up pieces between paper towels and squeeze all the water out before searing. Stir them in at the end with the cooked broccoli.

Chorizo Chicken 'n' Raisin-Thyme Dumplings

Serves 12

Talk about a big bowl of comfort. I grew up with all the mellow, warming flavors of the classic chicken 'n' dumplings and I wanted to give it a boost. Smoky chorizo sausage, loads of fall veggies, and sweet herbed dumplings make this extra tasty.

CHICKEN STEW

1 tablespoon extra virgin olive oil
1 pound fresh Spanish chorizo, casing removed,
*   sausage crumbled (see Note)*
One 3½- to 4-pound chicken, cut into 8 pieces
*   (2 wings, 2 legs, 2 breasts, 2 thighs), rinsed*
*   and patted dry*
Kosher salt and freshly ground black pepper
1 medium rutabaga, peeled and cut into ½-inch dice
2 fresh or dried bay leaves
4 sprigs fresh thyme
4 small carrots, peeled and cut into ½-inch dice
1 large sweet potato, peeled and cut into ½-inch dice
2 celery ribs, cut into ½-inch-thick slices
3 small parsnips, peeled and cut into ½-inch dice
2 cups fresh or frozen green peas

RAISIN-THYME DUMPLINGS

2 cups all-purpose flour
1 tablespoon baking powder
1 teaspoon table salt
½ teaspoon baking soda
½ teaspoon freshly grated nutmeg
1 teaspoon freshly grated orange zest
2 teaspoons fresh thyme leaves, chopped
¼ cup golden raisins, coarsely chopped
1 large egg, beaten
3 tablespoons unsalted butter, melted
¾ cup buttermilk

1. To make the stew: Heat a 12-quart stockpot or Dutch oven over medium heat. Add the oil, heat well, and add the crumbled chorizo. Cook, stirring occasionally, until browned, about 8 minutes. Use a slotted spoon to transfer the sausage to a dish.

2. Season the chicken pieces well with salt and pepper. Add half of the chicken to the fat in the pot and cook, turning once, until browned well, about 8 minutes. Transfer to another dish and repeat with the remaining chicken.

3. Pour out the fat from the pot and discard. Return the chicken and chorizo to the pot and add enough water to cover by 2 inches. Add the rutabaga, bay leaves, and thyme. Cover the pot and bring to a boil. Reduce the heat to maintain a steady simmer, then cook until the rutabaga is almost tender, about 10 minutes. Add the carrots, sweet potato, and celery. Cover and cook until the carrots are almost tender, about 15 minutes longer.

4. While the stew simmers, make the dumpling dough: Into a large bowl, sift together the flour, baking powder, salt, baking soda, and nutmeg. Stir in the orange zest, thyme, and raisins.

5. Make a well in the center of the flour and add the egg, melted butter, and buttermilk. Use a fork to blend the wet ingredients together, then quickly incorporate the dry ingredients to make a stiff dough.

6. Uncover the stew and add more salt and pepper to taste. Raise the heat to maintain a rapid boil. Stir in the parsnips and peas, if they're fresh. Adjust the heat to maintain a steady simmer.

7. Drop a few heaping teaspoons of the dumpling dough into the simmering stew, spacing them apart so that they don't touch one another right when they're dropped in. Once they're set on the outside, drop a few more teaspoons in. Continue until all of the dumpling dough is added. Cover and cook for 10 minutes. If you're using frozen peas, stir them in. Cover again and cook just until the dumplings are puffed and cooked through and the peas are hot, about 3 minutes longer. Check on the dumplings occasionally to make sure they don't overcook and dry out. Remove and discard the bay leaves and thyme sprigs and serve immediately.

NOTE

&Fresh, uncooked Spanish chorizo can be found in Spanish and specialty markets. If you can't find the fresh variety, you can use fully cooked links instead. Remove the casing and slice very thinly. Just be sure to buy Spanish, not Mexican, chorizo. You want the distinctive flavor from the smoked paprika in Spanish chorizo.

Super Fast Fried Chicken

Serves 4

Grandma Thelma was the Queen of Fried Chicken. When we went to dinner at her house, I'd start drooling the minute I walked in the door and smelled her juicy, crisp chicken. But I never actually helped her cook it. I didn't start frying chicken until I was in my thirties. Now that I'm the one in my family responsible for rescuing and preserving our family recipes, I've been working to perfect fried chicken. This is the version I've created for busy, busy nights when I'm craving homemade fried chicken. I don't have fried chicken all the time, but when I do, I want to remember Grandma Thelma. And this recipe helps me do just that.

> *Kosher salt and freshly ground black pepper*
> *2 pounds bone-in, skin-on chicken thighs (about 8)*
> *1 garlic clove, minced, then mashed to a paste*
> *   with the flat side of a chef's knife*
> *1½ cups all-purpose flour*
> *1 teaspoon sweet paprika*
> *½ teaspoon cayenne pepper*
> *½ teaspoon table salt*
> *⅓ cup peanut oil, plus more if needed*

1. Sprinkle kosher salt and pepper all over the chicken, then rub the garlic onto the chicken. Let sit for 15 minutes.

2. In a large resealable plastic bag, combine the flour, paprika, cayenne, and table salt. Add the chicken in batches and shake well until all the pieces are evenly coated. If you have time, let the pieces sit for 15 minutes.

3. Heat the oil in a 10-inch cast-iron or other heavy skillet over medium heat until it reaches 365°F. The oil's ready when a little flour dropped in bubbles and sizzles steadily.

4. Shake excess flour off a piece of chicken, then carefully place the chicken in the oil, skin side down. Repeat, adding just a few more pieces to the pan. You don't want to crowd the pan. Keep adjusting the heat to keep a steady sizzle and to maintain 365°F. Cover and cook until browned on the bottom, about 7 minutes, then carefully turn each

piece over. Cover and cook until browned and the meat is cooked through, about 8 minutes more.

5. Crumple up some paper towels and drain the chicken on them. Repeat with the remaining chicken, replenishing and reheating the oil between batches.

🫖 Setting the Stage

I was quiet and shy as a kid. Really! Actually, my mama's not so sure that that was the case, but I definitely remember being put in a theater class to get over my shyness. If you haven't already noticed, it worked. I fell in love with the stage and spent much of my childhood and teenage years in shows. Like all theater kids, I dreamed about makin' it big, but never considered it a reality until I saw my Uncle David on the stage in New York City.

As a child, I remember Uncle David, my dad's brother, as a dramatic character. He always sauntered into the room, his arms swinging confidently, throwing in a two-step here and there, bowing at the end. We all knew that he loved acting, but we never thought he'd up and move from his home in St. Louis to New York City to try it.

When he landed a role in *Bubbling Brown Sugar,* my whole family headed north to watch him perform. That show transformed my life—as did the fried chicken we ate afterwards. For whatever reason, Uncle David had some really good chickens in his fridge. Organic, fresh birds before you could easily buy organic, fresh birds. To celebrate the show, his mom, my Grandma Thelma, decided to fry 'em up, her specialty. She massaged salt into the cut-up chickens, then tossed the pieces with seasoned flour in a paper bag and let the meat sit in that bag for fifteen minutes to let the flour really stick to the chicken. I still remember her mumbling, "That's the most important step, gets the crust to stay on." Once the chicken went in the pan, she kept fiddling with it to get it right since she didn't have her special old cast-iron frying pan up there. Grandma Thelma's so amazing, she nailed that dish even without her pan. Those birds came out crisp and brown and juicy hot inside. It was so good that even thinking about it now makes me tear up a little. It was really that good.

Now I've ended up in New York City, cooking on television. I often think back on that first trip to the big city, to remind myself of just how lucky I am to have ended up doing what I love. I felt such a thrill as a kid, seeing Uncle David on stage, and such joy, eating Grandma Thelma's fried chicken with my family all gathered in this strange new place. I wouldn't have made it here without their inspiration and support and love. They've since passed on, but I remember them both every day.

Sunday Roast Chicken

Serves 4

Each chef has her own version of roast chicken. I tinkered with lots of techniques over the years and just love this one, which uses my desert-island ingredient—lemon!—with one of my favorite herbs. Of course, the brining is key to a juicy bird. It's easier than you think and makes a world of a difference. This dish is so special, it's good enough for company.

> Kosher salt
> 3 tablespoons packed brown sugar
> 2 quarts cold water
> One 3½-pound chicken
> 2 garlic cloves, minced
> 2 teaspoons freshly grated lemon zest
> 2 teaspoons finely chopped fresh thyme leaves
> 3 tablespoons butter, at room temperature,
>   plus 2 tablespoons cold butter
> 1 lemon, cut in half
> 1 cup dry white wine
> Freshly ground black pepper

1. Stir ⅓ cup salt and the sugar into the water until they dissolve. Place the chicken in a large resealable plastic bag and pour the brine over. Seal tightly and refrigerate for at least 3 hours and up to 9 hours.

2. Preheat the oven to 425°F.

3. Remove the chicken from the brine and rinse it well, inside and out. When you think you're done, do it one last time! Then pat it dry very thoroughly.

4. In a small bowl, mix the garlic, lemon zest, and thyme into the softened butter. Gently loosen the skin covering the breast and legs. Work the seasoned butter under the skin so that the butter covers the breast meat and thighs. Be very gentle with the bird. Don't tear the skin! Squeeze the lemon halves inside the cavity, then place the lemon halves inside. Tie the legs together with kitchen twine and push the wings behind the neck so that the chicken looks like it's relaxing and watching TV.

5. Place the chicken breast-side-up on a rack in a metal roasting pan. Roast until the juices run clear when the bird is pierced with a knife, about 1 hour.

6. Remove the chicken and the rack from the roasting pan. Set the pan over a burner on medium heat. Add the wine and cook, stirring and scraping the browned bits from the pan. Cook for a second, then remove from the heat. Add the cold butter and stir until incorporated. Season to taste with salt and pepper. Serve with the chicken, carving the chicken on a cutting board or serving platter just before serving.

Poached Chicken with Roasted Fennel and Frisée Salad

Serves 8

Poached chicken is so underrated. Okay, I'll admit, it's not pretty. But the succulent juiciness of the meat more than makes up for that. As a bonus, it's a really healthy, low-fat way to enjoy the white meat. I poach the chicken with a blend of aromatics, then echo those flavors in the salad and dressing. The double dose of anise—fennel and tarragon—comes in the form of seeds, bulbs, stems, and leaves. That, my friend, is how to eat whole foods.

1 quart cold water
2 garlic cloves, smashed
1 teaspoon fennel seeds, toasted (page 296)
1 teaspoon coriander seeds, toasted (page 296)
½ bunch fresh tarragon
Kosher salt
Four 6-ounce boneless, skinless chicken breasts
2 heads fennel, ½ cup fronds reserved, stalks discarded,
*   bulbs cored and cut into ¼-inch-thick slices*
1 tablespoon extra virgin olive oil
½ cup green olives (preferably Cerignola), pitted and
*   cut into thin slivers*
¼ cup thinly shaved red onion
2 heads frisée lettuce, separated into bite-size pieces
Tarragon Vinaigrette (recipe follows)

1. Preheat the oven to 425°F.

2. In a 5-quart saucepan, combine the water, garlic, fennel seeds, coriander, tarragon, and 1 teaspoon salt. Add the chicken and bring to a gentle boil over medium heat. Cover, reduce the heat to low, and simmer until just cooked through, about 15 minutes. Transfer the chicken to a plate and let cool. Pull into bite-size pieces. You can strain the broth and refrigerate it in an airtight container for another use.

3. While the chicken cooks, toss the sliced fennel with the oil and ½ teaspoon salt. Spread in a single layer on a half sheet pan and roast until tender and slightly charred, about 30 minutes. Let cool slightly.

4. Chop the reserved fennel fronds. In a large bowl, toss the chicken, roasted fennel, fennel fronds, olives, onion, frisée, and vinaigrette. Toss until lightly coated. Serve at room temperature.

Tarragon Vinaigrette

4 teaspoons sherry vinegar
¼ cup extra virgin olive oil
1 tablespoon minced shallot
1 teaspoon Dijon mustard
1 tablespoon mayonnaise
½ teaspoon kosher salt
¼ teaspoon freshly ground black pepper
2 teaspoons finely chopped fresh tarragon leaves

In a jar, combine the vinegar, oil, shallot, mustard, mayonnaise, salt, and pepper. Shake until well blended. Add the tarragon and shake again. You can also whisk the dressing in a small bowl and whisk again just before using.

Backyard BBQ Salad

Serves 4

My hometown of Nashville is the land of red-sauce barbecue. In other parts of the South, you'll find white barbecue sauce, which is basically a mixture of mayo and vinegar. I'm playing with that concept here and turning it into a fresh summer salad. This dressing would be fantastic in a slaw, too, especially if it's paired with good barbecue.

DRESSING
3 medium vine-ripened tomatoes
½ cup mayonnaise
4 teaspoons cider vinegar
4 teaspoons fresh lemon juice
2 teaspoons packed brown sugar
½ teaspoon kosher salt
¼ teaspoon freshly ground black pepper
Pinch of cayenne pepper

SALAD
4 boneless, skinless chicken breast halves
2 tablespoons Barbecue Dry Rub (page 157)
2 ears corn, husks and silk removed
2 romaine hearts, chopped
¼ small head red cabbage, finely chopped
1 yellow bell pepper, stemmed, seeded, and diced

1. To make the dressing: Trim the tops and bottoms of the tomatoes. Cut alongside the outer wall of flesh, the way you would cut the peel and pith off an orange, to remove just the outer walls of the tomatoes. Place the seed sacs in a strainer and press 1 tablespoon tomato water out of them. Dice the tomato outer walls and reserve; discard the cores.

2. In a small bowl, whisk together the tomato water, mayonnaise, vinegar, lemon juice, brown sugar, salt, pepper, and cayenne until smooth.

3. To make the salad: Heat an outdoor grill or grill pan to medium-high. Rub the chicken with the dry rub until well coated. Let stand while the grill heats.

4. Grill the chicken, turning once, until nicely browned and cooked through, about 12 minutes. Grill the corn alongside the chicken until charred in spots, about 12 minutes. When cool enough to handle, chop the chicken and cut the corn kernels off the cobs.

5. In a large bowl, toss the chicken, corn, tomato, romaine, cabbage, and bell pepper with the dressing until well coated. Serve immediately.

Matthew's Chicken Curry

Serves 4

This is one of my favorite dishes in the whole world. And that's because my husband, Matthew, makes it for me. Back home in D.C., he whips it up once a week and I can't get enough. It's packed full of rich curry flavors in a creamy coconut milk sauce. When we first married, he quickly realized that I was often too exhausted after a long day of cooking to come home and cook some more. So he took over the home kitchen and spoils me with his great cooking. Yup, I am a very lucky woman.

¾ pound boneless, skinless chicken breasts, cut into
*   1½-inch chunks*
¾ pound boneless, skinless chicken thighs, cut into
*   1½-inch chunks*
2 teaspoons ground coriander
1½ teaspoons cumin seeds, toasted and ground (page 296)
½ teaspoon ground turmeric
¼ teaspoon cayenne pepper
½ teaspoon kosher salt
1½ teaspoons freshly ground black pepper
3 tablespoons plus 1 teaspoon canola or other neutral oil
2 large yellow onions, very thinly sliced
1 serrano chile, stemmed, seeded, and finely chopped
2 tablespoons Chicken Stock (page 54) or water
4 garlic cloves, very thinly sliced
1½ teaspoons grated peeled fresh ginger
¾ cup coconut milk
¾ cup water
Toasted cashews, for garnish
Cilantro, for garnish
Steamed green peas, for serving
Cooked basmati rice, for serving

1. Put the chicken breast chunks in one bowl and the thighs in another. In a small bowl, combine the coriander, cumin, turmeric, cayenne, salt, and pepper. Divide between the bowls of chicken and turn the chicken pieces to evenly coat. Let stand for 20 minutes.

2. In a large, deep skillet, heat 1 tablespoon of the oil over medium-high heat. Add the chicken thigh chunks in a single layer and cook, turning the pieces occasionally, until nice and browned, about 2 minutes. Transfer to a plate. Repeat with another tablespoon oil and the chicken breast chunks, transferring them to another plate. You just want to sear the chicken, not cook it through.

3. Add another tablespoon of oil to the pan, reduce the heat to medium, and add the onions and chile. Cook, stirring occasionally, until onions are golden and melted, about 7 minutes. Reduce the heat to low and add the stock, stirring in the beautiful browned bits from the bottom of the pan.

4. Add the garlic, ginger, ¼ cup of the coconut milk and ¼ cup of the water. Stir well, bring to a simmer, and return the chicken thighs to the skillet. Cook for 20 minutes, then add the chicken breasts. Cook for 5 minutes, then stir in the remaining coconut milk and water. Cook 5 minutes longer or until stewy.

5. Top with cashews and cilantro. Serve with plain steamed peas and basmati rice.

Ginger Chicken Stir-Fry

Serves 6

One of the best things about writing a cookbook is meeting wonderful people in the process. When I was trying to figure out how to round out my recipe roster, my lovely and talented editor, Leslie, mentioned that she'd been stir-frying a lot at home. It's a technique I love for quick weeknight meals, so I decided to create one with summer vegetables. Peppery arugula heightens the heat of the chile for a zippy zing.

> *3 tablespoons soy sauce*
> *3 tablespoons canola or other neutral oil, plus more*
>   *for vegetables*
> *2 tablespoons packed brown sugar*
> *Freshly grated zest and juice of 2 limes*
> *1 fresh Thai chile, seeded and minced*
> *1 tablespoon grated peeled fresh ginger*
> *1 teaspoon freshly ground black pepper*
> *2 pounds boneless, skin-on chicken thighs*
> *2 small zucchini, cut in quarters lengthwise, seeded,*
>   *and sliced at an angle into thin 2-inch-long pieces*
> *2 medium carrots, cut in half lengthwise and sliced at an angle*
>   *into very thin 2-inch-long pieces*
> *Kosher salt*
> *1 small red onion, cut into ¼-inch dice*
> *3 garlic cloves, minced*
> *½ cup water*
> *2 cups firmly packed baby arugula, rinsed and dried*
> *Steamed rice, for serving*

1. In a large bowl, combine the soy sauce, oil, sugar, lime zest and juice, chile, ginger, and pepper. Add the chicken and turn well to coat. Marinate at room temperature for 30 minutes or cover and refrigerate overnight.

2. Heat a large skillet over medium-high heat. In a large bowl, toss the zucchini and carrots with just enough oil to coat. Season well with salt. Add to the hot skillet and cook, stirring, until just softened, about 2 minutes. Transfer to a plate.

3. Lightly coat the skillet with oil and add the onion. Cook for 1 minute, then add the garlic. Reduce the heat to medium and add just enough of the chicken to fit in a single layer. Cook, turning over once, until brown, about 3 minutes per side. Transfer the chicken to a plate and brown the remaining chicken. Discard any remaining marinade. Return the first batch of chicken to the pan and add the water.

4. Cover and cook until the meat is cooked through, about 10 minutes. Add the zucchini and carrots and cook for 1 minute, stirring. Add the arugula and toss until just wilted. Serve immediately with steamed rice.

Buffalo Wing Burgers

Serves 4

Best buffalo wings I ever had were in Paris. As in France. I know, I know. Crazy, right? But my fellow model friends and I were homesick, so we'd get together to cook good ol' American food. My friend Sherry had this amazing version that combined hot sauce and butter with honey. Some of the other girls freaked out about the honey, but I knew she was onto something. Her wings were sticky, sweet, and so yummy. I've never forgotten Sherry's wings and decided to turn them into a burger. Packing all that goodness including the celery sticks and blue cheese dressing!—between buns is super tasty and easy.

SPICY MAYO

¾ cup mayonnaise
1 tablespoon fresh lemon juice
1 tablespoon hot sauce (preferably Frank's)
2 teaspoons honey
½ teaspoon cayenne pepper

BURGERS

1 tablespoon unsalted butter
1 teaspoon olive oil, plus more for frying
⅓ cup minced yellow onion
½ teaspoon kosher salt
2 garlic cloves, minced
2 teaspoons hot sauce (preferably Frank's)
½ teaspoon dried thyme leaves
½ teaspoon crushed red chile flakes
½ teaspoon freshly ground black pepper
1¼ pounds coarsely ground chicken or turkey
4 brioche or potato buns, toasted if desired
Celery and Blue Cheese Slaw (page 37)

1. To make the mayo: In a small bowl, stir together the mayonnaise, lemon juice, hot sauce, honey, and cayenne until smooth. Refrigerate until needed.

2. To make the burgers: In a small skillet, heat the butter and oil over medium-high heat. When the butter is almost melted, add the onion and salt. Cook, stirring occasionally, for

2 minutes, then stir in the garlic. When the onion is golden and tender, stir in the hot sauce, thyme, chile flakes, and pepper. Transfer to a large bowl and cool to room temperature.

3. Combine the chicken with the cooled onions using slightly damp hands. You want it well mixed, but you don't want to squeeze it and make it tough. Form the mixture into four burgers ½ inch larger in diameter than the buns. Use your thumb to dimple the center of each patty.

4. Coat a large nonstick skillet with oil and heat over medium-high heat. Add the burgers and cook until browned, about 3 minutes, then carefully flip them. Cook until the other side is browned and the meat cooked through, about 3 minutes longer. The burger will feel firm and the juices will run clear.

5. Slather the spicy mayo on the buns. Divide the burgers among the bun bottoms and top with the slaw. Sandwich with the bun tops and serve immediately.

Pan-Seared Turkey
with Cranberry Pear Relish

Serves 12

Listen, I'm all about making beautiful dishes. And I love the look of a whole roasted bird. But I always break whole turkeys down into their parts now—even for the Thanksgiving feast. Here are my three great reasons for it: First, it's much easier to brine cut-up parts and refrigerate them than to cram a whole bird in the fridge. And yes, you must brine the turkey for juicy, delicious meat. Second, when you break down the bird, you can use the back and carcass to make homemade stock or gravy on that same day. If you do have leftover stock, you can whip up a quick soup or pot pie the next day. Third, and most important, cooking the bird in parts ensures that the pieces will all be cooked perfectly. The white meat will stay just as juicy as the dark.

When I made a version of this dish for *The Chew*'s Thanksgiving special, I instigated a great debate. To brine or not to brine, that was the question. I'm a briner. Mario Batali is, too. Michael Symon, however, is against it. Apparently, it's been an ongoing tussle between Mario and Michael. I'm on Mario's side for this one, but I get that some cooks don't want to brine. If that's the case, you can buy a kosher turkey, which is essentially brined for you.

1 quart water
½ cup packed brown sugar
10 whole allspice berries
10 whole cloves
10 whole black peppercorns
5 whole star anise
½ cup plus 2 teaspoons kosher salt
One 11- to 15-pound turkey, cut into 8 pieces
*   (2 wings, 2 legs, 2 breasts, 2 thighs)*
1½ cups fresh flat-leaf parsley leaves, finely chopped
¼ cup fresh sage leaves, finely chopped
4 garlic cloves, minced
3 tablespoons freshly grated lemon zest
1 tablespoon crushed red chile flakes
Extra virgin olive oil
Cranberry Pear Relish (recipe follows)

1. In a very large resealable plastic bag, combine the water, sugar, allspice, cloves, pepper-corns, star anise, and ½ cup salt. Seal tightly and shake to dissolve the salt and sugar. Add the turkey parts, seal tightly, and place in a large bowl. Refrigerate for at least 6 hours or up to overnight.

2. Preheat the oven to 400°F.

3. Remove the turkey from the brine, rinse well, and pat dry with paper towels. Discard the brine. In a small bowl, combine the parsley, sage, garlic, lemon zest, chile flakes, ½ cup olive oil, and 2 teaspoons salt. Carefully run your hand between the turkey skin and meat to loosen the skin, then rub the parsley mixture over the meat and under the skin. Cover and refrigerate for 3 hours.

4. Rub each piece of turkey with olive oil to lightly coat. Heat a heavy skillet over medium-high heat. Lightly coat the bottom with olive oil. Working in batches, sear the turkey parts until golden brown on all sides, about 3 minutes per side. Transfer the browned pieces to a half sheet pan and arrange in a single layer.

5. Roast until a meat thermometer inserted into the thickest part of each piece registers 170°F, about 45 minutes. Start checking the pieces after 40 minutes and transfer each piece from the pan to a platter as it's cooked through. Smaller parts, like the thighs, will be done earlier and the larger pieces, like the drumsticks, can take up to 1 hour. Serve with the cranberry relish.

Cranberry Pear Relish

Makes about 5 cups

>   1 medium yellow onion, finely diced
>   1½ cups sugar
>   ½ cup dry red wine
>   One 2-inch piece fresh ginger, peeled and grated
>   Two 3-inch strips lemon zest, removed with a vegetable peeler
>   1 teaspoon kosher salt
>   1 pound fresh or frozen cranberries, thawed if frozen (4 cups)
>   4 ripe Bosc pears, peeled, cored, and cut into ½-inch chunks

1. In a medium saucepan, combine the onion, sugar, wine, ginger, lemon zest, and salt. Bring to a boil over high heat, stirring to dissolve the sugar. Reduce the heat to maintain a simmer, then simmer for 15 minutes.

2. Stir in the cranberries and pears and simmer for 20 minutes or until the cranberries and onion have softened. The sauce will become a rich scarlet color.

3. Remove and discard the lemon zest. Let cool to room temperature before serving. You can cover and refrigerate the relish for up to 2 weeks.

Catering Like Carla

Save the turkey back and neck for making homemade stock. Simply follow the directions for Chicken Stock (page 54), swapping the whole chicken for the turkey back and neck.

Prick each cranberry with a pin or needle before cooking. This will keep the berries from bursting and getting mushy as they cook.

Duck Ragù over Butternut Squash Grits

Serves 10

Throughout the fall, I stew pots and pots of this ragù. When the weather starts to get chilly, I just want the cozy richness of braised duck in a spicy, smoky tomato sauce. With butternut squash grits, it's heaven. It's just as good over pasta, too. To balance the richness, I top the steaming stew with sharp arugula and salty ricotta salata cheese.

8 whole duck legs with the thighs, skin removed (4 pounds)
Kosher salt and freshly ground black pepper
¼ cup olive oil
2 large yellow onions, finely chopped
2 medium carrots, finely chopped
2 celery ribs, finely chopped
2 jalapeño chiles, stemmed, seeded, and finely diced
4 garlic cloves, minced
Two 28-ounce cans diced fire-roasted tomatoes
2 cups Chicken Stock (page 54) or store-bought
    unsalted chicken broth
2 cups Chianti or other dry red wine
2 fresh or dried bay leaves
Super Squashy Butternut Squash Grits (page 104)
Arugula, for garnish
Ricotta salata, for garnish

1. Remove excess fat from the duck legs and thighs and rinse them with cold water. Pat dry with paper towels and season with salt and pepper.

2. In a 12-quart heavy-bottomed casserole or Dutch oven, heat the oil over medium-high heat until almost smoking. Add half of the duck and cook, turning to brown on all sides, about 12 minutes. Transfer to a large dish. Repeat with the remaining duck.

3. Add the onions, carrots, celery, jalapeños, and garlic and season with salt and pepper. Cook, stirring occasionally, until softened, about 9 minutes. Add the tomatoes, stock, wine, and bay leaves, and bring to a boil. Return the duck to the pot and return to a boil. Cover and reduce the heat to maintain a steady simmer until the duck is tender, about 1 hour.

4. Transfer the duck to a dish. When cool enough to handle, pull the meat into bite-size pieces. Discard the bones and return the meat to the casserole. Simmer uncovered until the sauce is thickened, about 30 minutes. Season with salt and pepper to taste. Remove and discard the bay leaves.

5. Divide the grits among eight serving dishes. Top with the duck ragù and garnish with the arugula. Use a grater to grate the ricotta salata over the arugula.

Fish and Shellfish

Growing up in Nashville, I didn't have much fish or sea-food aside from catfish. My culinary school training and time in France taught me how to cook and flavor delicate fish and shellfish, even when the seasonings are bold, like Dijon mustard and capers. The best thing about seafood is that it cooks very quickly and can be infused with flavor, making it ideal for yummy weeknight meals and sophisticated dinner parties.

Grilled Tuna with Tomato-Olive Relish

Serves 4

No fuss, no muss. That's my motto for weeknight meals and weekend entertaining—and that's exactly what this dish is. It's a real winner because it's tasty, healthy, and fast. Super fresh sushi-grade tuna is always a treat, but it's the condiment that makes the dish. I love to put it over other simply grilled firm fish, and it works with steak and chicken, too. I can't wait for summer, when tomatoes are in season and full of flavor, so that I can keep a stash of this on hand. In fact, I start craving this relish at the end of spring, so I'll throw it together with first-of-the-season grape tomatoes cut in half. The relish keeps well for a day, so I'll make it one night and badda-bing badda-boom, the next night's dinner will be on the table in a flash.

TOMATO-OLIVE RELISH

1 pound plum tomatoes (about 3 large)
½ small red onion, finely diced (½ cup)
¼ cup good black or green olives, pitted and cut
*   into thin slivers*
2 tablespoons chopped fresh flat-leaf parsley leaves
2 teaspoons minced garlic
2 tablespoons extra virgin olive oil
1 tablespoon balsamic vinegar
½ teaspoon kosher salt
¼ teaspoon freshly ground black pepper

SIMPLY GRILLED TUNA

1 tablespoon extra virgin olive oil
Four 8-ounce center-cut sushi-grade tuna steaks
*   (each 1 inch thick)*
½ teaspoon kosher salt
¼ teaspoon freshly ground black pepper

1. To make the relish: Trim the tops of the tomatoes, then sit them on that flat side on your cutting board. Starting at the pointed tip, use a sharp knife to slice along the curve of the tomato to the bottom, removing the solid wall of flesh from the seeds in a nice flat fillet. Repeat the motion all around the fruit. At the end you should have three or four tomato fillets. You'll also have a central core of seeds that you can press for a small hit of

tomato water to drink and enjoy. Repeat with the remaining tomatoes, then finely dice the fillets.

2. Transfer the diced tomatoes to a medium bowl and stir in the onion, olives, parsley, garlic, oil, vinegar, salt, and pepper. Let sit at room temperature for at least an hour for the flavors to meld or refrigerate no more than a day in advance. (After that, the flavors start getting muddy.)

3. To make the tuna: Heat an outdoor grill or grill pan until it's very, very hot. As hot as you can get it.

4. Rub the oil all over the tuna with your fingers, then sprinkle with the salt and pepper. Put one steak on the hot grill. If it makes a sizzling sound, you can put the rest on. If it doesn't, get it off fast and get your grill hotter. When you're grilling something, it should make noise. Grill the tuna steaks until grill marks appear, 2 to 3 minutes, then carefully flip and grill the other side until the marks appear, another 2 to 3 minutes.

5. Transfer the tuna to your serving plates and top with the tomato relish. Serve immediately.

Spicy Hot Smoked Salmon

Serves 12

It's the ham of the sea. Seriously. After brining and slow cooking on the grill over wood chips, the fish gets incredibly smoky and dense. You've gotta have potato salad (page 41) on the side. Hoppin' John Salad (page 48), corn on the cob, grilled veg, and baked beans would be delicious, too. And that's just if you want to serve it as an entrée. I like to flake the fish for salads, quesadillas, stratas, sandwiches, and anything with cream cheese.

> ⅓ cup packed brown sugar
> ½ teaspoon freshly ground black pepper
> ½ teaspoon dry mustard
> 1 teaspoon Tabasco sauce
> 1 cup soy sauce
> 1 cup water
> 1 cup dry white wine
> 1 tablespoon freshly grated lemon zest
> 2 tablespoons fresh lemon juice
> 2 tablespoons olive oil
> 1 medium yellow onion, cut in half, then very
>   thinly sliced
> 3 garlic cloves, minced
> Six 8-ounce skin-on center-cut salmon fillets
>   (preferably 2 inches thick)
> 2 cups wood chips for smoking (preferably apple,
>   cherry, or alder)

1. In a large bowl, mix the sugar, pepper, and mustard. Stir in the Tabasco, soy sauce, water, wine, lemon zest and juice, and olive oil until the sugar and mustard dissolve. Add the onion and garlic. Slip the fish into the marinade and gently toss to evenly coat.

2. Divide the fish and marinade between two large resealable plastic bags. Seal the bags, then turn to ensure that all the fish is well coated. Place the bags in a rimmed dish and refrigerate for at least 12 hours and up to 48 hours, turning the fish every 6 to 8 hours.

3. Remove the fish from the marinade and pat off any excess. Transfer to a wire rack fitted into a half sheet pan and refrigerate uncovered for at least an hour to air-dry. The salmon should look glossy.

4. Meanwhile, in a medium bowl, cover the wood chips with cold water and let stand for at least 20 minutes.

5. Heat an outdoor grill to low (200°F). Drain the wood chips and scatter them over the coals in a charcoal grill or place in the smoking box of a gas grill. (If you don't have a smoking box in your gas grill, you can fashion your own: Fill a disposable aluminum pan with the chips, cover with foil, and poke holes in the foil. Set near the heating element.) Place the fish, skin side down, on the grill grate.

5. Cover and grill until the fish is just cooked through, about 20 minutes. Serve immediately or refrigerate for up to 2 weeks.

Crisp Salmon Cakes

Serves 4

When I was a kid, my dad made me salmon cakes with a recipe he got from his mom. I'd like to say that I looked forward to that meal, but even now, I shudder when I think of it. In his family's version, the first ingredient was canned salmon. Ugh. It was just all kinds of wrong. But I still love the memory of my dad cooking for me, so I created these to thank him. I've taken all the flavors that I like on a bagel with lox and put them into the cakes and sauce. Lemony and fresh and light—I'm sure my dad would like these, too.

One 1-pound center-cut skinless salmon fillet
1 tablespoon plus 1 teaspoon olive oil
Kosher salt and freshly ground black pepper
1 large lemon
½ cup panko bread crumbs
¼ cup finely diced red onion
2 tablespoons capers, rinsed, drained,
*   and finely chopped*
2 tablespoons finely chopped fresh dill leaves
2 tablespoons finely chopped fresh flat-leaf
*   parsley leaves*
1 large egg, lightly beaten
1 teaspoon coarse Dijon mustard
Garlic Aïoli (recipe follows)

1. Preheat the oven to 350°F.

2. Place the salmon on a baking sheet, rub with 1 teaspoon of the oil, and sprinkle with a pinch each of salt and pepper. Bake until just opaque on top but still translucent in the middle, about 13 minutes. Transfer to a large bowl and let stand until just cool enough to handle. Keep the oven on if you'll be cooking the cakes right away.

3. Zest the lemon, then squeeze 3 tablespoons juice.

4. With a fork, break the salmon into large chunks. Add the panko, onion, capers, dill, parsley, egg, mustard, lemon zest and juice, and ½ teaspoon salt. Fold and mix everything together until the salmon is all broken up and the mixture is almost pasty. Gently form

into 12 cakes (each 2 inches in diameter). You don't want the cakes packed too tightly; you want them to just hold together. At this point, you can cover the cakes with plastic wrap and refrigerate them overnight.

5. If the cakes were refrigerated, preheat the oven to 350°F.

6. Heat a large nonstick skillet over medium-high heat. Coat with the remaining tablespoon oil and add a single layer of cakes, spacing them apart. You'll have to work in batches. Cook until golden brown on the bottom, about 1 minute. Carefully flip them over and cook until lightly browned, about 1 minute. Transfer to a half sheet pan. Repeat with the remaining cakes.

7. Transfer the pan to the oven and bake until the cakes are cooked through, about 10 minutes. Serve hot with garlic aïoli.

Garlic Aïoli

Makes about ½ cup

> 2 garlic cloves, minced
> 1 large egg yolk
> 2 teaspoons fresh lemon juice
> ½ teaspoon Dijon mustard
> ½ cup canola or other neutral oil
> Kosher salt and freshly ground black pepper

In a medium bowl, whisk together the garlic, egg yolk, lemon juice, and mustard until well blended. Add the oil in a slow, steady stream while whisking continuously. Whisk until emulsified. Season to taste with salt and pepper.

Cod en Papillote with Roasted Tomato–Artichoke Ragout

Serves 4

Listen, I'm a busy girl, but I still love to entertain. This is my go-to when I want to impress my guests but not be tied to the stove. All the work is done before my doorbell rings and the rest is passive cooking. The pretty paper pouches trap all the yummy juices from the tomatoes and artichokes—and they look gorgeous on the dinner table.

2 teaspoons canola or other neutral oil, plus more
*   for the papillotes*
1 small yellow onion, finely diced
2 sprigs fresh thyme
Kosher salt
2 garlic cloves, minced
½ cup dry white wine
One 14.5-ounce can diced fire-roasted tomatoes
One 8-ounce jar artichoke hearts, drained and chopped
Four 6-ounce skinless center-cut cod fillets
Freshly ground black pepper
1 lemon, cut into 4 wedges
2 tablespoons chopped fresh flat-leaf parsley leaves

1. Heat the oil in a large skillet over medium heat. Add the onion and thyme and cook, stirring occasionally, until the onion is translucent and soft, about 5 minutes. Season with 1 teaspoon salt, then add the garlic. Cook, stirring, for 1 minute. Add the wine, bring to a boil, and cook until the liquid is mostly evaporated.

2. Add the tomatoes with their juices and simmer for 20 minutes. Stir in the artichokes and remove from the heat. Discard the thyme sprigs. You can refrigerate the ragout up to 1 day.

3. Preheat the oven to 450°F. Fold four large sheets of parchment paper (each about 14 inches square) in half to form rectangles, then unfold them and rub lightly with oil.

4. Divide the ragout among the parchment sheets, spooning it to one side of the fold. Season the fish with salt and pepper, then place on top of the ragout. Fold the other side

of the parchment over the fish to cover. Align the paper so the edges meet. Seal the three open sides by first making a 2-inch-long, ¼-inch-wide fold at one corner. Crease, and fold over again to seal. Continue folding the paper in 2-inch segments, slightly overlapping the folds, until the whole pouch is sealed. Repeat with the remaining packets. Make sure the paper is creased tightly; you don't want the pouches to open in the oven!

5. Place the packets on a half sheet pan and bake for 10 minutes. You want the fish to be opaque throughout, but (obviously) you can't see it in the packets. Ten minutes should be good, but if you're worried the fish isn't cooked through, open one packet and take a peek.

6. Cut an "X" in the top of each packet and fold the paper back. (Watch out for the hot steam!) Squeeze lemon juice onto the fish, then sprinkle with the parsley. Serve immediately.

Seared Cod in Spring Pea Broth with Minted Pea Pesto

Serves 4

This may look like a fish dish, but in fact the peas are the star and the cod is the supporting cast. Yet another perfect example of the versatility of peas, which I use in three ways here—as a soup, pesto, and garnish. (You can, of course, make the soup anytime to drink on its own.) In this dish, the subtle delicacy of cod highlights the delicious sweet peas in all their forms.

SPRING PEA BROTH

2 tablespoons unsalted butter
1 small yellow onion, thinly sliced
2 cups Chicken Stock (page 54) or Vegetable Stock
    (page 55) or store-bought unsalted broth
Kosher salt and freshly ground white pepper
1½ cups shelled fresh peas (from 1½ to 2 pounds pods)
¼ cup fresh mint leaves, coarsely chopped
2 tablespoons heavy cream
1 tablespoon fresh flat-leaf parsley leaves, coarsely chopped
1 teaspoon freshly grated lemon zest
2 teaspoons lemon olive oil or extra virgin olive oil

COD

Four 5-ounce skinless cod fillets
Kosher salt and freshly ground black pepper
1 tablespoon canola or other neutral oil
1 tablespoon unsalted butter, cut in quarters
½ cup Minted Pea Pesto (recipe follows)
4 lemon wedges, for garnish

1. Preheat the oven to 350°F.

2. To make the broth: In a medium saucepan, melt the butter over medium heat. Add the onion and cook, stirring occasionally, until tender and translucent, about 5 minutes. Add the stock and bring to a boil. Season with salt and pepper. Add the peas and reduce the heat to maintain a steady simmer. Cook until the peas are tender, about 8 minutes. Season again with salt and pepper. Set aside ¼ cup peas for garnish.

3. Working in batches if necessary, transfer the remaining broth and peas to a stand blender and puree until smooth. Reserve 1 teaspoon chopped mint. Add the remaining mint to the blender along with the cream and parsley. Puree again, then strain through a fine-mesh sieve. Pour the broth back into the saucepan and keep warm over low heat. Toss the reserved peas with the reserved teaspoon mint, lemon zest, and lemon oil. Season with salt and pepper.

4. To make the cod: Season the fish with salt and pepper. Heat a large skillet over medium-high heat. Add the canola oil, swirling to coat the bottom of the pan. Carefully put the fillets in the skillet, then add the butter pieces. Cook for 3 minutes, then carefully flip the fillets and cook for 2 minutes longer. Transfer the skillet to the oven and cook until the fish is opaque throughout, about 3 minutes.

5. Divide the hot pea broth among your serving bowls. Place the fish in the bowls, then top with the pesto. Garnish with the reserved peas and lemon wedges.

Minted Pea Pesto

Makes about 2½ cups

>   *Kosher salt*
>   *2 cups fresh or frozen peas*
>   *½ cup packed fresh flat-leaf parsley leaves*
>   *¼ cup packed fresh mint leaves*
>   *3 garlic cloves*
>   *¼ cup pine nuts, toasted (page 296)*
>   *¼ cup finely grated Parmigiano-Reggiano cheese*
>   *¼ cup extra virgin olive oil*

1. Bring a medium saucepan of water to a boil and generously salt it. Fill a large bowl with ice and water. Add the peas to the boiling water and cook the fresh ones until tender and the frozen ones just until thawed. Drain and immediately transfer to the ice water. Drain again, then transfer to a food processor.

2. Add the parsley, mint, garlic, pine nuts, and cheese. Pulse until a chunky paste forms. With the machine running, drizzle in the oil. Continue pulsing until well combined. Season to taste with salt. The pesto can be covered and refrigerated for up to 1 week or frozen for up to 1 month.

🐦 Starting From Scratch

When I'm creating a new dish, I start by choosing an ingredient that I just love. Take peas, for example. Then I think back to some of my favorite dishes and memories of that ingredient. As a kid, I loved when Mama made a well in my mashed potatoes and filled it with canned sweet peas dotted with margarine. (Being the daughter of a dairy farmer, Granny would have used butter all the way.) When I was working in London as a model, I always ordered fish with mushy peas in the local pubs. At first glance, I couldn't understand why they mashed up the peas. One bite with the fish and I totally got it. It was perfect with the fish that way. And for me, it was a perfect taste of home. When I started cooking professionally, I had fresh peas out of the pod for the first time. I didn't think I could love peas any more than I already did, but I was wrong. I went crazy for the fresh ones and now, whenever I'm working with peas, I start by thinking about the best ways to highlight their natural sweetness.

That ingredients-first approach also came from watching Granny happily take her garden's bumper crop and turn those vegetables into refreshing salads, rich braises, and tangy chow chow pickles. I refined what I learned from Granny and developed my own food philosophy while living and cooking abroad. Despite my very limited income in Paris, I tried to go out and eat well. In my journal, I noted my favorite dishes so that I could re-create them at home. By trying to make those dishes, I began to develop my philosophy of "less is more"—mainly because I had so little! Each ingredient I bought was precious; I worked to highlight the natural flavors without wasting a scrap. For example, the frisée lettuce there was beautiful, and relatively cheap, so I dressed it simply with a Dijon mustard vinaigrette to bring out its fresh bite. I'm sure that was the first time I had Dijon mustard, too. It seems like a lifetime ago . . .

Since then, I've continued to come up with new dishes by focusing first on quality ingredients, always starting with vegetables. Even though I'm a meat lover, I think about vegetables first when building flavor. They're my favorites! Their breadth and depth of flavors and textures can be put together in endless combinations that make for surprising dishes that still comfort. My seared pork tenderloin medallion recipe was created to be a great vehicle for my sweet root vegetable ragout, and my oat-crusted tofu is a really satisfying and sophisticated vegetarian main.

Once I start cooking, I taste and season every step of the way. Often, I'll end up throwing in an herb that I hadn't thought about using to begin with because I realize that a fresh bite's needed in the finish. Or I'll hold back on a spice that I planned on including because the dish already has enough going on. The real test of a dish's success, though, comes after I've plated the whole thing, sat down properly with real utensils, and taken a whole bite. If it makes me close my eyes and smile a big *mmm-mmm,* then I know it's good.

Miso-Poached Hake
with Cilantro-Orange Salt

Serves 4

As a contestant on *Top Chef*, I often had to come up with ways to get a lot of flavor fast. That's the beauty of miso. It's savory and flavorful—and it was in the *Top Chef* kitchen pantry. Because it can be quite salty but still delicate, I wanted to make a really light dish with subtlety and finesse. I love poaching hake in this broth, but any mild white fish haddock, cod, tilapia, halibut—works well, too.

MISO BROTH

5 cups water
⅓ cup white miso
⅓ cup chopped fresh cilantro stems
2 garlic cloves, smashed
One 1-inch piece fresh ginger, peeled and chopped
Three 4-inch strips orange zest, removed with
*   a vegetable peeler*
2 dried chiles de arbol, stemmed, cut in half, and seeded

CILANTRO-ORANGE SALT

1 tablespoon kosher salt
1 teaspoon freshly grated orange zest
1 teaspoon finely chopped fresh cilantro stems

1 small zucchini
1 large carrot, peeled and cut into matchsticks (page 296)
1 medium red bell pepper, stemmed, seeded, and
*   cut into matchsticks*
One 4-inch strip orange zest, removed with a vegetable peeler
2 tablespoons canola or other neutral oil
½ small head napa cabbage, shredded (2 cups)
1 scallion (green onion), trimmed and very thinly sliced
*   at an angle*
1 tablespoon coarsely chopped fresh cilantro leaves
Four 6-ounce skinless center-cut hake fillets

1. To make the broth: In a medium saucepan, stir together the water, miso, cilantro, garlic, ginger, orange zest, and chiles. Set over medium heat and bring to a simmer, stirring occasionally. Reduce the heat to low and steep for 45 minutes.

2. To make the salt: In a small bowl, combine the salt, orange zest, and cilantro stems. Use your fingertips to rub the mixture together. Salt can be kept in an airtight container for up to 2 days.

3. Trim the zucchini and cut in quarters lengthwise. Cut out and discard the seeds, then very thinly slice each zucchini quarter at an angle. Transfer to a large bowl, add the carrot, bell pepper, orange zest, 1 tablespoon of the oil, and ½ teaspoon cilantro-orange salt. Toss until evenly coated.

4. Heat a large skillet over medium-high heat until hot. Add half of the vegetables and cook, tossing, until the veggies are bright but still firm, about 1 minute. Transfer to a plate. Repeat with the remaining vegetables, then discard the orange zest.

5. In the same skillet, heat the remaining tablespoon oil over medium-high heat. Add the cabbage, scallion, and ¼ teaspoon cilantro-orange salt. Cook, stirring, until just wilted, about 30 seconds. Remove from the heat and stir in the vegetables and cilantro leaves. Reserve.

6. Using a ½-cup measuring cup, very carefully spoon out 1½ cups of the clear liquid from the top of the miso broth into a large, deep skillet. Be sure to avoid scooping any of the miso and solids. You want the broth to be really clear. Add ¼ teaspoon cilantro-orange salt and bring to a boil over medium-high heat. Reduce the heat to low so that the broth is just steaming.

7. Carefully slide the fish into the broth, cover, and poach just until a thin-bladed knife easily slides into the fish, about 6 minutes.

8. Divide the vegetables among four serving dishes. Arrange a fish fillet on top of each and spoon the poaching liquid all over. Top with a little cilantro-orange salt.

Poached Halibut with Roasted Vegetables and Mint Tea Broth

Serves 4

I don't drink coffee and I don't drink booze. What I love is tea. It's perfect for sipping and pairing with my meals, and it can be used in cooking, too. In this simple weeknight recipe, mint tea infuses the poaching liquid for the fish with its herbaceous freshness. This dish is super light, ideal for times when you're trying to trim down, but it's still intensely flavorful, too.

> *Olive oil cooking spray*
> *Kosher salt*
> *1 baby eggplant, cut into ¼-inch-thick rounds*
> *1 pint grape tomatoes*
> *1 small zucchini, cut into ¼-inch-thick rounds*
> *Freshly ground black pepper*
> *2 cups Chicken Stock (page 54) or Vegetable Stock*
>   *(page 55) or store-bought unsalted broth*
> *2 high-quality mint tea bags, paper tags removed*
> *4 garlic cloves, peeled*
> *½ bunch fresh basil, plus 8 leaves, thinly sliced*
> *Four 6-ounce skinless halibut fillets*
> *¼ cup pine nuts, toasted (page 296)*

1. Preheat the oven to 400°F. Lightly coat two half sheet pans with olive oil spray. Cut out a 10-inch round of parchment paper; reserve.

2. Lightly sprinkle an even layer of salt on the pans. Arrange the eggplant slices in a single layer on one half of one pan and scatter the tomatoes on the other half. Arrange the zucchini on the other pan. Lightly coat the tops of the vegetables with the olive oil spray and then sprinkle with salt and pepper.

3. Roast, one pan at a time, until the eggplant and zucchini are lightly browned and the tomatoes are blistered, about 10 minutes, then carefully flip the eggplant and zucchini and toss the tomatoes. Roast until the eggplant and zucchini are lightly browned on the other side, about 7 minutes. With a slotted spoon, carefully spoon the tomatoes on top of the eggplant to give it some of their flavorful juiciness.

4. While the vegetables roast, bring the stock to a boil in a 10-inch skillet. Add the tea bags, garlic, ½ bunch basil, and ½ teaspoon salt. Reduce the heat to low and simmer for 7 minutes. Remove and discard the tea bags.

5. Carefully place the fish in the skillet in a single layer and cover with the parchment paper round. Poach just until a thin-bladed knife easily slides into the fish, about 12 minutes.

6. Divide the vegetables among four serving dishes and carefully place a fish fillet on top. Strain the poaching liquid into a bowl through a fine-mesh sieve, season to taste with salt and pepper, and pour around the fish. Garnish with the pine nuts and sliced basil.

Roasted Snapper Bouillabaisse

Serves 4

This is my *Matrix* dish. You know the part in the movie where Neo says, "This is the one"? Well, this is it for me. I love this type of food and cooking for my everyday meals. It's elegant but simple to prepare, and the French flavors conjure so many happy memories. I once spent time cooking in Marseilles, home of bouillabaisse, and spent days preparing a classic version for the family I was cooking for. It was great, but this one's even better. I've kept the traditional sauce, but roasted the fish whole to serve with the fennel-and-clam tomato stew.

Unless you're feeling really ambitious, let your fishmonger prepare your whole snapper for you.

CROUTONS

4 tablespoons (½ stick) unsalted butter, at room temperature
One 10-ounce French country boule or rustic Italian round loaf

ROASTED SNAPPER

2 tablespoons freshly grated lemon zest
1 tablespoon fennel seeds
2 teaspoons fresh thyme leaves, plus 4 sprigs
Kosher salt and freshly ground black pepper
One 1¾-pound red snapper, gutted, cleaned, scaled,
  and fins trimmed
1 small yellow onion, very thinly sliced
½ lemon, very thinly sliced
3 garlic cloves, smashed

BOUILLABAISSE SAUCE

1 quart Chicken Stock (page 54) or store-bought
  unsalted chicken broth
1 tablespoon unsalted butter
Kosher salt
4 heads fennel, stalks discarded, fronds reserved, bulbs cut
  into quarters
2 medium leeks (white and pale green parts only), trimmed,
  cut in half lengthwise then into ¼-inch-thick half-moons,
  and thoroughly rinsed

4 sprigs fresh thyme, plus 1 teaspoon leaves
Freshly ground black pepper
1 tablespoon extra virgin olive oil
3 large plum tomatoes, cut in quarters lengthwise,
*   then each piece cut in half crosswise*
¼ cup dry white wine
2 garlic cloves, chopped
¼ teaspoon saffron threads
2 fresh or dried bay leaves
¼ teaspoon crushed red chile flakes
12 manila clams, scrubbed well
2 tablespoons finely chopped fresh flat-leaf parsley leaves

1. Preheat the oven to 400°F.

2. To make the croutons: Clarify the butter by placing it in a deep microwave-safe bowl. Microwave at 50% power in 30-second increments until the solids drop to the bottom of the bowl. The translucent golden liquid at the top is clarified butter.

3. Meanwhile, trim the tough crusts off the bread and reserve for another use. Cut the bread into ½-inch-thick slices, then cut each slice into 4 by 1-inch rectangles. They should resemble Jenga game pieces. Place the bread in a single layer on a half sheet pan and brush with the clarified butter. Bake until golden brown and crisp, about 10 minutes. Set aside to cool.

4. To make the fish: On a cutting board, chop and mash together the lemon zest, fennel seeds, thyme leaves, 2 teaspoons salt, and ½ teaspoon pepper. Cut four diagonal slits on each side of the fish. Stuff the lemon zest mixture into the slits. In a medium bowl, toss together the onion, lemon slices, garlic, thyme sprigs, ½ teaspoon salt, and ¼ teaspoon pepper. Stuff this into the fish's cavity.

5. Line a half sheet pan with foil and place the fish in the center. Pull the foil up around the fish like a loose tent so that the foil doesn't touch the top of the fish, and crimp the top and sides to seal completely. Roast for 30 minutes, then open the foil and roast for 30 minutes longer or until the fish is just opaque throughout. Raise the oven temperature to broil. Broil until the skin crisps, about 5 minutes.

6. While the fish cooks, make the sauce: In a large skillet, bring the chicken stock, butter, and 1 teaspoon salt to a boil. Add the fennel in a single layer, then scatter the leeks and

thyme sprigs over and around the fennel. Sprinkle with ½ teaspoon salt and ¼ teaspoon pepper. When the mixture returns to a boil, cover, reduce the heat to low, and simmer for 10 minutes. With a slotted spoon, carefully transfer the fennel and leeks to a plate. Strain the broth into a bowl through a medium-mesh sieve.

7. In the same skillet, heat the oil over high heat. Add the tomatoes and ½ teaspoon salt. Cook for 1 minute, then add the wine. Cook for 1 minute, stirring and scraping up browned bits from the pan. Add the garlic and cook for 1 minute, stirring. Add the saffron and cook for 1 minute, pressing the threads into the mixture. Add the bay leaves, chile flakes, and strained broth. Bring to a boil, cover, reduce the heat to low, and simmer for 25 minutes.

8. Strain the sauce into a bowl through a medium-mesh sieve, pressing hard on the tomatoes to extract as much liquid as possible. Return the sauce to the pan and add the reserved fennel and leeks in a single layer around the edge, leaving the center of the pan empty. Cover and bring to a simmer over medium-high heat. While the fish is broiling, add the clams, cover, and cook, shaking the pan occasionally, until they open, about 5 minutes.

9. Pick ¼ cup fennel fronds from the reserved fronds. Sprinkle over the clams along with the parsley and thyme leaves. Serve with the fish and croutons.

Lump Blue Crab Salad with Chilled Shiso Soup

Serves 4

Light, light, light. I crave the clean refreshing flavors of this chilled soup and salad combo when I want something really tasty that doesn't weigh me down. If you've never tried shiso before, you're in for a treat. These aromatic leaves have a faintly minty herbaceous flavor. You've got to use them for this soup; you can find them in a Japanese or Asian market, which should also stock mirin, rice vinegar, and Thai basil. If you can't find chayote, a delicate, crisp pale green fruit common in Mexico, for the salad, you can use jicama or a seedless cucumber instead. For a party, divide the soup and salad among Chinese soup spoons or shot glasses.

CRAB SALAD

8 ounces jumbo lump crabmeat, picked over for shells and cartilage
1 chayote squash, peeled, cut in half, pitted if necessary, and finely diced
¼ cup finely diced red bell pepper
½ habanero chile, stemmed, seeded, and finely chopped, plus more if desired
2 tablespoons finely minced lemongrass (white part only)
2 tablespoons very thinly sliced fresh Thai basil leaves
2 teaspoons grated peeled fresh ginger
1 teaspoon freshly grated lime zest
¼ cup fresh lime juice
¼ cup extra virgin olive oil
2 tablespoons rice vinegar
Kosher salt and freshly ground black pepper

CHILLED SHISO SOUP

1 cup packed shiso leaves
1 cup baby spinach leaves
1 tablespoon minced peeled fresh ginger
1 teaspoon minced garlic
2 tablespoons mirin
2 tablespoons rice vinegar
¾ teaspoon kosher salt
1 cup ice cubes
1 cup sour cream

1. To make the salad: In a large bowl, combine the crab, chayote, bell pepper, chile, lemongrass, basil, ginger, lime zest and juice, oil, vinegar, ½ teaspoon salt, and ¼ teaspoon pepper. Fold gently until well mixed. Taste and add more habanero, salt, and pepper to taste.

2. To make the soup: In a stand blender, combine the shiso, spinach, ginger, garlic, mirin, vinegar, and salt. Puree until smooth. Add the ice and puree until well blended. Add the sour cream and blend on low speed until well combined.

3. Divide the cold soup among four dishes. Spoon the crab salad in the center of each dish.

🍷 It's Gon' Be Okay

Here's what professional chefs know that home cooks don't: No matter what happens in the kitchen, it's gon' be okay. Sometimes, cooking is all about the recovery. Ideally, everything goes smoothly from the moment you pick up your perfect ingredients right on time to the instant your gorgeous plate of food goes before guests at its ideal temperature. More often than not, though, something goes wrong along the way. It's the nature of cooking and what doesn't kill you will make you a stronger cook.

That's a lesson I learned the hard way when working as a private chef for a family in the Bahamas. I was already in desperate straits, without any staff and without enough ingredients, when I called my friend Donna and told her, "I need you to come to the Bahamas. Here's my shopping list." When she asked when she should arrive, I replied, "Tomorrow. Your flight leaves at noon." Donna, amazing friend that she is, simply said, "Got it! See you tomorrow." We had worked together for years catering events in Washington, D.C., so I knew I could trust her to help me please this impossible-to-please boss.

Donna showed up right in time because I decided to do spiny lobster for dinner that night. Each evening, I had to prepare a three-course dinner and the lobster was going to come out after the soup. Because we had to cook for so many people, I decided to roast the lobsters in the rickety propane oven. Bad idea. When I opened the oven door to check on the lobsters, I singed my eyebrows on the *whoosh* of flames that burst out. I slammed the door shut and began screaming, "Donna! Donna! The oven's on fire!" After a minute, I took a deep breath and told myself, "It's gon' be okay. I can do this." We put out the fire, rescued the lobsters, and finished them on the stovetop. They were delicious—as if they'd been smoked.

That was the origin of my "gon' be" philosophy. Over the years, I've experienced so many moments when I've had to remind myself that my food's gon' be okay, no matter what. Even when clients say they want dinner in an hour then change their minds and say they want the food out in five minutes: It's gon' be okay. More than a decade later, that philosophy came back to the Bahamas when I was on *Top Chef All-Stars*. Nothing quite like cooking in a competition on an island and having a deep-fryer go up in flames to remind you that everything's gon' be okay. It's definitely as much about attitude as it is about how the food tastes. Of course, I give you tips throughout this book to help you out of culinary disasters. But what you need to remember is that you're just sharing love by making good food. If you're cooking to please yourself and prove how good you are by putting out perfect dishes, you're never going to believe that everything's gon' be okay. If you're cooking for others, to make them happy and feel good, you'll relax in the kitchen and know that the meal's gon' be okay—and the time you have together will be even better.

Lobster Bisque

Serves 6

Is there anything more special than lobster bisque? I don't think so. I've got one shortcut here—using lobster tails instead of whole crustaceans. Same delicious depth of flavor and a lot less work. Making the stock from scratch is a little time consuming, but essential to this elegant dish. Homemade stock adds a dimension of flavor that no store-bought brand can match, no matter how fancy. The stock recipe here is the foundation of all seafood stocks. You can swap in a half-pound of shell-on shrimp or a pound of clams for the lobster and simmer them only until they're cooked through.

STOCK

1 quart water
2 lobster tails (each about ½ pound)
2 celery ribs, coarsely chopped
1 carrot, coarsely chopped
1 yellow onion, cut into quarters
1 leek, trimmed, coarsely chopped,
     and thoroughly rinsed
1 fennel bulb, cut into quarters
3 garlic cloves, minced
2 fresh or dried bay leaves
4 sprigs fresh flat-leaf parsley
6 whole black peppercorns
Kosher salt

BISQUE

4 tablespoons (½ stick) unsalted butter
1 medium yellow onion, chopped
2 shallots, minced
2 garlic cloves, minced
½ cup all-purpose flour
¼ cup dry sherry
2 tablespoons tomato paste
3 cups half-and-half
1 teaspoon kosher salt
¼ teaspoon freshly ground white pepper

¼ teaspoon sweet paprika
⅛ teaspoon cayenne pepper
1 cup crème fraîche

1. To make the stock: In a 4-quart saucepan, combine the water and lobster tails. The water should just cover the tails; add more water if needed. Transfer the tails to a plate. To the water, add the celery, carrot, onion, leek, fennel, garlic, bay leaves, parsley, peppercorns, and a pinch of salt. Bring to a boil.

2. Add the lobster tails, reduce the heat to low, and simmer just until the lobster is cooked through, about 10 minutes. The tail shells will start to turn pink as they cook and may take as long as 15 minutes, but you don't want the meat to overcook and become tough. It should be just opaque throughout.

3. Transfer the lobster to a plate to cool. While the tails cool, raise the heat to high and boil the stock until reduced by half. Strain the stock into a bowl through a fine-mesh sieve. Discard the solids. You should have 2 cups stock.

4. Remove the lobster meat from the shells and discard the shells. Coarsely chop the meat and set it aside.

5. To make the bisque: In a 4-quart saucepan, heat the butter over medium-high heat for 2 minutes. Add the onion, shallots, and garlic, reduce the heat to medium, and cook until the onion becomes translucent, about 7 minutes.

6. Alternately sprinkle the flour and lobster stock, 1 tablespoon at a time, over the vegetables while stirring continuously. Once all the flour has been added, whisk the remaining lobster stock into the vegetables. Whisk in the sherry and tomato paste until well blended. Bring to a boil, then cook over medium heat, stirring continuously, until thickened, about 10 minutes.

7. Reduce the heat to low and whisk in the half-and-half, salt, pepper, paprika, and cayenne. Simmer for 10 minutes, stirring occasionally. Add half of the lobster meat and cook until the meat is heated through, about 2 minutes. Taste and adjust the seasonings.

8. Divide the bisque among serving bowls and top with a dollop of crème fraîche and the reserved lobster meat. To serve as a fancy appetizer, use shot glasses. Arrange a piece of lobster meat on top. Serve immediately.

Lobster Rigatoni

Serves 4

One of the greatest things about being on *The Chew* is getting to know my cohosts. They're great friends and amazing cooks and teachers. Mario Batali regularly reminds our viewers to avoid oversaucing pasta. In America, we've learned to treat our noodle dishes incorrectly by drowning them in sauce. In this quick, simple dish, which I developed for a beginners' cooking class, I use fresh tomatoes with lobster to lightly coat the pasta with flavor.

If you're intimidated by cooking whole lobsters, you can simply cook lobster tails for the meat, or even buy cooked fresh lobster meat from a reputable fishmonger. So often, we only prepare lobster for special occasions, but it can be used in a special weeknight meal, too. When it's in season, it can actually be affordable. I love making luxury accessible and that's what this dish is all about. And, of course, this is tasty with shrimp, too.

> *Kosher salt*
> *¼ cup extra virgin olive oil*
> *1 large yellow onion, finely chopped (1½ cups)*
> *1 garlic clove, minced*
> *½ teaspoon crushed red chile flakes, plus more to taste*
> *1 pound rigatoni*
> *¾ cup dry white wine*
> *1 pound plum tomatoes, peeled, seeded, and chopped*
> *1 cup cooked lobster meat chunks (½ pound)*
> *Freshly ground black pepper*
> *1 cup freshly grated Pecorino Romano cheese*
> *½ cup thinly sliced scallions (green onions)*

1. Bring a large pot of salted water to a boil.

2. While the water is heating, heat the oil in a large skillet over low heat. Add the onions and cook, stirring occasionally, until golden, about 8 minutes. Add the garlic and chile flakes and cook, stirring occasionally, until the garlic is softened, about 4 minutes.

3. Add the rigatoni to the boiling water and cook according to the package's directions until al dente. Drain well in a colander, then return to the pot.

4. While the pasta cooks, add the wine to the onions and bring to a boil over medium-high heat. Cook until the wine has almost completely evaporated, about 8 minutes. Stir in the tomatoes and cook until the mixture thickens slightly, about 5 minutes. Add the lobster and heat until warmed through. Season to taste with salt and pepper.

5. Stir the lobster and sauce into the rigatoni. Add the cheese and toss gently until well combined. Divide among serving plates and garnish with the scallions.

Desserts

Here's what dessert is: It's that big tight hug your old friend gives you when it's time to go. The conversation was great and the laughs even better, but it's that good-bye hug that makes the visit. A delicious dessert *makes* a meal, no matter how tasty your savory menu. Ending on a satisfying sweet note can be as simple as cookies or as elaborate as three-tiered napoleons. For a short (short!) period of time, I was worried about being pigeon-holed as a chef who does only desserts really well and I began to shy away from pastry. Well, that was silly. I love making desserts—and eating them, too. For years, I've tinkered with ingredients and techniques to get my cakes, cookies, pies, tarts, and other tasty creations just right. I like my desserts sweet, but not too sweet; I like texture, especially crunch; and I like playing with new, unexpected flavors in the classics. All of the recipes that follow are meant to be shared and lingered over with a cuppa tea. After your guests are stuffed full of sweets, be sure to give 'em big hugs good-bye, too!

Flaky Butter Crust

Makes two 9-inch crusts

Homemade pie crust is just the best, especially when it's flaky and tender and buttery. Here's my secret formula for the perfect crust. Well, it's not so secret now that I'm putting it here, but I'm so happy to share it. The real secret to making great crust is practice. You'll start to get the feel of it after a few pies. But even the practice ones will taste great.

> *1 tablespoon sugar*
> *½ teaspoon table salt*
> *⅓ cup water*
> *½ pound (2 sticks) cold unsalted butter,*
>   *cut into ½-inch dice*
> *2¼ cups all-purpose flour, plus more*
>   *for rolling*

1. In a small bowl, dissolve the sugar and salt in the water. Refrigerate until very cold, about 30 minutes. During that time, refrigerate your butter, flour, mixer bowl, and paddle, too.

2. Make sure your butter's cut into ½-inch dice. Bigger pieces will make your dough puffy. In the chilled bowl, combine the cold butter and flour. With your hands, toss the butter in the flour until each cube is lightly coated.

3. With the chilled paddle, beat the flour-butter mixture on low speed to just break up the butter, about 30 seconds. Add the water mixture all at once and raise the speed to medium-low. Beat just until the dough comes together in big chunks, then immediately turn off the mixer.

4. Divide the chunks of dough in half and very gently pat each group into a round 1-inch-thick disk. Wrap each tightly in plastic wrap and refrigerate until firm, about 1 hour, before rolling. You can refrigerate the disks for up to 1 day or freeze for up to 3 months.

Granny's Five-Flavor Pound Cake

Serves 12

Best. Cake. Ever. I'm not just saying that because of my fond food memories. This easy cake is moist, complex in flavor, and totally foolproof. When it bakes, the smell of the five extracts in the buttery dough will have you droolin'. Just ask any of my fellow chefs from my first cooking job after culinary school. I was an extern—basically free labor—at a fancy restaurant. But I was so excited to be there and even more excited to bake Granny's cake for them. One taste and everyone agreed we had to serve it in the restaurant. I immediately called Granny and told her that "Granny's Five-Flavor Pound Cake" had been printed on the menu. She was so proud. This was our family dessert, the cake we begged her to send us when we moved away, the cake she always served at Christmas. Whenever she mailed one to me, she wrapped it in layers and layers of paper and plastic wrap. It was the best gift—one that I'm happy to share.

Nonstick baking spray
3 cups all-purpose flour
1 teaspoon baking soda
1 teaspoon table salt
8 tablespoons (1 stick) unsalted butter, cut into
    tablespoons, at room temperature
2½ cups sugar
6 large eggs, at room temperature
1 cup sour cream, at room temperature
1 teaspoon vanilla extract
1 teaspoon rum extract
1 teaspoon coconut extract
1 teaspoon lemon extract
1 teaspoon almond extract

1. Preheat the oven to 350°F. Spray a 10-cup Bundt or tube pan with nonstick baking spray.

2. Sift the flour into a large bowl, then measure 3 cups sifted flour back into the sifter. Return any remaining flour to your flour container. Add the baking soda and salt to the sifter and sift into a clean bowl.

3. In the bowl of an electric mixer fitted with a paddle, cream the butter and sugar on medium-high speed until pale and fluffy, about 3 minutes. Stop and scrape down the sides and bottom of the bowl. With the mixer on medium, add the eggs one at a time, completely incorporating each egg before adding the next. Stop and scrape down the bowl.

4. With the mixer on low speed, add the flour in thirds, alternating with the sour cream and beginning and ending with the flour. Continue beating for 2 minutes on medium speed, stopping to scrape the sides and bottom of the bowl occasionally. Add the extracts one at a time, completely incorporating each before adding the next. Continue beating until the batter is shiny, about 4 minutes.

5. Pour the batter into the cake pan. Bake until the cake is golden and a toothpick inserted in the center comes out clean, about 1 hour. It will smell really, really good.

6. Let the cake cool in the pan on a wire rack for 10 minutes, then unmold onto the rack. Let the cake cool completely. The cake will keep in an airtight container for up to 1 week.

Cinnamon-Raisin Bread Pudding with Bourbon Sauce

Serves 16

I can't imagine anything more comforting than a nice slice of custardy bread pudding. I like to make mine light and tender on the inside, not all bready, so I use a lot of liquid in proportion to soft egg bread. I also don't sweeten the bread mixture much before baking—I save that step for the end when I soak the hot pudding with a super simple bourbon caramel sauce. When you get a mouthful, you'll feel so warm and cozy inside. Just how I like it!

BREAD PUDDING

1 tablespoon unsalted butter
One 1-pound loaf challah or other sweet
*   egg bread, cut into ½-inch dice*
8 large eggs
1 cup sugar
2 quarts whole milk
2 teaspoons ground cinnamon
½ teaspoon freshly grated nutmeg
2 teaspoons vanilla extract
1 cup dark raisins

BOURBON SAUCE

1 cup heavy cream
8 tablespoons (1 stick) unsalted butter
½ cup sugar
¼ cup bourbon

1. To make the bread pudding: Preheat the oven to 350°F. Butter a 13 by 9 by 2-inch baking pan.

2. Spread the challah cubes on a half sheet pan. Bake until light brown and crisp, about 8 minutes. Transfer the pan to a wire rack and let cool. Turn off the oven.

3. Meanwhile, in a large bowl, whisk the eggs and sugar until well combined. Whisk in the milk, then the cinnamon, nutmeg, and vanilla. Add the raisins and cooled bread. Stir

until well mixed, then carefully pour into the baking pan. Spread in an even layer; the mixture will come up to the top. Gently press the bread and raisins to submerge them in the liquid. Let stand at room temperature for 1 hour or cover tightly and refrigerate up to overnight.

4. Preheat the oven to 350°F.

5. Bake the bread pudding, uncovered, until puffed, golden brown, and a skewer inserted in the center comes out clean, about 1 hour.

6. While the bread pudding bakes, make the sauce: In a small saucepan, heat the cream until bubbles begin to form around the edge of the pan. Keep warm. In a medium saucepan, combine the butter and sugar. Cook over medium heat, stirring continuously, until it turns golden brown and is bubbling. Add the cream in a slow, steady stream while stirring continuously. Be careful! The mixture will bubble up and is very, very hot. When the cream is fully incorporated, remove the sauce from the heat and stir in the bourbon.

7. Transfer the bread pudding pan to a wire rack and let cool for 15 minutes. Use a long fork to prick holes all over the top of the pudding. Spoon ½ cup of the hot bourbon sauce over the bread pudding and let it soak in. Continue adding the sauce, ½ cup at a time, letting each addition absorb before adding the next, until the pudding seems completely saturated and can't take any more sauce. If you have any leftover sauce, you can serve it alongside the pudding, which should be served warm.

Catering Like Carla

🍀 You can make the whole bread pudding with the sauce in it and cover and refrigerate it. It cuts into very neat squares when cold. Reheat the squares in the microwave just before serving.

Pecan Shortbread 'Nana Puddin'

Serves 12

One of the great things about being from the South is getting to know other chefs from there and compare notes—and tastes—of how we reinterpret the classics we grew up eating. I'm a big fan of my colleagues' work, even when I wonder what the heck they're thinking. When I was tasting one chef's banana pudding, I kept digging around for the cookies. The pudding was amazing, very banana-y and tasty, but it was just pudding! For me, banana pudding has to have a cookie layer, sliced bananas, and whipped cream. It just does. My good friends Cheryl and Griff Day of Savannah's Back in the Day Bakery agree. Their version blew my mind. In each bite, I tasted buttery cookies along with my pudding. So, so good. They inspired me to come up with my own version—and to incorporate my own cookies!

I swapped out the vanilla wafers of my childhood puddin' for homemade pecan shortbread and made the pudding itself airy and light. Each bite combines banana-creamy and cookie-crunchy and gives me a little taste of my happy years in Nashville.

BANANA PASTRY CREAM
¼ cup cake flour or all-purpose flour
1¼ cups granulated sugar, or ¾ cup granulated sugar
*   and ½ cup superfine sugar*
¼ teaspoon table salt
¼ cup half-and-half
6 large pasteurized eggs, separated, at room temperature
1½ cups whole milk
1 vanilla bean, pod split, seeds scraped
¼ cup banana nectar (preferably Looza brand)
2 tablespoons dark rum
1 tablespoon unsalted butter, cut up
1 teaspoon cream of tartar

40 Pecan Shortbread cookies (page 264), plus more crumbled for garnish
3 to 4 ripe bananas
½ cup heavy cream, whipped to soft peaks

1. To make the pastry cream: In a large bowl, sift together the flour, ¾ cup granulated sugar, and salt. In a small bowl, whisk together the half-and-half and egg yolks until well blended. Whisk the yolk mixture into the flour mixture until well combined.

2. In a small saucepan, combine the milk and vanilla seeds and pod. Heat over medium-low heat until bubbles begin to form around the edge of the pan. Add the hot milk and vanilla to the yolk and flour mixture, a little at a time, while whisking continuously. When the bottom of the mixing bowl is warm, whisk in the remaining milk. Whisk in the banana nectar.

3. Pour the mixture into a large saucepan and cook over medium-low heat, stirring continuously. Be sure to scrape along the bottom of the pot and along the sides. Continue cooking and stirring until the custard thickens, increasing the speed of your stirring as the custard gets thicker. You want to actually boil the custard but not burn it, so keep stirring while it bubbles and gets really thick, about 15 minutes. Remove from the heat and stir in the rum.

4. Strain the custard through a fine-mesh sieve into a large bowl. Fold in the butter until fully incorporated. Press a sheet of plastic wrap directly against the surface of the custard. Refrigerate until cold.

5. In the bowl of an electric mixer fitted with a whisk, combine the egg whites and cream of tartar. Whisk on low speed until combined, then raise the speed to medium and whisk until frothy. With the machine running, whisk in ¼ cup of the superfine or remaining granulated sugar. Continue whisking and gradually add the remaining ¼ cup sugar. Whisk until stiff but not dry peaks form. Gently fold into the chilled pastry cream until fully incorporated.

6. You can assemble the pudding in one large trifle dish or in individual parfait glasses. You want at least two sets of layers and can do three if you'd like. Here's the layering order: pudding, shortbread, banana slices; end with a pudding layer. Dollop whipped cream on top and sprinkle crumbled shortbread over the whipped cream right before serving.

Catering Like Carla

The assembled pudding can be covered and refrigerated up to overnight. The longer it sits, the softer the cookie layer gets. You don't want to chill it much longer than that or the bananas will start to turn brown.

When you strain the custard, don't throw away that precious vanilla pod! It's expensive! Plus, it still has a lot of flavor left in it. Rinse and dry the pod well. When it's completely dry, bury it in your sugar jar to make vanilla sugar or in your kosher salt to perfume your savory dishes.

Pecan Shortbread

Makes about 20 dozen

When I was ready to call it quits with catering, I decided my next business would celebrate the one food I love most: cookies! Cookies are all love. A little sweet bite to make you feel better, even if you're already feeling great. At Alchemy by Carla Hall, my tiny cookie bites company, my pecan shortbreads are always a hit. The version here makes bigger rounds, but the flavor's just as fantastic. Nutty and crisp, these buttery sweets are one big hug.

> 4 cups pecans, toasted and ground (page 296)
> 2 cups all-purpose flour
> 1½ teaspoons table salt
> ½ pound (2 sticks) unsalted butter, softened
> 2 cups sugar
> 2 large egg yolks
> 2 teaspoons vanilla extract
> ½ teaspoon almond extract

1. In a large bowl, whisk together the pecans, flour, and salt.

2. In the bowl of an electric mixer fitted with a paddle, beat the butter and sugar on medium speed until just mixed, stopping to scrape the sides and bottom of the bowl occasionally. The mixture should still be grainy; it shouldn't be pale yellow and fluffy. Beat in the egg yolks, vanilla, and almond extract until blended.

3. Stop and scrape the bowl. With the mixer on low speed, gradually beat in the pecan mixture. Beat just until the dough sticks together.

4. Transfer the dough to a parchment paper–lined half sheet pan and flatten into a disk. Cover and refrigerate until just firm. Divide the dough in quarters and shape each piece into a log 1 inch in diameter. Wrap each log tightly in plastic wrap. Refrigerate for up to 3 days or freeze for up to 3 months.

5. When ready to bake, preheat the oven to 350°F. Line baking sheets with parchment paper.

6. Cut one log into ¼-inch-thick slices. Place on the baking sheets, spacing the rounds 1 inch apart. Bake until the edges are browned and the tops are golden brown, about 12 minutes.

7. Transfer the pans to wire racks and let cool. Repeat with the remaining dough on clean parchment paper.

Catering Like Carla

❧I always keep a log or two of this dough in the freezer. That way, I can cut off a few slices and bake them whenever I want. You can cut and bake the slices directly from the freezer. Just be sure to keep the logs well wrapped in there so they don't pick up any off flavors from the other stuff you've got in the freezer.

Double Lemon Chess Pie

Makes one 9-inch pie

Everyone in the South makes chess pie. And my friend Liz Clardy's mom's is the best. I've tinkered with her version to make it just the way I like it. Too often, this pie can go from tangy custard on top to doughy crust on the bottom. That's a formula for my not liking a pie. So I blind-bake the crust first—that is, I bake the dough until it's golden brown and crisp—then I add the filling and bake the pie again. And I've made my filling even tangier than most with a splash of white balsamic vinegar. There's a subtle sweetness in that variety of vinegar that pairs so nicely with the sugary, lemony filling.

> *All-purpose flour, for rolling*
> *1 disk Flaky Butter Crust (page 257)*
> *6 tablespoons (¾ stick) unsalted butter, melted*
> *¾ cup granulated sugar*
> *⅓ cup packed light brown sugar*
> *5 large eggs*
> *1½ tablespoons stone-ground yellow cornmeal*
> *1½ tablespoons cornstarch*
> *2 tablespoons freshly grated lemon zest*
> *3 tablespoons fresh lemon juice*
> *2 tablespoons white balsamic vinegar*
> *1 tablespoon vanilla extract*
> *⅛ teaspoon table salt*

1. Preheat the oven to 425°F.

2. Lightly dust your work surface and rolling pin with flour. Swirl the disk of dough in the flour to lightly coat the bottom. You want to make sure your dough can move. Roll the disk from the center out, then rotate the disk a quarter turn and roll again. Keep rolling and turning to form a 12-inch round, lightly, lightly flouring the surface and top of dough. You want just enough flour to keep the dough from sticking; don't overflour!

3. Once you have your beautiful thin round, gently fold it in half, then again into quarters. Transfer it to a 9-inch pie plate, arranging it so that the point of the dough triangle is in the very center. Gently unfold the dough and press it into the plate. Don't stretch the

dough at all; that will make it shrink later. If you want to move it to center it, lift it and move it instead of pulling it.

4. You should have a ½-inch overhang all around the edge. Gently tuck that under so that the edge of the dough is flush with the rim of the plate. To make a decorative crimped edge, pinch a small section of the edge with your index finger and thumb while pushing your other index finger in between to form a little flute. Be sure to press the dough down against the rim of the pie plate as you're crimping. At this point, you can cover it with plastic wrap and freeze for up to 1 week. If the dough got soft, you should freeze it until firm anyway, about 10 minutes.

5. Line the dough with parchment paper, then fill with dried beans. Bake until just set, about 20 minutes. The bottom of the dough may look just a little wet, but the rest of the crust should look and feel dry. Carefully remove the weights with the parchment. Return the crust to the oven and bake until golden brown, about 12 minutes.

6. While the crust bakes, make the filling: In a large bowl, whisk together the butter, granulated sugar, and brown sugar until well blended. Whisk in the eggs, then whisk in the cornmeal, cornstarch, lemon zest and juice, vinegar, vanilla, and salt until well blended.

7. Slide out the oven rack with the hot crust and pour in the filling. Carefully slide the rack back in. Reduce the oven temperature to 350°F.

8. Bake until the custard is just set in the center and the top is golden brown, about 45 minutes, covering the edge with foil if it starts to burn.

9. Transfer the pan to a wire rack and let cool. Serve at room temperature.

Apple–Sweet Potato Upside-Down Pie

Serve 12

When I began learning how to make classical French cuisine, first in culinary school then at high-end restaurants, I didn't think I'd ever connect those techniques to my down-home favorites. Well, never say never. I've taken my three favorite Thanksgiving pies—apple, sweet potato, and pecan—and rolled 'em into one rustic French tart. The beauty of tarte tatin, which is essentially an upside-down skillet pie, is how quickly it comes together. (Homemade pies take time. I think they're well worth the time, but sometimes, I just don't have that many hours before I want dessert!) All you have to do is cook the filling a little on the stovetop, top it with crust, and pop it in the oven. The fun part is flipping it over when it's done: gorgeous caramelized fruit on top, buttery brown crust under. Yum. Instead of plain ol' sugar, I sweeten the apple–sweet potato combo with a syrupy brandy glaze brightened by lime.

BRANDY GLAZE
½ cup brandy, rum, or bourbon
½ cup dark maple syrup
¼ cup packed brown sugar
Freshly grated zest and juice of 1 lime
3 tablespoons unsalted butter
½ teaspoon table salt

TARTE TATIN
All-purpose flour, for rolling
1 disk Flaky Butter Crust (page 257)
1 tablespoon canola or other neutral oil
1 tablespoon unsalted butter
8 tart medium apples, peeled, cored, and cut into quarters
1 large sweet potato, peeled and cut into pieces the same
*   size as the apple quarters*
1 cup pecans, toasted and chopped (page 296)

1. Preheat the oven to 400°F. Line a baking sheet with parchment paper.

2. To make the brandy glaze: In a small saucepan, bring the brandy to a boil. Cook until reduced by half. Stir in the syrup, brown sugar, lime zest and juice, butter, and salt. Adjust

the heat to maintain a steady simmer, then simmer, stirring occasionally, for 5 minutes. Remove from the heat.

3. To make the tart: On a lightly floured surface, with a lightly floured rolling pin, roll the disk of dough into a 9¼-inch round. Transfer to the baking sheet and refrigerate until ready to use.

4. Heat a 9-inch cast-iron or other heavy ovenproof skillet over medium heat. Add the oil and butter and swirl to coat the bottom of the pan. Add the apples and sweet potato and turn to coat, then arrange all the pieces in a tight, single layer. Cook, rotating the pan and turning the pieces occasionally, until browned, about 7 minutes.

5. Pour half of the glaze over the apples and potatoes, then sprinkle with half of the pecans. Place the rolled-out dough on top of the apples and tuck the edges of the dough into the edges of the pan. Immediately transfer to the oven.

6. Bake until the crust is golden brown and the apples and sweet potato are soft enough for a toothpick to slide through them easily, about 1 hour.

7. Transfer the skillet to a wire rack and let cool for 5 minutes. Center a large, rimmed serving dish over the skillet, then hold on to both the pan and dish and quickly and carefully flip both together over quickly. Lift off the skillet. Be sure to wear oven mitts because the skillet and its contents are extremely hot!

8. Sprinkle the remaining pecans over the tart and serve warm with the remaining brandy glaze and vanilla ice cream.

Catering Like Carla

🍤 You can refrigerate the glaze for up to a week. Just reheat it until bubbling before using it in the tart. Of course, the glaze is delicious over ice cream, too!

Spring Tart with Strawberry-Rhubarb Curd

Makes one 9-inch tart

This elegant dessert started with my fascination with lemon curd. While browsing the goods at the Fancy Food Show (a huge industry event that showcases new edible treats), I was on a mission to find the best lemon curd. I began thinking about playing with other flavors for curd. A few months later, I had to come up with a dessert for an event for President Obama. It was the height of strawberry-rhubarb season, so I wanted to do a trio of sweets with that classic combo. And it hit me: strawberry-rhubarb curd! Sadly, the president didn't get to try my dishes (security and what not). It's a shame because I think he would've really liked them. The curd, especially. The rhubarb complements the lemon's tartness with its own floral tang, and strawberries mellow it all out with their juicy sweetness. Together, those three fruits make a delicious and stunning sunset-hued tart filling.

PÂTE SUCRÉE

1 large egg yolk
2 tablespoons heavy cream
½ teaspoon vanilla extract
1½ cups all-purpose flour, plus more for rolling
¾ cup confectioners' sugar
¼ teaspoon table salt
10 tablespoons (1¼ sticks) cold unsalted butter,
*   cut into ½-inch dice*

STRAWBERRY-RHUBARB FILLING

½ pound strawberries, hulled
2 large stalks rhubarb, trimmed and chopped
1 teaspoon powdered unflavored gelatin
5 tablespoons fresh lemon juice
8 large egg yolks
1¼ cups granulated sugar
1 tablespoon freshly grated lemon zest

12 Lime Meringues (page 273), for serving (optional)

SPECIAL EQUIPMENT

9-inch tart pan with removable bottom

1. To make the pate sucrée: In a small bowl, beat together the egg yolk, cream, and vanilla until well mixed. In a food processor, pulse the flour, confectioners' sugar, and salt until just mixed. Transfer to a large bowl, add the butter, and toss with your fingers until each butter cube is coated. Return it to the food processor and pulse until the mixture is sandy with just a few pea-size butter pieces left. Pulse while adding the egg yolk mixture, then process just until the dough forms a ball. Form into a 1-inch-thick disk, wrap tightly in plastic wrap, and refrigerate for 1 hour.

2. On a lightly floured surface with a lightly floured rolling pin, roll the dough into a 12-inch round. Carefully transfer to a 9-inch tart pan with a removable bottom. Trim the edge flush with the rim of the pan by running a paring knife around the top. If the dough has torn at all, patch the tears or holes with the scraps. Freeze until firm while you heat the oven.

3. Preheat the oven to 350°F.

4. Line the dough with parchment paper, then fill with dried beans. Bake until the dough is dry to the touch, about 15 minutes. Very carefully remove the paper with the beans. Bake again until the crust is really brown, about 25 minutes.

5. Transfer the pan to a wire rack and let cool.

6. To make the filling: In a stand blender, puree the strawberries until liquid and very smooth, or use a juicer, if you have one. Strain through a fine-mesh sieve, squeezing out as much juice as possible from the solids. You should have ¾ cup juice. Blend or juice more strawberries if needed. Repeat with the rhubarb to get ¾ cup juice. You don't need to clean out the blender between uses. Discard all the solids.

7. In a small bowl, sprinkle the gelatin over 2 tablespoons of the lemon juice and let stand to soften, about 5 minutes.

8. Meanwhile, in a medium bowl, beat the egg yolks with the sugar until well mixed. In a medium saucepan, combine the lemon zest, strawberry juice, rhubarb juice, and the remaining 3 tablespoons lemon juice. Bring to a simmer over medium-high heat; remove from the heat. Whisk a few spoonfuls into the yolk mixture. Continue whisking and adding a few spoonfuls until the bottom of the bowl is warm. Whisk the remaining hot juice into the yolk mixture.

9. Return the juice-yolk mixture to the saucepan and cook over low heat, stirring continuously, until it registers 160°F on a candy thermometer and is thickened, about 10 minutes. Stir in the softened gelatin until it melts. Strain through a fine-mesh sieve into the cooled crust and spread into an even layer.

10. Refrigerate until set, at least 4 hours and up to overnight.

11. Cut into wedges and serve at room temperature with the meringues, if desired.

Catering Like Carla

You can also make smaller tarts with this recipe. Simply cut out the size round you need and adjust the crust baking times accordingly.

Lime Meringues

Makes about 9 dozen

I always want my meringues to be memorable. Unlike the dry, crisp kind, mine are hard on the outside and chewy in the middle, almost like a pavlova. I make them that way because I loved gummy bears as a kid and still enjoy treats with a sugary chew. Foamy dry meringues just don't satisfy me. And the lime balances the sweet with its bright, tropical acid. I don't really like a plain ol' meringue; I want it to taste like something. It's a surprise when a meringue is yummy! I created these as a topping for my Spring Tart with Strawberry-Rhubarb Curd (page 270), but they're great on their own, too.

> 6 large egg whites
> ¼ teaspoon cream of tartar
> ½ cup superfine sugar (see Note)
> 1 teaspoon freshly grated lime zest
> 1 tablespoon fresh lime juice
> ⅛ teaspoon table salt

1. Preheat the oven to 250°F. Line three baking sheets with parchment paper. Using a 1½-inch round cookie cutter or stencil, trace circles on the parchment paper, spacing them ½ inch apart. Flip the parchment paper over. You should be able to see the circles through the paper. If you don't have that many baking sheets, go ahead and make 3 parchment paper sheets as described above. Later, bake in batches, very carefully sliding the parchment sheets off and onto the same baking sheet.

2. In the bowl of an electric mixer fitted with a whisk, combine the egg whites and cream of tartar. Beat on medium-high speed until soft peaks form.

3. With the mixer running, gradually add the sugar. Continue beating, stopping to scrape the sides and bottom of the bowl occasionally, until stiff peaks form, about 2 minutes. Pinch the mixture between your fingers. If you feel the grit of the sugar, you have more work to do. Just keep beating until the whites are stiff and the sugar completely dissolved. Add the lime zest and juice and salt and continue beating until shiny.

4. Fill a pastry bag fitted with a small plain tip with half of the meringue batter. Using the circles on the parchment as a guide, pipe 1½-inch rounds. Start from the outside edge

and spiral in, ending by lifting the bag up to create a happy little spiral. Repeat with the remaining batter.

5. Bake until cream-colored and dry to the touch, about 40 minutes, rotating the sheets halfway through.

6. Transfer the pans to wire racks and let cool. Serve immediately. (These chewy meringues don't keep well.)

NOTE

❧If you can't find superfine sugar, you can make your own: pulse granulated sugar in a dry food processor until very fine.

Catering Like Carla

❧If you're making smaller strawberry-rhubarb tarts, you can make the meringues the same size as the top of the tarts. When ready to serve, center the meringue on top like a little cap.

A What? A Tomato Compote with Tomato-Strawberry Sangria Sauce!

Serves 4

If ever there was a doubt that the tomato's a fruit, this dessert is the definitive answer. I got such a rush when I was developing this recipe. I knew I wanted to do something sweet with tomatoes, but I couldn't figure out what. When I'm stuck like that, I just need a minute to get really still and think. I had a box of strawberries and spied a bottle of red wine on the counter and started playing, and it just came to me. When I tasted this sauce for the first time, I just gasped. It's perfect! It had all the rich complexity of sangria with the vegetal sweetness of grape tomatoes. Little bursting fruits in a syrupy sauce are, in a word, amazing. That moment—when you discover something you really love in the kitchen—that's when cooking becomes love and the food just hugs you.

SANGRIA SAUCE

¼ cup sugar
2 tablespoons fresh lemon juice
2 tablespoons balsamic vinegar
2 tablespoons dry red wine
1 pound strawberries, hulled and cut into quarters
1 pound vine-ripened tomatoes, cored and
    cut into quarters

TOMATO COMPOTE

½ teaspoon canola or other neutral oil
1 cup grape tomatoes, cut in half lengthwise
1 tablespoon sugar
1 tablespoon unsalted butter

Crème fraîche or vanilla ice cream, for serving

1. To make the sauce: In a large nonstick skillet, stir together the sugar, lemon juice, vinegar, and wine until well combined. Bring to a boil over medium-high heat, then stir in the strawberries and tomatoes. Reduce the heat to maintain a steady simmer. Simmer, stirring occasionally, until the tomatoes are very soft, about 20 minutes. Strain through a fine-mesh sieve, reserving the liquid.

2. To make the compote: Wipe out the skillet. Heat over high heat, then coat the bottom with the oil. Add the tomatoes and cook, shaking the pan, until they just start to blister, about 1 minute. You don't want them to start breaking down. Remove from the heat and add the sugar and butter. Shake the pan to toss until the mixture is bubbly and caramelized and the tomatoes are glossy and glazed.

3. Divide the sauce among four serving dishes with scoops of ice cream in the center. Spoon the tomato compote on top.

Blackberry-Tarragon Parfait

Serves 6

It's funny how some recipes start. This dessert began as a traditional tiramisu, but mascarpone is too often heavy and bland. I made a flavorful, light mascarpone mousse instead and decided to use it as the star of a dessert. It became the perfect vehicle for fresh summer berries, and tarragon gives it a lovely herbaceous note. To top it off, lemon crumble adds a bright crunch.

LEMON CRUMBLE

¾ cup all-purpose flour
¼ cup packed dark brown sugar
2 tablespoons granulated sugar
2 teaspoons freshly grated lemon zest
Pinch of salt
6 tablespoons (¾ stick) cold unsalted butter,
*   cut into small pieces*

BLACKBERRY-TARRAGON COMPOTE

1½ pints blackberries, berries cut in half
1 tablespoon fresh tarragon leaves, chopped,
*   plus whole leaves for garnish*
½ to 1 teaspoon fresh lemon juice
Granulated sugar

MASCARPONE MOUSSE

3 large pasteurized eggs, separated
½ cup granulated sugar
Pinch of salt
8 ounces mascarpone cheese (1 cup)
1 teaspoon vanilla extract

1. To make the lemon crumble: Preheat the oven to 375°F. Line a half sheet pan with parchment paper.

2. In a medium bowl, combine the flour, sugars, lemon zest, and salt. Add the butter and work together quickly with your fingers until the crumble comes together. Spread out on the pan.

3. Bake until crisp and golden, about 15 minutes.

4. Transfer the pan to a wire rack and let cool completely. Break into small crumbles.

5. To make the blackberry compote: In a medium bowl, combine the blackberries, tarragon, lemon juice, and a pinch of sugar. Taste and add more lemon juice and sugar if desired. Let stand for at least 20 minutes.

6. To make the mascarpone mousse: In a large bowl, whisk the egg yolks, ¼ cup of the sugar, and the salt until lemony yellow and very light. Whisk in the mascarpone until well incorporated.

7. In a clean bowl, whisk the egg whites with 2 tablespoons sugar. Continue whisking while you gradually add the remaining 2 tablespoons sugar. Continue whisking until medium peaks form. Gently fold the egg whites into the mascarpone mixture. Stir in the vanilla.

8. To assemble: Divide the blackberry compote among six parfait glasses. Top with the mascarpone mousse, then sprinkle the lemon crumble over the mousse. Garnish with tarragon leaves.

Catering Like Carla

The crumble can be kept at room temperature in an airtight container for up to 1 week.

The compote can be covered and refrigerated for up to 1 day.

The mousse can be covered and refrigerated for up to 2 days.

If making ahead, assemble and garnish just before serving.

Butterscotch Mousse with Vanilla Salt

Serves 12

Granny was the ultimate Southern hostess. She always kept pretty little tins of candy in her sitting room. I loved the long candy sticks, but hated the butterscotch rounds. You remember? The ones in yellow wrappers? Mama, however, couldn't get enough of those. She'd pop them in her mouth and I could smell the butterscotch from across the room. I had no idea what butterscotch was. I just knew I hated it.

Fast forward a few decades and I'm a professional chef who still hasn't tasted butterscotch. I just had a mental block against it. One night, I went out to dinner with a group of other chefs and somebody ordered the butterscotch pudding. Everyone at the table started raving, "Oh. My. God. This is so delicious!" I took a tiny spoonful and realized they were right. It was so, so good. That was when I discovered that butterscotch is essentially caramel and butter—a combo I adore. I had to learn how to make it. I tinkered until I came up with a silky light mousse, which I paired with crunchy nuts. When I served the mousse in tuile cups at a catering event, everyone went crazy for them! This dessert is such a well-balanced blend of sweet and salty, crisp and creamy. And every component can be made ahead of time. All you have to do is put the pieces together when it's time to serve.

VANILLA SALT
¼ dried vanilla bean
¼ cup kosher salt

BUTTERSCOTCH MOUSSE
⅔ cup packed dark brown sugar
3 tablespoons cornstarch
½ teaspoon table salt
1½ cups half-and-half
2 large egg yolks
3 tablespoons unsalted butter, cut into small pieces
1 vanilla bean, pod split and seeds scraped
2 teaspoons dark rum
1 cup heavy cream

12 Almond Tuiles (page 284), shaped into cups if you like or left flat
½ cup Candied Almonds (page 8), coarsely chopped

1. To make the vanilla salt: Coarsely chop or break the vanilla bean into two pieces. Combine 1 piece and 2 tablespoons of the salt in a spice grinder. Pulse until the vanilla is very finely chopped and blended with the salt. Transfer to a small bowl. Repeat with the remaining vanilla and salt. This makes more than you'll need just for this dessert. Store any remaining in an airtight container for up to 1 week and use any way you'd like. It's good on any caramel or chocolate desserts and on savory dishes such as roast pork.

2. To make the mousse: In a medium bowl, whisk together the sugar, cornstarch, salt, and ½ cup of the half-and-half until smooth. Press through a fine-mesh sieve into a medium saucepan to break up any remaining lumps of sugar. Whisk in the egg yolks and remaining 1 cup half-and-half.

3. Cook over medium heat, stirring continuously with a rubber spatula, until thick and bubbling, about 7 minutes. Remove from the heat and whisk in the butter, vanilla seeds, and rum until well combined. Transfer the pudding to a medium bowl and press a sheet of plastic wrap directly against the surface. Refrigerate until cold, at least 3 hours and up to overnight.

4. Whisk the cream until soft peaks form. Whisk a quarter of the whipped cream into the pudding to loosen it. With a rubber spatula, fold in the remaining whipped cream until completely incorporated. Pipe or spoon the mousse into the tuile cups, if you made them, or glass cups if you didn't. Top with the candied almonds and sprinkle with a little vanilla salt. Garnish with tuiles if not using tuile cups.

Catering Like Carla

❧ The mousse can be covered and refrigerated for up to 3 days.

❧ When I was catering, I usually made these as tuile cups filled with the mousse. Occasionally, my tuile cups would be especially lacy. To ensure that the mousse didn't spill out through the cups, I'd brush a very thin layer of melted dark chocolate over the bottom and sides of the cups. When the chocolate hardens, it creates a seal. Be sure to brush very lightly. You don't really want to taste the chocolate at all; it's just there to reinforce the cup.

Almond Tuiles

Makes about 3 dozen

I first leaned how to make these in culinary school and was so excited by my ability to turn out such delicious, delicate cookies. And then I got over it. I'll be honest, making these lacy tuiles is a bit of a pain. The dough is easy enough, but then you need to spread the balls flat before baking to get a thin, elegant round. I'll never forget the time I was cooking at the Henley Park Hotel and we had to make a ton of tuiles. We put our extern in charge of them because the lowest person on the totem pole always got the tuiles. She stayed late to finish them and did a fantastic job. She put the tray of them on top of the ice cream machine and was relieved to be done with them. Later that day, when we were spinning the ice cream, the tray went sliding to the floor and the tuiles crashed and shattered like glass. It was one of those sad slow-motion moments when you watched the shards of cookie spray up in the air. We've all had those moments, right?

Have I convinced you to not try these by now? Well, you still should. You don't need to make nearly as many as our poor extern did. Plus, the dough keeps forever. You can make only as many as you need or want to eat at any given time. When you're doing a dozen or so, it's actually a lot of fun. Crackly caramelized almond thins are absolutely worth the effort.

8 tablespoons (1 stick) unsalted butter
½ cup granulated sugar
⅓ cup light corn syrup
1½ cups almonds, finely ground (see Note)
2 tablespoons all-purpose flour
½ teaspoon table salt
1 teaspoon vanilla extract

1. In a large saucepan, combine the butter, sugar, and corn syrup. Heat over low heat, stirring occasionally, until the butter melts and the mixture is well blended.

2. Stir in the almonds, flour, salt, and vanilla until well combined. Remove from the heat and let cool to room temperature. The batter can be refrigerated in an airtight container for up to 2 months.

3. Preheat the oven to 350°F. Line two half sheet pans with Silpats or other nonstick silicone baking mats.

4. Form the tuile batter into 1-inch balls and place on a pan 3 inches apart. (You'll be able to fit five balls on a pan: one near each corner and one in the center.) Using a small off-set spatula or wet fingertips, flatten the balls into thin 3-inch-diameter disks. Bake until golden brown, about 8 minutes. While one pan bakes, prepare the batter for the next pan. Once the second pan goes in the oven, shape the first pan's tuiles as instructed below. Keep going from one pan to the other, forming the batter, baking, and shaping. The baking time may shorten as the pans get hot.

5. To make tuile cups, use an offset spatula to immediately transfer the hot tuile to an inverted shot glass. Gently press the sides of the tuile against the glass to form a cup. Repeat with the remaining tuiles. If the tuiles harden before you have a chance to shape them, return to the oven for a few seconds to make them pliable again. You can also leave the rounds flat or drape them over a thin rolling pin to make cradles. Cooled tuiles will keep in an airtight container for up to 1 week.

NOTE

☙ To grind almonds fine, pulse them in a food processor. Stop before they turn pasty and start to clump; they should just be very, very finely chopped. Freezing them first helps prevent clumping.

Catering Like Carla

☙ You can make these with any type of unsalted nut: pistachios, pecans, peanuts. Just be sure to grind the nuts very fine. Large pieces will cause the tuile batter to tear.

Chocolate Espresso Napoleons

Serves 6

When I was living in Paris, I used to walk down the Champs-Élysées to admire the stunning displays in the patisseries. As a model, I was there for the fashion gigs, but I was always window-shopping for food. The napoleons were especially pretty: towers of delicate pastry with luscious cream in between. This chocolate stack is an homage to classic French pastries, but I've used flaky phyllo dough in place of the traditional puff pastry. The phyllo has a delicate, crisp texture that pairs perfectly with the chocolate-coffee cream.

CHOCOLATE ESPRESSO PASTRY CREAM

1½ cups whole milk
2 tablespoons instant espresso powder
¼ cup finely chopped semisweet chocolate
5 large egg yolks, at room temperature
¾ cup sugar
3 tablespoons cornstarch
1 tablespoon unsweetened cocoa powder
½ teaspoon table salt
1 teaspoon Kahlúa or other coffee liqueur
½ teaspoon vanilla extract
1 tablespoon unsalted butter
1 cup plus 1 tablespoon heavy cream

CINNAMON-CHOCOLATE WAFERS

¼ cup sugar
2 tablespoons unsweetened cocoa powder
½ teaspoon ground cinnamon
6 large (18 by 14-inch) sheets phyllo dough
6 tablespoons (¾ stick) unsalted butter, melted,
    plus more if needed

½ cup pine nuts, toasted (page 296)
Whipped cream, chocolate shavings, and/or chocolate-covered
    coffee beans for garnish

1. To make the pastry cream: In a medium saucepan, heat the milk on medium until bubbles just begin to form around the edge. Stir in the instant espresso until dissolved, then stir in the chocolate until melted.

2. Meanwhile, in a medium bowl, whisk the egg yolks and sugar until very thick. Whisk in the cornstarch, cocoa powder, and salt until smooth and fully incorporated. Continue whisking while adding the hot milk in a slow, steady stream. When fully incorporated, return the mixture to the saucepan.

3. Cook over low heat, whisking constantly, until the mixture thickens, about 5 minutes. It should have the consistency of pudding. Stir in the Kahlúa, vanilla, butter, and 1 tablespoon of the heavy cream until fully incorporated. Press a sheet of plastic wrap directly on the surface and refrigerate until cold.

4. When cold, whisk the remaining 1 cup heavy cream until medium-soft peaks form. Whisk a quarter of the whipped cream into the chocolate pudding to loosen it. Gently fold in the remaining whipped cream until fully incorporated. Refrigerate until ready to serve.

5. To make the wafers: Preheat the oven to 375°F. Line a baking sheet with parchment paper.

6. Combine the sugar, cocoa powder, and cinnamon in a small bowl.

7. Keep the phyllo covered with a damp paper or kitchen towel while working. Lay one sheet of phyllo on your work surface, then brush with melted butter. Sprinkle one-third of the cocoa mixture over the phyllo. Repeat two more times, then stack the remaining three sheets on top, brushing with butter between each sheet.

8. Using a ruler, trim the edges, then cut the stack into three even strips. Cut the strips into sixths to form eighteen rectangles. Place the phyllo on the baking sheet, spacing ½ inch apart. Place another sheet of parchment on top, then top with another baking sheet.

9. Bake until the wafers are golden brown and crisp, about 15 minutes. Remove the pan on top and the parchment and transfer the pan with the wafers to a wire rack. Let the phyllo cool completely.

10. To assemble, top one-third of the phyllo with one-third of the pastry cream and pine nuts. Repeat the layering twice. Garnish with whipped cream, chocolate shavings, and/or chocolate-covered coffee beans and serve immediately.

Catering Like Carla

🍴The pastry cream can be covered and refrigerated for up to 3 days.

🍴The wafers can be kept in an airtight container for up to 3 days.

🍴Assemble just before serving.

🂠 Ingredients That Need Friends

On one episode of *The Chew,* we turned the show into a pajama party and played the popular sleepover game, Truth or Dare. When it was my turn, I chose dare and was confronted with a truth I don't easily admit: There are some flavors I really don't like. Coffee and alcohol are at the top of the list. My dare was to eat a boozy fruit cake with a cup of espresso. On live television, I actually gagged. With my mouth open. I couldn't swallow either, I was so overcome with disgust at the flavors.

Here's the thing with not liking certain flavors: You have to remember that you may actually like them in other forms. For example, I can't kick back a shot of either espresso or alcohol, but I use those flavors all the time in my cooking. I just think they need friends; they can't come to my food party alone. I love coffee with chocolate in desserts and often use wine and liquor in savory and sweet sauces. Blue cheese falls into this category for me, too. I can't nibble a hunk of it plain, but I love it tossed into salads or mixed with other milder cheeses. So before you swear off a recipe because it includes an ingredient you don't like, check out its friends first. You may just want to hang out with them all together.

Chocolate Decadent Bites

Makes about 40 bites

I'm not really into chocolate. I mean, I like it, but I don't go gaga over it. And yet I love these little bites! And there's coffee in them, a flavor I don't like unless it's playing with others. Here, it's BFF with chocolate. I enjoy this combo because it's not too sweet and the strong coffee lends a depth of richness to the bittersweet chocolate. The texture hovers somewhere between truffle and cake. Rich chocolate ganache sandwiched between fudgy chocolate cake makes for a memorable bite your friends will swoon over. Note that this makes a big batch, ideal for parties or to give as a homemade gift.

CHOCOLATE CAKE

¾ pound (3 sticks) unsalted butter, cut up,
    plus more for the pan
¾ cup all-purpose flour, plus more for the pan
¾ pound bittersweet chocolate (68% cacao), chopped
1 teaspoon instant espresso powder
1 teaspoon table salt
9 large eggs
1½ cups sugar
2 tablespoons vanilla extract
2 cups pecans or walnuts, toasted and finely chopped (optional)

CHOCOLATE GANACHE

1 pound bittersweet or semisweet chocolate, finely chopped
2 cups heavy cream
2 tablespoons liqueur (such as Frangelica, Chambord,
    or Grand Marnier), optional

1. To make the cake: Preheat the oven to 350°F. Butter a half sheet pan and line it with parchment paper. Butter the parchment and dust with flour, tapping out excess.

2. In a medium saucepan, melt the butter and chocolate over low heat, stirring occasionally. Stir in the espresso powder. Let the mixture cool.

3. Sift the flour and salt into a small bowl.

4. In the bowl of an electric mixer fitted with a paddle, beat the eggs and sugar on medium-high speed until thick and a pale-lemon color, stopping to scrape the sides and bottom of the bowl occasionally. Beat in the vanilla until blended. Reduce the mixer speed to low and gradually add the flour until just incorporated. Add the melted chocolate in a steady stream. Continue beating until thoroughly blended, stopping to scrape the sides and bottom of the bowl occasionally. Stir in the nuts, if using.

5. Spread the batter in an even layer in the baking pan. Bake until a toothpick inserted near the edge comes out clean, about 40 minutes. Transfer the pan to a wire rack and let cool completely.

6. While the cake cools, make the ganache: Place the chocolate in a large bowl. Heat the cream in a small saucepan until steaming. Pour over the chocolate, then gently stir with a wooden spoon until smooth. If using, stir in the liqueur until fully incorporated.

7. Invert the cake onto the wire rack. Peel off and discard the parchment paper. Place a large board or pan, flat side down, on top of the cake. Invert the board, cake, and rack together. Remove the rack, then cut the cake in half crosswise to form two 12 by 8-inch rectangles. Place the rack over a rimmed baking sheet and place one cake layer on it.

8. Spread half of the chocolate ganache to cover the cake layer on the rack. Sandwich with the top layer, smooth side up. Pour the remaining ganache all over cake, spreading to evenly cover the top and sides. Refrigerate until firm, at least 2 hours and up to 2 days. Cut into bite-size pieces and serve.

Catering Like Carla

❧ You can mix up the type of chocolate you use to your taste. I use 68% cacao chocolate for the cake because I don't like my desserts too sweet. But if you prefer a sweeter dessert, use a lower percentage semisweet chocolate. For a more intense bitterness, use a higher percentage bittersweet. If you're using semisweet for the cake, you can use bittersweet for the ganache and vice versa. But I wouldn't go all the way to milk chocolate (and certainly not white chocolate); those varieties wouldn't taste right.

Pantry

You need good ingredients if you're gonna cook well. I try to buy the freshest possible organic produce from farmers' markets. At my local grocery stores, I look for sustainable meat, fish, and shellfish. Here are just a few of my favorite must-haves.

Let's start with my desert island ingredient, the one thing I'd take with me if stranded. Lemons! This is going to be the one time I apologize for using lemon in nearly every dish I cook because I recognize that this is a character flaw. But you know what? I'm not really sorry. I just don't want to be told what I already know: I use citrus in everything. I love it! It adds a bright acidity and aromatic freshness to savory and sweet dishes. Lemons can be pricey, but always pick up a few at the market and keep them in the fruit drawer of your fridge.

Salt: kosher for savory cooking; iodized table for baking.

Sugar: white granulated; white superfine; confectioners'; light or dark brown (I usually use light).

Tomatoes: canned whole and diced; tubes of tomato paste (much better than cans because you can use just a little at a time). Once, when my sister and I cleaned out our mama's pantry, we found more than twenty-five cans of tomatoes. You don't need that many, but it's always good to keep some on hand.

Legumes: dried beans; dried lentils; dried black-eyed peas; canned beans. These are in the running to be desert island ingredients, too, because I enjoy cooking and eating them so much. Dried lentils cook quickly, but other beans don't, so it's good to keep canned ones in case you don't have time to soak and simmer dried ones.

Fresh herbs: thyme, parsley, rosemary, sage, cilantro, mint, dill, basil—those are a few of my favorites. I especially love thyme—I must be French somewhere deep in my heart. Always keep thyme around, if only so you can say to yourself when you're super busy, "I have thyme!" I encourage you to keep fresh herbs in the fridge all the time. If you get 'em, you'll use 'em!

Dairy: Unless stated otherwise, I use whole milk, whole-milk ricotta, regular sour cream, plain whole-milk yogurt, regular cream cheese, and full-fat cheeses. It's all about moderation.

Honey: I prefer a middle-of-the-road honey, not too light and not too dark, and love looking for local varieties. Be sure to buy 100 percent honey made with only honey; it sounds "duh," but some companies sell fake stuff and call it honey-flavored syrup. (Look out for the same thing with maple syrup! The only ingredient should be "maple syrup.") Jarred honey will keep in the pantry for months. If it crystallizes and begins to harden or separate, just microwave in 10-second increments and stir to bring it back together. To infuse honey, stick a sprig of fresh rosemary, thyme, or sage in the jar. I love drizzling that over peanut butter on whole-grain toast for breakfast.

Tips and Techniques

Over the years, I've figured out the best and most efficient ways for me to complete basic kitchen tasks. These are some of the fundamentals that'll make you look like a pro while cooking. Here's how I roll in the kitchen:

To season, you need to use salt. I know, duh! But this is the *most* important thing you need to learn to cook well! I always use kosher for seasoning savory dishes. Remember that salt is a compliment. If you don't use it, you ain't gon' get any compliments. But add too much and it becomes an insult. It's like going to your high school reunion and having an old classmate tell you how good you look. The first time, it's a lovely thing to hear. The second time, even. But if she keeps telling you again and again, you start to wonder, "What? Did I not look good before?" And then it's not so nice anymore. Salt is the same way. You have to use just the right amount, and the only way to know is by tasting as you cook. If you're worried that you're using too much salt for your health, I encourage you to actually measure the pinches that you sprinkle over the food. You'd be surprised: there's less than you think between your fingertips. Of course, check with your doctor about how much salt you should be consuming and do what doc says.

Hey, you salt lovers out there—yes, I'm talkin' to y'all—listen up. When you have a dish that has a really savory element, like bacon or ham hocks, you want to add only a little salt while you're cooking. You've already got a lot of salt in there and you need somewhere to go with a dish. Once you oversalt, you can't go back. Just keep tasting and seasoning, keeping in mind that you're concentrating flavors as food cooks. But you still need to season the dish before it's completely done. The time to put the salt in is in the kitchen, not at the table.

To dice an onion, trim off the top but keep the root end on. Cut the onion in half through the root end. Place one half flat on a cutting board and use your noncutting hand to hold both sides of the onion halfway between the trimmed side and root end. (You do need to have hands big enough to reach around the onion to do this.) Slice into the onion, cutting from the trimmed top to the root end but not slicing through the root end. Turn the onion 90 degrees, hold it together again, and cut across the slices to form small dice.

To dice zucchini, yellow squash, and cucumbers, I want to avoid including the seeds in the dice. They're watery and will dilute the flavor of the dish, and make the texture mushy.

Trim just enough of each long side to make four flat edges. Sit the vegetable flat on one side, then cut along one side of the seeds to remove one seedless side of squash. Cut along the opposite side to remove another side. Turn the squash a quarter turn and slice off the remaining two sides. Discard the center with the seeds and dice the planks of squash.

To peel a carrot, I run a peeler up and down half the length of the carrot, working all around, then flip the carrot around and run the peeler up and down the other half. Remember, a peeler has blades going in both directions. By running the peeler both up and down, you can peel the carrot a lot faster. This doesn't really work with super sharp or Y-shaped peelers, though. They take off too much carrot if you go in both directions.

To cut a carrot into matchsticks, I cut a thin slice off one side, lengthwise, then sit the carrot down on that flat side. Starting from the tip, I cut ⅛-inch-thick slices at a sharp angle, so that each slice is quite long. Then I cut each of those slices into ⅛-inch-thick matchsticks.

To grate citrus zest, buy a Microplane zester. Go run out and get one if you don't have one. It's the best money you'll ever spend on a small kitchen tool. It's best for removing citrus zest—you want to remove just the aromatic outermost layer of peel. The rhythm I keep when zesting is "shooka, shooka, turn; shooka, shooka, turn." In case you missed that, each "shooka" is a light grating, so you want to go over a single area twice before turning the fruit to get more.

To thinly slice basil and mint leaves, stack a few leaves, then roll them tightly as if rolling a cigarette. Not that I've ever rolled a cigarette. Okay, as if you're rolling a sleeping bag or jelly roll. Then use a sharp knife to thinly slice across the roll.

To mince garlic, run a clove along a Microplane zester. It'll quickly give you the finest, most even mince. If you don't want the smell of garlic on your fingers afterwards, just rub your fingers against a stainless-steel spoon.

To seed a jalapeño chile, trim off the stem end. Sit the chile cut side down flat on the cutting board, then cut along the walls to remove the flesh in sections. The seeds attached to the ribs in the center will come out as a single seed pod.

To toast spices or nuts, heat them in a small dry skillet over medium heat until they're just fragrant and golden. (You can use the oven if you have it on anyway or are doing a huge batch on a baking sheet.) Watch the spices or nuts very carefully to make sure they don't burn. When you're done with the spices, make sure you get all the seeds out of the pan. One little burnt seed will jack you up and turn everything bitter. If you want to grind them, cool completely then pulse in a spice grinder.

To sear meat, cook just a few pieces at a time in a hot pan, and let each side get nice and brown and crusty before turning to the next side. You don't ever want to crowd the pan and start steaming the meat. It's the brown that adds flavor to the dish. If you rush the searing process, you'll end up with a gray stew. And that isn't food that hugs you—that's food that pushes you away.

To drain fat from fried foods, ball up paper towels to form a "rack" for the food. The paper soaks up the oil and the crumply shape prevents the crust from sitting flat against a surface, which causes the food to steam and get soggy.

Acknowledgments

For a number of years now, I've come to understand that there are no mistakes in the universe. Everything—and I mean everything—happens for a reason. The seemingly random and sometimes tough paths that have gotten me to this point—the point of actually being a part (and only a part) of this cookbook—never seemed to have gone in a straight line. If someone had told me twenty-five years ago that someday I would have my own cookbook, I would have thought her crazy. However, I have always been aware that the right and perfect people have been put on my path to guide me and to take me by the hand to the next place where I'm supposed to be. I would like to thank you for your warm hugs—be it physical or virtual.

Thank you to:

My husband, Matthew Lyons, who has given me the gift of unwavering support while I struggled to stay on the path of my passion in food, most times without money and always with "borrowing" our personal kitchen appliances and tools for use in someone else's kitchen. And, of course, Noah, for being part of this adventure.

My mother, Audrey Hall, for allowing me the freedom to shoot for happiness and being one of my biggest cheerleaders. My sister Kim and my brother-in-law Gus; my daddy George; my grandma Thelma; my brother Daniel; my niece (and assistant!) Nyemale; and all my wonderful aunts, uncles, cousins, nieces, and nephews.

Genevieve Ko, for her organization, tireless work, understanding of who I am, and her insight in writing this manuscript that captures my essence. Thanks also for sharing your family with me on all those long nights of recipe testing.

Janis Donnaud, my literary agent, for being full of heart and wisdom and sometimes brutally honest while lighting a fire under me to be the best "me" I could be. Jessica Weiner, my manager, for tying together all the pieces and people.

My editor, Leslie Meredith, for taking the time to prepare the recipes in my proposal for our initial meeting and for seeing the cookbook writer in me. Also, the Free Press team for their infectious excitement and expertise in making the manuscript into an actual book: Martha Levin, publisher; Dominick Anfuso, editor in chief; Suzanne Donahue, associate publisher; Carisa Hays, director of publicity; Meg Cassidy, senior publicist; Donna Loffredo, associate editor; Erich Hobbing, design director; and Eric Fuentecilla, art director.

The Dream Team that magically came together at the last minute before the photo shoot: Greg Powers, photographer; Ceci Loebl, food stylist; and Grace Knott, prop stylist.

The chemistry we had and our effortless way of working together was nothing short of a blessing. I'd like to pre-order you all for the next shoot, please.

The staff at Alchemy by Carla Hall: Lee, Nancy, Daniel, Ralph, Brandy, and last but not least, Verlette Simon, who runs it all in my absence. Thanks for making me look good by baking perfect cookies and treats and catching whatever challenges I throw at you.

My business roommate, Susan Soorenko of Moorenko's, for being a taster whenever we needed an outside opinion and for all that delicious ice cream that pairs beautifully with our sweet treats.

The Chew cast and crew: Clinton, Daphne, Mario, Michael, Gordon, and everyone behind the scenes—and I mean each and every last one of you—make every day loads of fun. The *Top Chef Season 5* and *Top Chef All-Stars* folks for good times and great memories.

My culinary instructors and the first executive chefs I worked under, Jon Dornbush and Richard Thompson, whose leadership and direction kept me in the food game and whose voices I continue to hear in my head . . . still.

My family and friends from home in Nashville to here; my former clients from the Lunch Bunch to Alchemy; and all the other souls I bumped into while traveling the path of food memories and discovery.

And last but not least, Granny, who taught me to dream and to be happy in whatever I do. It's her hands that I see when I make biscuits and rolls and the dishes that I grew up on; it's her voice that I hear when I teach someone to make something for the very first time; and it's her energy that I feel when I nurture someone with a hug by cooking for them.

—Carla Hall

Carla isn't just as nice as she seems—she's nicer. And that doesn't even begin to describe how much grace, joy, and energy she brings to her cooking and to everyone she meets. Thank you for being so open in sharing your delicious recipes and all your food memories. And thanks to your family for sharing meals and family memories with me.

I'm grateful to Janis Donnaud and my agent, Angela Miller, for bringing me and Carla together. Many thanks to Leslie Meredith, Donna Loffredo, Suzanne Fass, and the rest of the Free Press team for this fantastic book and to Greg, Ceci, and Grace for the stunning photos.

As always, thank you to David, Charlotte, Natalie, Vivien, and Izzy for your love and support.

—Genevieve Ko

Index

K

Kim (sister), 3, 191

L

Lamb Roast, Persian
Marinated, with
Cucumber-Yogurt
Sauce on Grilled Pita,
183–84
Leek and Goat Cheese Tart
with Pink Peppercorn
Crust, 134–35
legumes, stocking of, 293
lemon(y):
Crumble, for Blackberry-
Tarragon Parfait,
279–80
Double, Chess Pie,
266–67
Roasted Beets and
Arugula with Herb
Cheese, 33–34
Lemongrass, Fennel and
Napa Cabbage Slaw
with Ginger and,
38–39
Lentil and Oat Salad, 145–46
Leslie (editor), 208
Lime Meringues, 273–74
Lobster:
Bisque, 250–51
Rigatoni, 253–54
Lump Blue Crab Salad with
Chilled Shiso Soup,
247–48

Lyons, Matthew (husband),
xiii, 164, 176

M

Mac and Cheese, Creamy,
127–28
Mama's Hamburger
Help-Me Meal,
164–65
Maple-Glazed Bacon, 16
Matthew's Chicken Curry,
205–6
Meat, 155–84
Beer-Braised Pulled
Barbecued Brisket,
157–58
Cuban Pork Loin with
Marinated Red Onions
and Queso Blanco
in Grilled Tortillas,
172–74
Granny's Slow-Cooked
Sunday Smothered
Pork Chops, 167–68
how to sear, 297
Mama's Hamburger
Help-Me Meal,
164–65
Marinated Flank Steak
with Roasted Red
Pepper Tapenade,
161–62
Osso Buco, 180–81
Persian Marinated Lamb
Roast with Cucumber-
Yogurt Sauce on
Grilled Pita, 183–84

Pork Tenderloin
Medallions with Root
Vegetable Ragout,
169–70
Roasted Filet of Beef,
159–60
Swamp Thing: Braised
Pork Shoulder in
Smoked Pork-Corn
Broth, 176–78
Meringues, Lime, 273–74
Minted Pea Pesto, for
Seared Cod in
Spring Pea Broth,
233–34
Miso-Poached Hake with
Cilantro-Orange Salt,
237–38
Mousse, Butterscotch, with
Vanilla Salt, 281–82
Mozzarella and Sun-Dried
Tomato Pesto Grilled
Sandwich, 130–32
Mushroom(s):
Creamed Chicken with
Broccoli and, 191–92
Tart, Rustic, 137–38
Mustard-Marinated Grilled
Veggies, 143–44

N

Napa Cabbage and Fennel
Slaw with Ginger and
Lemongrass, 38–39
Napoleons, Chocolate
Espresso, 286–88
nuts, *see* specific nuts

Pan-Seared, with
Cranberry-Pear Relish,
213–16
Turkey Sausage and
Cornbread Dressing,
108–9

U

Uncle David, 198

V

Vegetables:
Mustard-Marinated
Grilled, 143–44
Roasted, for Poached
Halibut and Mint Tea
Broth, 240–41
Summer, in Green Chile
Broth, 66–68
Vegetable Stock, 55
vegetarian dishes, 125–54
Black Bean Patties with
Mango Relish and
Tropical Vinaigrette,
149–50
Creamy Mac and Cheese,
127–28
Garlicky Spinach Soufflé,
139–40
Goat Cheese and Leek
Tart with Pink

Peppercorn Crust,
134–35
Grilled Cheese Trio:
Broccoli Pesto and
Cheddar; Sun-Dried
Tomato Pesto and
Mozzarella; Arugula-
Artichoke Pesto and
Havarti, 130–32
Mustard-Marinated
Grilled Veggies,
143–44
Oat and Lentil Salad,
145–46
Pecan and Oat-Crusted
Tofu, 147–48
Roasted Red Pepper
Risotto, 151–54
Rustic Mushroom Tart,
137–38
Spring Pea Flan,
141–42
Summer Vegetables in
Green Chile Broth,
66–68
Vinaigrette(s):
Apple Cider, for Mixed
Greens and Pan-
Roasted Butternut
Squash Salad, 31–32
Champagne, for Arugula
and Shaved Fennel
Salad with Goat
Cheese Croutons,
26–27
Chocolate, for Mixed
Greens, Strawberries,

Pecans, and Ricotta
Salata, 29–30
Lemon, for Lemony
Roasted Beets and
Arugula with Herb
Cheese, 33–34
Spicy Cumin, for
Roasted Carrot Salad,
35–36
Tarragon, for Poached
Chicken with Roasted
Fennel and Frisée
Salad, 201–2
Tropical, for Black Bean
Patties with Mango
Relish, 149–50

W

Walnuts, Sweet and Spicy,
7–8
Watermelon Gazpacho with
Cucumber, Jicama,
Sweet Peppers, and
Basil, 63–64
Willan, Anne (chef), 7

Y

Yogurt-Cucumber Sauce,
for Persian Marinated
Lamb Roast on Grilled
Pita, 183–84

About the Authors

Carla Hall is a co-host on the ABC talk show *The Chew*. She attended L'Academie de Cuisine in Maryland, was a caterer, and is owner and executive chef of Alchemy by Carla Hall, an artisanal cookie company based in Washington, D.C., where she lives with her husband, Matthew Lyons, and stepson, Noah. Her sweet and savory cookies can be found in specialty markets, select Whole Foods, and at alchemybycarlahall.com.

Genevieve Ko is a food writer whose cookbooks include, most recently, *Home Cooking with Jean-Georges*. She also has been a food editor at *Good Housekeeping, Gourmet,* and *Martha Stewart Living.*